The Globalization of Anthropology

Carol E. Hill and

Marietta L. Baba, VOLUME EDITORS

Tim Wallace, SERIES EDITOR

Contents

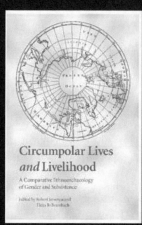

GLOBAL CONNECTIONS AND PRACTICING ANTHROPOLOGY IN THE 21ST CENTURY

CAROLE E. HILL
University of North Carolina–Asheville

MARIETTA L. BABA
Michigan State University

This chapter examines the major themes in the chapters that compromise this volume by discussing how the practice of anthropology across nations and regions of the world is changing as a result of globalization. Several themes are delineated that reflect a unity of purpose and concern about the development and structure of practicing and policy anthropology in the 21st century. Divergent viewpoints among the chapters are also examined. Through comparing and contrasting the major points of the chapters, four major interconnected themes are discussed. They are: 1) local/global transformations: challenge to the traditional; 2) the power of practicing anthropology in local/global contexts; 3) academic and practicing transformations, and 4) the closing gap between colonized and colonizer nations. These themes have important implications for the future of global practice and present challenges to the organization and uses of the products of anthropological inquiry. Key Words: globalization, applied anthropology, practice, colonization, power

This volume represents a 15-year effort by the editors to achieve a systematic understanding of the practice of global anthropology. It is the latest product of the activities of the first global Commission on Anthropology in Policy and Practice, chartered by the International Union of Anthropological and Ethnological Sciences in 1993. Prior to the establishment of this commission, an international network of applied/practicing anthropologists had been in the process of formation for at least three years. In the spring of 1990, representatives of the British Association for Social Anthropology in Policy and Practice (BASAPP) and the Society for Applied Anthropology (SfAA) met together in York, England, to discuss the creation and expansion of an international network to expand communications and cooperation among applied and practicing anthropologists across different nations and regions. Later that year, the American Anthropological Association's (AAA) Board of Directors suggested that an international commission of applied and practicing anthropologists be established within the International Union of Anthropological and Ethnological Sciences (IUAES), the largest anthropological organization in the world with member associations from more than 70 nations. Their objective was to form a global network of practicing/applied anthropologists

NAPA Bulletin 25, pp. 1–13, ISBN 1-931303-28-2. © 2006 by the American Anthropological Association. All rights reserved. Permissions to photocopy or reproduce article content via www.ucpress.edu/journals/rights.htm.

working in diverse public and private sector settings, in order to facilitate cross-national communication and the sharing of knowledge, and to create a synergy through international collaboration.

A small planning committee was subsequently formed that initially included delegates from the AAA, the SfAA, and the BASAPP. Marietta Baba represented the AAA and the National Association for the Practice of Anthropology, Carole Hill was the SfAA representative, and Sue Wright represented BASAPP. This committee contacted IUAES member organizations in several countries to request participation in a larger planning effort. Anthropological organizations in Canada, France, Mexico, and Russia (then USSR) expressed interest in this effort and sent delegates to a planning meeting at the 1991 Annual Meetings of the AAA in Chicago, Illinois. A proposal for an IUAES Commission on Anthropology in Policy and Practice was drafted, circulated, and finalized at this meeting. It was approved by the IUAES in 1993 (Baba 1999).

The first meeting of the IUAES Commission on Anthropology in Policy and Practice held its first scientific session at the 1993 IUAES Congress in Mexico City with anthropologists from 12 nations (and the United Nations) presenting papers to a substantial audience. Papers were presented by authors from Australia, Canada, Costa Rica, France, Great Britain, India, Israel, Japan, Mexico, Nigeria, Russia, and the United States. Each author wrote about the organization and function of applied anthropologists in their respective countries. The Commission decided to publish the papers from this first session, resulting in one of the most diverse collections of papers ever assembled on global applied/practicing anthropology. Delegates from member nations were eager to have access to a publication that would provide information on the practice of anthropology in the First, Second, and Third Worlds. Dr. Mario Zamora, General Editor of Studies in Third World Societies, College of William and Mary, offered to publish the papers as a volume in this series. His offer was accepted by the Commission, and thus began a three-and-a-half-year effort to publish the papers (Baba and Hill 1997). Unfortunately, Dr. Zamora passed away before the book was published. While the College of William and Mary honored their publishing commitments, they eventually decided to discontinue the series. In the late 1990s, unsold volumes from the series were shipped to Dr. George Appell in Maine, who was commissioned as reseller of the series' titles, and they have languished there ever since.

PURPOSE AND ORGANIZATION OF THE VOLUME

The chapters in this volume reflect the second effort of the global applied/practitioner community to communicate their practice of anthropology across the nations and regions of the world. Each chapter presents the viewpoints of practitioners and applied anthropologists from ten nations (Canada, China, Ecuador, Egypt, Great Britain, India, Israel, Portugal, Russia, and the United States). These nations were selected both to provide continuity with the first volume for the purposes of comparison (i.e., Canada, Great Britain, India, Israel, Russia, and the United States) and to include new voices (i.e., China,

Ecuador, Egypt, and Portugal). The sequencing of chapters reflects an alphabetical ordering of nations generally categorized as Third, Second, and First World countries.

Each chapter describes the state of practicing and policy anthropology in the author's home country and provides insights into the critical questions and issues facing applied anthropologists in each nation today within the context of globalization. The authors were asked to focus their chapters on specific topical areas, including the following:

1. History and organization of applied/practicing anthropology
2. Substantive foci of applied/practicing anthropology in the country (i.e., local problems, issues, and domains of work)
3. Role and power of anthropology in local/global linkages and policy formation, including changes brought about by globalization
4. Nature of linkages between academic and applied/practicing anthropology
5. Case studies representative of applied/practicing anthropology in the authors' respective nation

The chapters are organized according to these themes, thereby framing their discussions within the contemporary context of applied/practicing anthropology within a historical perspective. They clearly demonstrate that any history of applied anthropology is inextricably linked to the history of the discipline as a whole, even in countries where relations between applied/practicing and academic anthropologists have been contentious. It should be noted, however, that several of the chapters reveal that the distinction between applied/practicing and academic anthropology is blurred in many nations. Chapter 11 discusses, in some detail, why they are certainly not cross-national categories.

Each chapter presents original information that allows us to systematically compare and contrast applied/practicing anthropology from a global perspective. They each describe the state of applied/practicing anthropology in nine countries, providing data for an analysis of the changing nature of anthropology on a worldwide scale. Since the early 1990s, the pace of globalization, with its new forms of linkages and communication, are rapidly reshaping the discipline of anthropology here in the United States as well as abroad.

World events in the past decade have made it clear that we are living in a compressed world. Events in one area of the world, even those that may have appeared to be localized at one point in time, now reverberate across the globe. The emerging complex dynamics that connect global and local processes have intensified—the world has become, in many ways, a single place. The chapters in this volume provide new information about applied/practicing anthropology, documenting many of the changes taking place within the discipline as a result of globalization. They chronicle, in some detail, the current work of applied/practicing anthropologists, much of which is unpublished. Many of the authors also give personal accounts of their own work, placing it within the context of general patterns in the field.

We use these chapters, those in our first book (1997), and published information on global anthropology as data from which to develop general propositions about the impact of globalization on applied and practicing anthropology. These propositions are discussed in Chapter 11 of this volume.

Several recurrent themes embedded in the chapters provide a foundation for an assessment of the status of the global practice of anthropology. Several of these themes reflect a unity of purpose and concern about the development and structure of practicing and policy anthropology in the 21st century. The chapters also represent diverse national perspectives about the goals, roles, and statuses of anthropology in global change processes. There are, therefore, divergent viewpoints within the themes. Through comparing and contrasting the major points of the chapters, we have delineated four major interconnected themes: (1) local/global transformations: challenge to the traditional; (2) the power of practicing anthropology in local/global contexts; (3) academic and practicing transformations; and (4) the closing gap between colonized and colonizer nations. These themes have important implications for the future of global applied/practice and present challenges to the organization and uses of the products of anthropological inquiry.

Local/Global Transformations: Reversing Power Relations

Changing political and economic relationships among nations and within nations in the 21st century are changing the structure of anthropological application and practice. More anthropologists are working with larger projects that are multidimensional and multidisciplinary in nature. Much of the work in the 20th century was designed in one locale (often North America or western Europe) and expanded elsewhere. Now, by contrast, nations around the world are increasingly defining their own problems and projects to fit local situations. The social and cultural problems discussed in these chapters, many resulting from global–local dynamics and dislocations, are remarkable similar. They include migration and resettlement, poverty, environmental and ecological problems, health and labor problems, land use and ownership, national and local identities and politics, and ethnic/indigenous collective rights.

The authors seem to agree that tackling these problems demands approaches that combine new configurations of power and organization, from the local level through national and international policies. Several of the chapters give examples of how local people and groups are becoming the primary power sources for change. In fact, it appears that local groups are increasingly reversing the traditional flow of dominance from traditional global structures to local levels. The production of knowledge and exchange of knowledge among local groups is resulting in an emerging new model of practice, mixing perspectives and concepts from all areas and regions of the world (Mursic 2005; World Anthropologies Network Collective 2005).

Uquillas and Larreamendy (Chapter 2) discuss a new applied perspective on development practices in their innovative project in Ecuador. They explain how their project fosters the exchange of knowledge between indigenous peoples and anthropologists. The project, PRODEPINE, funded by the World Bank, is designed to build pro-poor forms of social capital and promote "ethno-development" among indigenous and Afro-Ecuadorian groups in the country. Since its inception in 1993, the project has given power to indigenous groups to mobilize local resources and to direct new ones to the poorest populations and have them manage these "in accordance with their own vision of what their problems and solutions are." The authors suggest that this new approach is redefining the meaning of tradition and modern knowledge as both are used to increase the resources and capital of the poor in Ecuador.

Yamskov (Chapter 6) discusses critical social and political issues involving power and preservation of local cultures in Russia. He participated in a major cultural preservation project in areas inhabited by ethnic groups, aimed at providing information about environmental pollution to the Russian government. In the past, the Soviet government developed policies that attempted to modernize certain ethnic groups in central Asia. Indeed, nomadic peoples in such regions often were forcibly settled in order to "modernize" their economic practices. National policies of the early 1990s, however, were aimed at environmental restoration and attempted to revitalize the traditional cultures of the Bruyats, a nomadic group located in one of these polluted areas. This represents a change of policy in Russia that incorporated anthropologists in order to enhance the power of local groups.

Jianmin and Young (Chapter 5) likewise review projects in China whose main objective is to promote cultural preservation and ecological, social, and economic development in rural areas predisposed to major impacts of globalization. Changes such as privatization and the introduction of capitalism are taking place even in the most remote communities. Local farmers are playing a significant role in defining and implementing new programs. The Chinese government employs anthropologists to monitor, record, and organize these communities to prepare or cope with these major changes.

In addition, el-Aswad (Chapter 4) summarizes changes in the configuration of knowledge and power between local groups and national development by stating that "anthropologists [in Egypt] have moved away from the classical view of development . . . to discuss the interrelationship between local and global forces and development processes." In his chapter, el-Aswad discusses how anthropologists are moving toward a conceptualization of research problems as "praxis" that are conceived multilaterally rather than being based on the hegemonic practices of international agencies and governments in the past.

While interdisciplinary applied/practicing projects have integrated research methods with other disciplines, the majority of the chapters, especially those on Ecuador, Canada, Portugal, Great Britain, Russia, and Egypt, discuss alternative and interdisciplinary methods being used in applied/practicing work. Use of these methods, such as participatory action research, participatory learning, and other action approaches, reflect the changing flow of knowledge and power from local to global. While some of the methods are not new (see, e.g., Peterson 1978 and Schensul 1986), what's new is the pervasive use of them on a global scale. Local groups are increasingly viewed as active participants in their own fate. They are participating in their own destiny through the utilization of these alternative methods. This trend is blurring the boundary between academic anthropology, applied/practicing anthropology, and their subjects, producing a convergence of previously divergent areas of the discipline.

The tensions reported in the chapters among agencies, organizations, and groups on the global, national, and local levels are encountered by most applied/practicing anthropologists. The conflicts generally center on decision-making power regarding the content and processes that govern the impact of change programs on local cultures. In 2005, in an effort to recognize and preserve local cultures, UNESCO (United Nations Educational, Scientific and Cultural Organization) approved a cultural diversity pact aimed to promote ethnic traditions and minority languages and protect local cultures from the negative effects of globalization (the U.S. did not support the pact). These negotiations between local peoples and national and international institutions and organizations generally focus on issues of knowledge, power, voice, and cultural boundaries, the second theme of the chapters.

The Power of Practicing Anthropology in Local/Global Contexts

A central issue discussed in a majority of the chapters involves the roles and power of applied/practicing anthropologists in mediating the struggle between global and local forces and the effect their work has on policy formulation. Although the literature has been replete for decades with articles discussing these issues, they continue to concern many practitioners of the discipline. Mahapatra (Chapter 4) states that anthropologists in India "have not been able to contribute significantly to the regeneration of the inherent capacities of the tribal people to fight for their interests and to claim their legitimate share in the polity and economy." Afonso (Chapter 10) reports that anthropologists working on applied projects in Portugal were powerless to influence policy; she cites several cases in which the contract agencies were only interested in ethnographic reports as "information producers" that would be used in any way they wished for solving social problems.

Other chapters focus on the changing situations of local peoples vis-à-vis national and international political and economic policies. Ervin and Holyoak (Chapter 9) point out several critical issues that need to be addressed in order to resolve issues relating to the situations of local peoples, including aboriginal self-government, land use, multiculturalism, migration, resettlement, and industrial development. One salient issue for practitioners centers on the role of anthropologists and other social scientists in deciding the fate of indigenous peoples. Who determines the fate of local groups—the groups themselves, or "outsiders" (including anthropologists), whose voices will be heard in policy deliberations about the preservation of local culture and knowledge?

Mahapatra (Chapter 4), Uquillas and Larreamendy (Chapter 2), Yamskov (Chapter 6), and el-Aswad (Chapter 3) suggest that anthropologists working for international organizations are having success in affecting social policies. In Ecuador, for example, bilateral and international cooperation agencies are paying more attention to the environmental and social dimensions of development. According to Uquillas and Larreamendy, the aim of these agencies "is not only to find ways to redistribute income but also to increase beneficiaries' participation in decision making, adapting development programs to local conditions, in social, cultural, and ecological terms." This approach, they argue, leads to a greater role for NGOs in development. Likewise, international agencies are becoming more involved in Egypt with attention increasingly being paid to local voices. El-Aswad states that in Egypt, foreign agencies give more attention to people's participation in implementing projects and thus are more interested in small projects with specific objectives that help local communities. Nonetheless, el-Aswad points out some of the more dramatic and less-than-positive consequences of globalization on the people of Egypt. He discusses ways in which anthropologists and other social scientists are working with governmental agencies to ameliorate some of these effects.

Several chapters make clear that the practice of anthropology certainly is not or should not be value-free. Contrasting his views with those of Radcliffe-Brown, Mahapatra states that he has:

> realized bitterly through this life that only research does not solve the problems, as policy makers and administrators in our country do not attach much weight to the findings and recommendations of the social scientists, including anthropologists, even when the same administrators and policy makers have sponsored relevant research or supported social science research institutes. Therefore, I have also come to realize that we have to fight for the right causes and against the wrong programmes and decisions with the added role of a social activist. Social science researchers are just not enough by themselves. [Mahapatra 1992:328]

In his chapter, he places these active roles of anthropologists within the framework of human rights. Emphasizing his perspective, he quotes Bose, a highly respected anthropologist, who states that "an Indian anthropologist should not be value-neutral, if he is to apply scientifically acquired anthropological knowledge."

Ervin and Holyoak (Chapter 9) make an equally strong argument for advocacy anthropology or a "value-added" dimension for practice. They suggest that the policy anthropologist should "take a stand" on the critical human issues that face all nations. Indeed, they argue that the only legitimate role for anthropologists in the globalization process is that of advocate and activist for our process designed to reproduce students who have the knowledge and skills both to take a stand on policy matters, and, second, a critique of the extreme relativist position that is currently dominating mainstream anthropology. Both of these solutions involve action on the part of academic and applied/practicing anthropologists. Indeed, most of the chapters indicate that where schisms between local and national/international agendas once existed, change toward some type of amelioration appears to be occurring within the global context.

Academic and Applied Transformations

The relationships between anthropologists who practice anthropology and those who work in traditional academic settings have, in the past, often been uneasy in many countries (Hill and Baba 2000). In 1997 Shore and Wright (Great Britain) discussed the awkward, if not often openly hostile, relationship that policy anthropologists have had with traditional anthropologists in Great Britain. They suggested that a bridge needed to be built between the two so they could get beyond the dualism that now exists in British anthropology. Shore and Wright (1997) suggested, along with most authors in our first global practice volume, that the usefulness of anthropological knowledge is being held hostage by the culture of the discipline itself. Fiske and Chambers (1997) labeled these relations a "dance of distance and embrace" between academic and practicing anthropology in the United States. In First World countries, the relationship for at least the past 50 years has been more "distance" than "embrace." The balance, however, is changing as we enter the 21st century, as is discussed in Chapter 11.

On the other hand, anthropological work in some countries often is framed in terms of alternative ideologies and context, one in which a schism between academic and applied/practicing anthropology is relatively mild or even nonexistent. Nahmad (1997) explores how anthropology in Mexico has a long tradition of making the results of its inquiry useful. Nahmad begins his article with a historic rendering of the life and work of Manuel Gamio, considered the first Mexican applied anthropologist. Gamio's concern for the economic and political conditions of the Indians led him to advocate their rights as a government administrator and as a university professor. Nahmad acknowledges Gamio's ties to American anthropology and credits the theoretical assumptions of Boas for Gamio's approaches to solving Indian problems in Mexico. Gamio's Mexican and Latin American Indianism greatly influenced the subsequent generation of Mexican anthropologists whose studies begin with the premise that their work was to be made useful for their country.

The history of anthropology in China, Russia, Mexico, Ecuador, and Egypt described in this volume demonstrates that the practice of anthropology in these countries dominates the discipline and, in effect, *is* the discipline. Earlier, Bozzoli (1997) argued that educators in Costa Rica choose to educate and enculturate students in the ethics and practice of public service. The goal of all research in the social sciences within Costa Rica is to solve basic human problems through the application of research results in practice. This holds true especially for anthropology because of its focus on the issues and problems of native peoples. She says that to be an anthropologist in Costa Rica is to be a practicing anthropologist. Forline (2004) makes similar points about anthropology in Brazil. He states that activities such as policy formulation, community development, and advocacy "have never been termed as a special component of Brazilian Anthropology. Thus, while unnamed, applied anthropology in Brazil has been part and parcel of the profession almost since its inception" (2004:2). As a consequence, in these countries, graduate education rarely makes a distinction between academic and applied anthropology, negating the tension that exists in Western (developed) countries (also, see Mursic 2005 and Ntarangwi 2005).

Anthropology in Israel is relatively young and much of the work can be categorized as applied. Nevertheless, practitioners have struggled to win acceptance and to organize as applied anthropologists. The discipline was established, for the most part, by British anthropologists who transferred their model of academic anthropology. Nonetheless, Shabtay and Kalifon (Chapter 7) argue that while applied anthropologists have had some trouble being recognized by their colleagues and that few anthropologists in academia identify themselves as applied anthropologists, the practice of anthropology in Israel has always been present. They guide us through a historical journey of Israel and demonstrate that because of the nation's unique history and geographical position, applied work began in Israel. Indeed, it is difficult to understand how Israeli anthropologists practice their vocation without understanding the context of their concern with solving human problems in their country. Issues of immigration, land settlement, the urban poor, and health have been the focus of applied research for several decades in Israel. Shabtay and Kalifon end their chapter by setting forth a future agenda for practicing anthropologists in Israel. They suggest that, in addition to new research problems, applied anthropologists should build upon their newly found strength and create more programs for the training of students. In addition, they suggest that a network between anthropologists who choose to practice outside academia and those who remain in the university setting needs to be established.

Afonso (Chapter 10) and Shabtay and Kalifon (Chapter 7) suggest that the gap between applied and academic anthropology is constructed in their countries. For example, Afonso points out that applied anthropology in Portugal is often linked with colonialism and, as a consequence, she suggests that it will take time for the discipline to overcome its negative image of application. Recently, however, she finds that more anthropologists are participating in applied research and, at the same time, maintaining positive relations with the academy. She states, "Although . . . applied anthropology in Portugal is still in its infancy, it is important to mention that a progressive openness toward a diversified range of topics, clearly motivated by practical problems of contemporary societies, . . . is emerging among academic anthropologists, even if they are being framed by theoretical concerns." Pink (Chapter 8) chronicles a similar trend in Great Britain due, for the most part, to increasing social problems generated by globalization. Anthropologists are now being recruited by governmental organizations to address these societal issues and problems. Pink also documents a "healthy presence in public and private sectors in Great Britain." However, the boundary between theoretical and applied/practicing continues to remain rather rigid as anthropology beyond the academy continues to have a low profile. These descriptions stand in sharp contrast to those descriptions of the history of practicing anthropology in countries with strong traditions of using anthropology to solve their problems.

Indeed, it is clear that the academic/applied/practice model in anthropology has not and does not exist in all nations of the world. Yamskov (Chapter 6) states that applied anthropology is present in Russia, just not in a Western sense. In countries where the Western model exists, the divide between academic and applied/practicing anthropology appears to be narrowing. Possible reasons for such convergence are discussed in Chapter 11.

Bridging the Disconnect of Colonizer and Colonized Nations

The final trend we delineate from the chapters concerns shifts in power distribution and the direction of the flow of power and knowledge between the countries we term colonizers and the ones we call colonized. Anthropology is a product of Western science. It has a long history in Europe, China, Russia, Canada, and the United States. These countries are considered the major players in the colonization (or neo-colonialization) of other countries in the world. They were the colonizers; they dominated or controlled, in some fashion, Africa, India, Asia, the Middle East, and Latin America (the colonized) for long periods in recent history. The colonized became the subjects of anthropological investigations; indigenous anthropologists in these countries were, for the most part, trained in anthropology or by anthropologists from the dominant nations. While the chapters in this volume do not represent all areas of the world, they do represent a broad spectrum of nations that were historically colonizers or colonized over the past three centuries. The differences across these nations, both in the issues that concern applied/practicing anthropology and in anthropology in general, appear to crystallize around the roots and power of the discipline within a specific country, as well as the international interests of a specific nation and its relationships with other nations.

Traditional academic anthropology became entrenched as a scholarly discipline in nations that used its knowledge to colonize and rule indigenous peoples in dominated countries in the 19th century. Until recently, a majority of anthropologists in the colonizer nations did not consider themselves to be applied/practicing anthropologists; their professional expectations were to study other peoples, mostly in other countries, and to publish the results of their findings. If indigenous peoples existed in a dominant nation, such as in the United States or Canada, they were studied in much the same fashion as in other nations. The chapters in this volume and the previous publication (Baba and Hill 1997) indicate that it is, for the most part, in the colonizer nations that the practice of anthropology often conflicts with academic anthropology. McDonald has recently pointed out that "as American academics' prestige goes up, their public engagement goes down" (2002:1). He cites Nader (1999), who suggests that, since the Civil War, American academics have shifted away from public engagement in the form of advocacy or applied research. It appears that the academic tradition became the dominant model in colonizer nations, separating itself from putting knowledge to work for the country. Anthropological work was not thought of as an obligation of citizenship; rather it was distinguished from public work (with the possible exception of the World War II era).

In contrast, many of the countries whose peoples were studied and had a history of colonization are guided by a model that assumes that the practice of anthropology is the main focus of the discipline. Anthropology in the colonized countries often developed under the rule of other nations. Using their indigenous peoples as subjects for study by foreigners became a point of contention in the colonized nations. This conflict eventually resulted in a different kind of anthropology—an anthropology in which the goal was not so much to publish (as is still the case in the mainstream of the colonizer nations) as to preserve and protect indigenous peoples or as an act of national citizenship. The usefulness of anthropological research for furthering the policies of governments was made apparent in the colonized nations. As these nations gained independence, the role of anthropology continued to be viewed as one of utility, but not in the service of outside forces. The discipline came to be structured differently than in colonizer nations. The conflict that exists between academic and applied anthropology failed to develop in nations such as Ecuador, Egypt, India, Brazil, Costa Rica, and Mexico.

While Russia and China have a history of colonizing other nations, their governments tightly controlled the work of their anthropologists, including their theoretical perspectives, and they mostly worked with groups within their own geographic region. The goal was to study and control people in their own territories. As a consequence, anthropology was, for the most part, applied, as in the colonizer countries, even after the renewal of the discipline in a modern sense. The Western model of splitting theoretical and applied anthropology generally was not adopted in these countries.

CHALLENGES TO TRADITIONAL KNOWLEDGE AND POWER

The local and global processes analyzed in this volume bring home the fact that the discipline is being structured and restructured just as all other groups in a world of time/space compression. If we have learned anything from our international colleagues, it is that all anthropology is practical in specific national contexts. Taking a lead from the practice of anthropology in non-Western nations, we find that the discipline is developing a more integrated and whole model—one that transcends 20th-century schisms.

Emerging data on global anthropology suggests that a new model of anthropological practice is emerging. Mahapatra (Chapter 4) makes this point clear in his chapter by stating that the Western model of anthropology is no longer dominant in India. He, along with other authors, discusses the prevalence of local, "homegrown" models for solving problems. Likewise, Ribeiro (2004, 2005) suggests that anthropologists now must consider the qualitative and quantitative growth of anthropological production outside traditional hegemonic centers. Hill has summarized these changes by stating that:

> The changing nature of the discipline is compelling new alliances and collaborations with the public, industry, governmental, and non-governmental organizations, and universities. Anthropology is reaching out to the discipline's traditional "subjects" as a resource for survival in the 21st century. Critical contracts with minority and international populations, other disciplines, policymakers, and the public are essential for the continuation and transformation of the anthropological imagination.... The resulting new forms of these collaborative efforts will create a type of "civil anthropology." [1999:278]

Specific consequences of the impact of global change on applied/practicing anthropology are discussed extensively in Chapter 11.

Finally, the chapters in this volume give us hope for the shared futures of applied/practicing and theoretical/academic anthropology. Our discipline is creating new hybrids and convergences as traditional, organizational, and functional distinctions blur, reversing the flow of knowledge and power within the discipline and among anthropology and the world.

REFERENCES

Baba, Marietta L.
   1999   Creating a New Community of Practicing Anthropologists. Human Organization 57(3):315–318.

Baba, Marietta L., and Carole E. Hill, eds.

    1997 The Global Practice of Anthropology. Studies in Third World Societies, No. 58. Williamsburg, VA: College of William and Mary Press.

Bozzoli de Wille, Maria Eugenia

    1997 Anthropology of Practice in Costa Rica and Central America. *In* The Global Practice of Anthropology. Marietta L. Baba and Carole E. Hill, eds. Pp. 81–95. Studies in Third World Societies, No 58. Williamsburg, VA: College of William and Mary Press.

Fischer, Michael M. J.

    2003 Emergent Forms of Life and the Anthropological Voice. Durham, NC: Duke University Press.

Fiske, Shirley J., and Erve Chambers

    1997 Status and Trends: Practice and Anthropology in the United States. *In* The Global Practice of Anthropology. Marietta L. Baba and Carole E. Hill, eds. Pp. 283–309. Studies in Third World Societies, No 58. Williamsburg, VA: College of William and Mary Press.

Forline, Louis

    2004 Applying Anthropology in Brazil: Professionalism and the Commitment to Social Action. Practicing Anthropology 26(3):2–5.

Hackenberg, Robert A., and Beverly H. Hackenberg

    2004 Notes Toward a New Future: Applied Anthropology in Century XXI. Human Organization 63:385–399.

Hill, Carole E.

    1999 Challenging Assumptions of Human Diversity: The Teaching Imagination in Anthropology. *In* The Social Worlds of Higher Education. Bernice A. Pescosolido and Ronald Aminzade, eds. Pp. 271–279. Thousand Oaks, CA: Pine Forge Press.

Hill, Carole E., and Marietta L. Baba, eds.

    2000 The Unity of Theory and Practice in Anthropology: Rebuilding a Fractured Synthesis. NAPA Bulletin 18. Washington, DC: American Anthropological Association.

Mahapatra, L. K.

    1992 Professional Reminiscences and Musings. *In* Science, Culture and Development: L. K. Mahapatra Felicitation Volume. N. K. Behura and K. C. Tripathy, eds. Bhubaneswar: Paragon Publishers.

McDonald, James H.

    2002 The Applied Anthropology Reader. Boston: Allyn and Bacon.

Mursic, Rajko

    2005 Slovene Ethnologists Standing at the Crossroads. Anthropology News 46:8, 10.

Nader, Laura

    1999 Thinking Public Interest Anthropology, 1890's–1990's. General Anthropology 5(2):1, 7–9.

Nahmad, Salomon

    1997 Mexican Applied Anthropology: From Founder Mario Gamio to Contemporary Movements. *In* The Global Practice of Anthropology. Marietta Baba and Carole Hill, eds. Pp. 229–244. Williamsburg, VA: College of William and Mary Press.

Ntarangwi, Mwenda

    2005 African Anthropology Struggling Along. Anthropology News 46:9.

Peterson, John H., Jr.

    1978 The Changing Role of an Applied Anthropologist. *In* Applied Anthropology in America. Elizabeth M. Eddy and William L. Partridge, eds. Pp. 165–181. New York: Columbia University Press.

Ribeiro, Gustavo

    2004 Practicing Anthropology in Brazil: A Retrospective Look at Two Time Periods. Practicing Anthropology 26(3):6–10.

    2005 A Different Global Scenario in Anthropology. Anthropology News 46(7):5–6.

Robertson, Roland

    1992 Globalization: Social Theory and Global Culture. London: Sage.

Schensul, Stephen L.

    1987 Perspectives on Collaborative Research. *In* Corroborative Research and Social Change. Donald Stull and Jean Schensul, eds. Pp. 211–219. Boulder CO: Westview Press.

Shore, Cris, and Susan Wright

1997 Colonial Gaze to Critique of Policy: British Anthropology in Policy and Practice. *In* The Global Practice of Anthropology. Marietta L. Baba and Carole E. Hill, eds. Pp. 139–154. Studies in Third World Societies, No 58. Williamsburg, VA: College of William and Mary Press.

World Anthropologies Network Collective

2005 Establishing Dialogue among International Anthropological Communities. Anthropology News 46:8–9.

APPLIED ANTHROPOLOGY IN ECUADOR: DEVELOPMENT, PRACTICE, AND DISCOURSE

Jorge E. Uquillas and Pilar Larreamendy
The World Bank

Applied anthropology in Ecuador has been influenced by both global and local contexts, particularly the development paradigms which have been in fashion in the last four or five decades and the political orientation and consequent academic curriculum of universities offering academic training in this field. Using the concept of "localized modernities," this chapter analyzes how anthropology has contributed to the development process in Ecuador, a country characterized by a great social and cultural diversity. Responding to official efforts to build a unified nation-state and to integrate indigenous peoples under the banner of "indigenism," the practice of anthropology in the country initially focused on learning about the socioeconomic and cultural characteristics of indigenous communities and helping them to access some basic public goods and services. However, in more recent times, as a result of a changing international context favorable to the recognition of indigenous peoples rights and to the high degree of social organizations and mobilization of indigenous peoples, anthropologist have adapted their discourse and practice, largely becoming allies of indigenous peoples in their efforts not only to maintain their own cultures but also to participate in the political process. The case of PRODEPINE is presented as an example of how applied social scientists have contributed to strengthen indigenous peoples' social organization, as well as to improve their access to land and territories and key financial resources. Key Words: Ecuador, development, localized modernities, indigenism, applied anthropology

Current perspectives of applied anthropology are related to development practices on both the global and local scale. Our analysis is based on information of localized practices and discourses in the field of social sciences, which is redefining the meanings of traditional and modern knowledge and technology. Not all anthropologists become academics but all have academic training, whereas the development discourses are influenced by international institutions and localized practices. Therefore applied anthropology is determined by local contexts. We pretend to rethink anthropological theory and methodology in the context of applied development. Therefore, we focus on how anthropology understands development research and implementation, and the implications

NAPA Bulletin 25, pp. 14–34, ISBN 1-931303-28-2. © 2006 by the American Anthropological Association. All rights reserved.
Permissions to photocopy or reproduce article content via www.ucpress.edu/journals/rights.htm.

when promoting "modernization," "development," and "poverty reduction." This raises the question of to what extend applied anthropology is one of the results of the globalization process and to what extent it is the result of local processes.

This chapter is a reflection of two social scientists, an anthropologist and a sociologist, engaged in academic work and applied development experience in Ecuador. We will discuss the development of applied anthropology in Ecuador within a global context. The theme of local/global development will frame our documentation of the current achievements and challenges of local applied anthropology in a multicultural context increasingly linked to globalization. The chapter begins by providing the conceptual framework for our developmental work in Ecuador including a discussion of the relationship between anthropology and development. The subsequent section contains a brief review of anthropology in Ecuador. This proceeds with reference to the academic curriculum of both the Universidad Católica del Ecuador and the Universidad Politécnica Salesiana. We analyze the trajectory of anthropology in Ecuador including the findings of qualitative data collected through a survey among anthropologists working as academics and as development practitioners. The following section provides information about Ecuadorian indigenous peoples' emergence as social actors, and the public policy environment. The last section is a case study of the Ecuadorian Indigenous and Afro-Ecuadorian Development Project (PRODEPINE), focusing on the influence of and implications for applied anthropology.

THEORETICAL FRAMEWORK: LOCAL AND GLOBALIZED PROCESS IN DEVELOPMENT

The notion of "localized modernities" is presented as a way to analyze how ethnography and anthropology contribute to development research and practice (Arce and Long 2000:3). This leads us to consider two main questions: first, how the process of exchange of knowledge between indigenous peoples and anthropologists takes place, and second, how applied anthropology influences the international development agendas and practices.

According to Arce and Long (2000), since the 1970s, international nongovernmental organizations (NGOs) have supported community organizations to improve the local socioeconomic conditions, thus redefining their development agenda. In the 1990s, participatory approaches were used to ensure sustainable poverty reduction and community development. The local partners of development were community-based organizations and local NGOs. This holistic view of poverty reduction implied the involvement of local knowledge and skills to create conditions for accurate research and to define ways to link advocacy and local community leadership. Anthropology, which has historically been instrumental in providing heuristic explanations of local communities, is capturing their distinctive knowledge and helping to interpret the interaction between local and global knowledge and experiences.

In Ecuador, the array of methods and tools used by anthropological analysis is not only helping the analysis of the events occurring in the field within a culturally diverse population but also responding to the demands of global development. The increasing participation of indigenous peoples in politics has been closely related to the emerging international standards of indigenous rights and sustainable development. International development agencies, governments, and academic institutions have become the domain of anthropological practice. In addition, applied anthropologists are involved in the formulation of indigenous peoples' political plans and the redefinition of a representative democracy.

Standard interpretations of the concept of development carry implications of desirable social, economic, and political change. Whereas traditional development practice was monocultural, implying the predominance of some values and traits over others, the new perspective considers culture as a dimension of development that is no longer an obstacle but an asset. Failures of development efforts in the Third World have demonstrated the resistance by non-Western societies to imposed development patterns.

Social scientists seek to understand the social and environmental issues linked to development. Concurrently, bilateral and international cooperation agencies, which originally gave priority to technical and economic factors, are currently paying greater attention to the environmental and social dimensions of development. Their aim is not only to find ways to redistribute income but also to increase beneficiaries' participation in decision making, adapting development programs to local conditions, in social, cultural, and ecological terms. This new orientation of development assistance has meant less work with government agencies and greater reliance on NGOs. Ecuador was not an exemption to this trend. Between 1980 and 1994 it showed an increase in the number of NGOs working on development from 51 to 376, influencing the development discourse and practice and gradually involving social scientists as part of their teams. The process of an increased number of NGOs working on development was concomitant to the emergence of indigenous organizations, a process that will be analyzed in the following section.

ANTHROPOLOGY IN ECUADOR

Ecuador is a country characterized by ethnic, social, economic, and regional diversity. From its very beginning, anthropology in Ecuador faced the difficult task of explaining and giving meaning to these diversities in the context of an official nation-building objective. In this respect, we can say that anthropology in Ecuador has always been "applied." In any case, the history of Ecuadorian anthropology and its "application" cannot be fully described and understood based solely on the relationships between the state and the indigenous populations. It has to be also interpreted considering the international political context.

The Precursors: "Americanism" and Studies outside Academia

The history and development of the discipline of anthropology, especially applied anthropology, in Ecuador is related to other trends in Latin America and to their relationship with European and North American anthropology. Until the early 1950s, social thought in Ecuador developed outside academia but close to the political context influenced by the above-mentioned nation-building objective, where integration was the predominant idea. This period, which spans from the end of the 19th century until the early 1950s, is consistent with the wider movement defined as "Americanism" or to be more precise "Latin Americanism." While Asian and Oriental cultures were the object of academic studies, the reflection on the Americas and their cultures was delegated to the several "societies" (of history, geography, etc.). These societies, whose origins dated back to the 18th century, were not only think tanks but also planning agencies for the expansion of colonialism. The Americanists' profile combined the roles of academics as well as those of explorers, travelers, and government agents; in any case, Americanists were producers of abundant and detailed ethnographic data. This trend of studies made itself visible through the institutionalized organization of Congresses. They progressively became the ideal framework of organization and legitimization of an anthropological knowledge that resided outside the universities and was closer to the centers of power and political decision making.

In Ecuador, this period witnessed the constitution of the Ecuadorian Society of the American Historical Studies and its Boletín de la Sociedad de Estudios Históricos Americanos, an institution that in 1920 was converted into the National Academy of History; it was the first official institution related to anthropology as a discipline. In the postwar period, Ecuador increasingly participated in international events, and social research moved gradually toward the inclusion of indigenous peoples in national development and in shaping the national identity.

The Post–World War II Context and the Rise of *Indigenism*

The production of anthropological knowledge was influenced by three important and wider processes: (1) a systematic treatment of what was considered the "indigenous problem," (2) the institutionalization of a national culture, and (3) the inclusion of social sciences in universities. Meanwhile, the intellectual center of reference moved from Europe to the United States and new cultural actors appeared: Intellectual elites from civil society were substituted by state intellectuals and culture planners. The first professional anthropologists made their appearance, and the universities and their centers of specialization assumed the task that once belonged to "societies."

A comprehensive and exhaustive history of the relationships between Latin American states and indigenous peoples is beyond the scope of this chapter. However, it is important to underline that the international context, with the appearance of the United Nations and other international organizations, plays a fundamental role in shaping the identity of Ecuadorian anthropology as the discipline par excellence related to indigenous people. The organization of the Indigenist Congress of Patzcuaro (Mexico 1945) is a landmark in the history of anthropology all over Latin America. During this Congress, the Inter-American Institute for Indigenous Policy (Instituto Indigenista Interamericano) was created. Its Ecuadorian branch opened in 1946. Its purpose was to support the systematic and institutional attempt by the Ecuadorian Government to integrate indigenous peoples within modernization and development programs.

In the 1950s the Ecuadorian Institute of Anthropology and Geography (IEAG) was created as a private, nonprofit organization supported by the Government; its goal was to supply professional services to governmental initiatives aimed at the indigenous and peasant populations and to provide state interventions with research and field data. The IEAG has supported the creation of the Peasant Social Security, and between 1951 and 1952 it designed several plans of intervention in indigenous communities; it also created the Ethnographic Museum, and in 1956 it began publishing the periodical *Llacta*.

In 1954 the Andean Mission started its work of development in Ecuador, where it was organized by a Commission of the United Nations.[1] Parallel to the above, there was another intervention openly directed toward the study of rural and indigenous communities, characterized by the presence and active involvement of the state. Its institutional body was the Casa de la Cultura Ecuatoriana (CCE), created in 1946 following a Mexican model. The CCE promoted those cultural expressions considered as autochthonous and conforming to the "national being." This trend of study is based on the concept of folklore and essential to these studies was the work and research conducted in Ecuador by the Brazilian linguist Paulo Carvalho Neto. This trend considered indigenous traditions and customs as the "authentic" roots of the national culture. This influence is evident starting from 1956, when the Ecuadorian Institute of Folklore was created. This institute included a multidisciplinary team and soon established itself as a real cultural movement at the national level that for a long period determined the public "taste" around the national identity.

After World War II, North American universities were organized around the category of "area studies," that is to say according to a geographic area that presented linguistic, historical, and cultural coherence. Modernization and development were the dominant topics in the social sciences and research was a tool for intervention. Several institutions or centers of Latin American studies were opened, usually ascribed to different faculties of social science. These centers were highly specialized and put a strong emphasis on field research. Their impact is still evident in the Andean region. In Ecuador, its influence, in the 1970s and 1980s, created a tremendous increase in the production of ethnographic indigenous studies on the Andes and Amazon; this partly explains the massive presence of foreign researchers in the country.

In Ecuador, the first attempt to formalize the teaching of anthropology at the university level was made in 1965 with the creation of the School of Sociology and Anthropology in the main state university (Universidad Central del Ecuador). This school was part of a new College of Basic Sciences, created under agreement with the University of Pittsburgh and whose objective was to start a pilot experience along the lines of U.S. universities and colleges. This model, associated with the USAID Alliance of Progress, was strongly opposed by the Ecuadorian Federation of University Students and was eventually closed. The School of Sociology and Anthropology, which later was reduced to teaching sociology, had a significant influence on a generation of social scientists in Ecuador.

A formal Faculty of Anthropology was established in 1971 by the Catholic University of Quito, and since 1976 it has maintained a regular and specialized program of anthropological studies. In 1980 the degree of archaeology was established by the Escuela Superior Politécnica del Litoral (ESPOL), with a corresponding Center of Archaeological and Anthropological Studies (CEAA). The establishment of these two formal degrees marks the start of anthropology as a discipline in the country.

In the 1940s and 1950s the United States was actively engaged in starting and leading a process of modernization within the Latin American countries. Regional particularities—especially as far as indigenous cultures were concerned—were to be respected wherever they did not constitute an obstacle to national development. This same attitude was adopted, in the 1940s and 1950s, by several Latin American governments which promoted programs of applied anthropology—of course with different characteristics—related to indigenous populations. This was especially strong in Mexico, where the term *indigenismo* was coined to refer to this type of policy.

Modern *indigenism* can thus be defined in this respect as the whole of governmental policies aimed at integrating indigenous people within the national society; the ultimate goal of these policies was the constitution of a nation-state with a single and strong national identity. The task of "integrating" indigenous peoples was given to anthropologists.[2] However, and unlike the case of Mexico (which is considered a leader within Latin America as far as indigenist policies are concerned), in Ecuador an official, coherent, and steady indigenist policy has never been adopted by any government. Therefore, anthropologists have not been particularly active in politics. It was not until the early 1980s that applied anthropology began to gain a wider influence in the country, especially because anthropologists had been very close to the indigenous peoples; they had become involved with indigenous daily lives and with their political and ethnic claims, and they strongly supported indigenous peoples' efforts to organize themselves, leading to an ethnic movement, which in 1990 made its sudden appearance on the national political scene. In this context, anthropologists' main contribution has been to redefine the relationships between the state and the indigenous movement, as well as to improve the design and implementation of development programs within indigenous areas.

Indeed, the 1980s witnessed the consolidation of professional anthropology in the country. Ecuador started to be considered as a privileged site of "fieldwork" by students coming from European and North American universities. Their academic production was not visible in the country, since it was published in their home countries; however, their presence helped to mobilize local institutions and resources. Additionally, since 1980, a fundamental role has been played by the Central Bank of Ecuador, according to the belief that state entities have the responsibility to preserve the national cultural and archaeological heritage through museums and publications.

Modern Indigenism and the Emergence of "Applied" Anthropology

In the 1980s, the strong link between institutionalized anthropology and indigenous ethnic and political claims became evident, and development projects became increasingly concerned with indigenous communities. This decade was marked by social unrest and by the organization of indigenous people, which reached its climax with the 1990 indigenous uprising. In this decade, several anthropologists and other professionals in social sciences actively committed to influence the state policy toward indigenous peoples and formed numerous social organizations. The involvement of anthropologists in this decade took the shape of concrete initiatives with indigenous peoples.

One such fundamental initiative, if not the most important, was the constitution of the Institute of Applied Anthropology in 1987, converted in 1995 into the School of Applied Anthropology of the Universidad Politécnica Salesiana. This determined a change in the history of applied anthropology. Since 1975 in Ecuador, prior to launching the School of Applied Anthropology, the Salesians had the leading indigenous editorial work, Abya Yala, a publishing house of ethnographic research and indigenous peoples' topics. Abya Yala's aim was to support indigenous organizations by promoting publications and dissemination of ethnographic and ethnological research of both local and foreign anthropologists. These publications also included bilingual texts and documents intended to reach wider audiences among indigenous peoples. Abya Yala promoted an impressive exchange among anthropologists, linguistics, and missionaries that also contributed to the enhancement of international networks of indigenous leaders, scholars, researchers, and development practitioners.[3]

Anthropologists in Ecuador have generally worked as professionals outside universities, mainly because the socioeconomic conditions of the country have not allowed them to make a living only as academics. Yet the academic programs of study did not openly prepare students for a job other than research. The formal constitution of the School of Applied Anthropology means that for the first time in the country, an academic institution designs programs of study openly preparing anthropologists to work as professionals outside the academic milieu and to be actively committed to changing the unequal structures of society. In other words, anthropology was institutionalization as an "applied" discipline, in contrast with purely academic approaches.

Initially, this commitment means a strong emphasis on indigenous populations and development projects. Through the years, the emphasis of the School of Applied Anthropology has notably changed toward the concept of "culture" and a wider application of a cultural perspective to other nonindigenous fields of study and application, such as urban contexts, institutions, political parties, study of peers, as well as the recognition that the concepts of "diversity" and "alternality" are not relegated to indigenous populations only, but they equally apply to the national society as such.

Interestingly, in Ecuador, the two Schools of Anthropology have been supported by the Catholic Church: the Jesuit Order (Universidad Católica del Ecuador [PUCE] in the mid-1970s) and the Salesian Order (Universidad Politécnica Salesiana [UPS] in the late 1990s). This fact, which is not coincidental, is telling us that since the 1970s the academic approach to indigenous studies has been of vital concern to the Catholic Church. The Catholic Church's interest in anthropology has largely been related to the liberation theology and the educational methods of Paulo Freire addressing the poorest and least advantaged people in society.

The Jesuits (PUCE) put a significant emphasis on Marxist theory to define the indigenous condition. Indigenous peoples were seen primarily as peasants and the analysis of indigenous "religiosity" was part of the curriculum. The peasant condition of the indigenous peoples defined as a class condition entailed the indigenous "mode of production." This involved looking at indigenous knowledge and culture, as was the case of the influential study of indigenous peoples in the highlands (páramos) and their integrated management of ecological floors (Salomon 1981). A number of professors were committed to the leadership of the emerging indigenous organizations that were demanding primarily land rights in the central highland provinces.

Despite the coincidences of the two orders that resulted in a sustained support for the formation of professionals in anthropology, there are distinct perspectives on what could be considered as producing scientific knowledge. Whereas on the one hand the PUCE dismisses applied anthropology as unscientific, on the other hand the UPS argues that to produce scientific knowledge requires addressing the historical excluded ("others") and providing them with the instruments and methodologies to work in the field. This is an unresolved debate and there are gravitating questions about whether applied anthropology is "less scientific" than the nonapplied version or not.

However, it is important to highlight that for all the anthropologists interviewed for this chapter, graduated students of both universities, the main opportunities offered by the local market are in development projects implemented by governmental and nongovernmental institutions. The practice of anthropology in development means a focus on social issues, particularly the satisfaction of basic needs (in terms of health, education, housing, nutrition) (interviews by the authors, December 2003). In the practice of anthropology of development, social scientists are critical analysts. Thus, they carry out studies such as (1) the interrelationship among the environment, the sociocultural milieu, markets, public policies, and technological systems; (2) the economic, cultural, and social impacts of development; and (3) participatory approaches to policy making and the building of a more equitable society (Uquillas and DeWalt 1989).

There are multiple examples of anthropologists working for multilateral and bilateral development agencies. Just to exemplify the types of studies, we have the following: the indigenous traditional justice system, the production of baseline studies of rural development (for the Inter-American Development Bank [IDB]), and social diagnostics for the design and evaluation of projects (World Bank projects). The interviews confirmed that they are working in or have worked in development projects, and among the most cited were for the Netherlands (SNV), Spain (Agency of Spanish Cooperation), Canada, Germany (GTZ), Switzerland (COSUDE), and the United States (USAID). Workers for multilateral and bilateral agencies also include post-graduated professors (e.g., FLACSO and Universidad Andina). The anthropologists working for the governmental institutions are also numerous; this is the case for those working for the National Council for the Development of Nationalities and Peoples of Ecuador (CODENPE), the Ministry of Tourism producing a diagnostic for eco- and ethno-tourism, the Ministry of Social Affairs, and the Women's National Council, among others. Anthropologists have also supported legal and policy reforms such as the case of the Constitutional Reform (1998), which recognized the rights of indigenous and Afro-Ecuadorian peoples and nationalities, and policies on land titling for ancestral populations.

According to the interviews, national and international NGOs offer work mainly as consultants in the fields of education, health, services provision, local income-generating activities, environment, and development. NGOs generally have few anthropologists as part of their staff and contract consultants according to the demands of the projects. According to the testimonies gathered in the field, social scientists are no longer perceived as "theorists" but rather as individuals capable of providing a more effective delivery of development within multidisciplinary teams. Moreover the increasing number of professionals of different ethnic groups provides bridges between the beneficiaries and development practitioners (interviews by the authors, December 2003 to January 2004).

In sum, the emergence and enforcement of applied anthropology has been an overlapping process that responds to local demands of the increasingly organized community members and the need to have multidisciplinary teams capable of a more efficient delivery of development products. Global development agendas have influenced the types of local jobs offered to anthropologists. Local events such as the years of political unrest along with the prominence of the indigenous social movement have, in turn, led to a gradual interest of governments to institutionalize the indigenous and Afro-Ecuadorian development agendas (Larreamendy 2003).

INDIGENOUS PEOPLES AND DEVELOPMENT POLICIES

In Ecuador, indigenous and Afro-descendant peoples together represent almost 20 percent of the population, although estimates vary widely.[4] There are 13 officially designated, non-Hispanic ethnic groups or nationalities in Ecuador.[5] The country's rural indigenous and Afro-Ecuadorian population is concentrated in 288 of the country's 966 *parroquias* (parishes, the smallest division in the country). The largest nationality comprises the highland Quichua-speakers, who constitute more than 90 percent of Ecuador's indigenous peoples. Ecuadorian indigenous peoples, as those in the rest of Latin America, have faced struggles due to their historical marginal position (Albó 1994; Hendricks 1988). The emergence of indigenous organizations and the underpinning revitalization of indigenous ethnicity has been the result of overlapping processes where other social actors such as NGOs and the Catholic Church have had a critical role (Botasso 1982; Breton 2001; Brysk 1994; Lehman 1990; Muratorio 1981).

State policy regarding indigenous peoples has not been clearly defined and has numerous ambiguities, but certain general trends may be distinguished. Since the creation of Ecuador in 1830, attempts have been made to integrate indigenous peoples into the general society by promoting acculturation. However, at times certain forms of social exclusion persisted, such as limitations on indigenous collective property, citizenship rights (for example, by not allowing illiterate persons to vote or be elected), land ownership, and the right to maintain their own forms of government.

Since the 1980s there has been a gradual shift toward greater openness to the interests and demands of indigenous peoples. Although agrarian legislation has many gaps, significant progress has been made in acknowledging indigenous land rights. Bilingual education has been legitimized, with autonomous management by indigenous organizations (Selverston-Scher 2001). Opportunities have been created for the training and legal recognition of second- and third-tier organizations, from community associations to provincial federations to regional and national organizations. The 1998 National Constitution states that the country is multicultural and recognizes a broad array of collective rights for those self-identified as indigenous peoples and nationalities, clarifying previously recognized rights to ancestral lands and separate forms of cultural identity and self-governance, including the establishment of indigenous "jurisdictions" in areas of their domain. Moreover, the inclusion of indigenous people in national society in the context of cultural diversity is increasingly a reality.

Despite having been known as the "lost decade" because of the low growth and consequent poverty increase, the 1980s saw an increase in the number and influence of development programs managed by indigenous organizations (Bebbington et al. 1992). The reduction of state intervention on rural development was supplanted by NGOs with development agendas that took into account participatory and self-development perspectives (Martínez 2000). During the 1980s and 1990s the generalized detrimental living conditions in Ecuador coincided with a gradual emergence of indigenous peoples as prominent social and political actors. By the early 1990s 35 percent of Ecuador's population lived in poverty and another 17 percent was highly vulnerable to poverty.[6] Overall, the relationship between poverty, household characteristics, and social indicators varies considerably both across and within regions and areas.

The above-described process overlaps with the emphasis attributed to the "Indian condition," which has shifted from being framed by social class toward a focus on ethnicity. The indigenous demands have been focused on the recognition of "multiethnicity" and "multicultural" demands. The indigenous discourse is a "demonstration of ethnicity in action" (Diskin 1991:157) seeking to pose indigenous demands and to alter the relationship between the state and the ethnic groups or, in other words, seeking social change. The indigenous demands, although focused on the recognition of cultural distinctiveness such as bilingual and intercultural education, implied the redefinition of citizenship and participative democracy. In other words, the indigenous demands were renovating a citizenship definition that involved the revitalization of a collective ethnicity framed by the daily life practices (Escobar 1995a, 1995b). Development programs entailed from productive to socio-organizational community practices and that formulated a new "indigenous political discourse." It is in this context that indigenous development is posed as different from past development practices.

The emergent indigenous movement brought a concern for ethnic collective rights and politics of identities, and engaging the cultural became crucial to indigenous politics (Radcliffe 1998). The recognition of distinct indigenous cultures within a nation evidences that there are different national identities and responses to development means and contents. Culture and power are interrelated and reaction to the status quo implies a need to redefine indigenous development. What is indigenous development? Does it differ from other development?

Social Organization of Indigenous Peoples

In the mid-1990s, Convention 169 of the United Nation's International Labor Organization (ILO) was ratified. This international document has been the threshold for the 1998 Constitutional reform which stated that Ecuador is multicultural and recognizes the collective rights for those self-identified as indigenous peoples and nationalities, clarifying previously recognized rights to ancestral lands and separate forms of cultural identity and self-governance, including the establishment of indigenous "jurisdictions" (*circumscripciones territoriales*).

Currently in Ecuador there are about 2,500 grassroots indigenous organizations (communes, centers, and cooperatives) at the community level. Historically, the first effort was to build community-level organizations, which in turn organized into higher-tier associations or local and regional federations in a pyramidal scheme, ending with the formation of national federations. Illustrative of this trend is the case of the Shuar, who in the early 1960s organized at the community level as "centers" and then formed second-tier organizations called "associations," and these in turn created the Shuar Federation. The Shuar Federation joined other ethnic federations in the eastern lowlands to form the Confederation of Amazon Indigenous Peoples of Ecuador (CONFENIAE), and this in turn joined forces with highland and coastal federations and organized the National Council of Ecuador's Indigenous Nationalities (CONAIE).[7]

After the May 2002 elections, the Pachacutik Indigenous Movement political party and their allies gained control of 26 municipalities (12 headed by indigenous mayors) and increased representation in the municipal councils (*consejos cantonales*) and parish councils (*juntas parroquiales*). They have built on the experience of Guamote, a municipal government controlled by indigenous peoples since 1992, which has evolved into a model of indigenous governance (*poderes locales*). Guamote has been able to coordinate actions among its local indigenous federations, to have a municipal government under indigenous control, to have a local development committee, and to create its unique version of an indigenous lawmaking body, the Indigenous Parliament (see also Bebbington and Perreault 1999; Torres 2000).

The following section focuses on the analysis of a development project which shows the case of a project financed by a multilateral agency where the influence of the ethnodevelopment is evident in the entire project cycle.

THE INDIGENOUS AND AFRO-ECUADORIAN PEOPLES DEVELOPMENT PROJECT: A CASE STUDY OF ANTHROPOLOGY IN ACTION

The Indigenous and Afro-Ecuadorian Peoples Development Project is financed by a loan from the World Bank and the International Fund for Agricultural Development (WB PRODEPINE, 1998–2004). This project illustrates how social scientists, particularly anthropologists, contribute to development as cultural brokers, as development agents, and as critical analysts of the process of development (for more details, see Uquillas and Van Nieuwkoop 2003). The project is the first stand-alone investment operation financed by the World Bank that focuses exclusively on indigenous peoples and other ethnic minorities. It is the first time that Ecuador borrowed resources specifically for investments to benefit poor indigenous and Afro-Ecuadorian populations, channeling resources directly through indigenous organizations with a minimal role of the government. It is also the first time that indigenous federations and the Ecuadorian government implemented "development with identity," or "ethnodevelopment." This vision builds on the positive qualities of indigenous cultures and societies—such as their sense of ethnic identity, close attachment to ancestral land, and capacity to mobilize labor, capital, and other resources for shared goals—to promote local employment and growth. PRODEPINE has invested in local capacity building, small-scale demand-driven rural subprojects, land tenure regularization, cultural heritage activities, and institutional strengthening of the official institution dealing with indigenous peoples.[8]

Enabling Conditions for Project

By the mid-1990s a combination of factors led to the establishment of PRODEPINE. First, indigenous peoples' level of organization and capacity for social mobilization had grown substantially. Second, in 1994 the Government of Ecuador (GoE) created the National Secretariat of Indigenous and Ethnic Minorities (SENAIME) and initiated a series of contacts with donors to request support for SENAIME and its proposed operations to benefit indigenous peoples and Afro-Ecuadorians. Third, partly in anticipation of the United Nations International Decade of the World's Indigenous People, in 1993 the World Bank started its own Indigenous Peoples Development Initiative. Thus, the institution was relatively well positioned to respond to requests such as that from Ecuador. Fourth, the existence of a strong ethnicity–poverty relationship as found by the Bank Poverty Assessment (1995) stressed the need for a targeted poverty intervention focusing on Ecuador's indigenous and Afro-Ecuadorian population. The fact that other rural development projects proved to have difficulties reaching out to this population further emphasized the need for a new approach.

Indigenous Organizations as Executing Agencies

While the national-level indigenous organizations were legitimate representatives of the project's intended beneficiary population, it was recognized that their particular strength was in the political and public policy arena. Given the project's orientation toward generating direct benefits for indigenous communities, it adopted a strategy of also working directly with second-tier indigenous organizations (as stated previously, under this definition were a broad range of organizations linking communities with the national federations), which are usually based in small urban or rural towns accessible to their community-level member organizations. Since second-tier organizations have a closer relationship with indigenous communities, they are in a better position to know local needs and demands, are inclined to focus on providing services to their members rather than merely representing them politically, and in general have a more pragmatic agenda. During implementation, executing agencies included not only second-tier organizations but also some third-tier organizations and even a few municipalities where indigenous mayors and councillors have been elected recently.

This strategy of making the project known at the regional level, including the second-tier organizations in project preparation, and aligning project design to their pragmatic agenda created a substantial "pull" effect of second-tier organizations speaking in favor of the project at relevant meetings and forums. Because the credibility of the national indigenous organizations depends to a large extent on effective linkages with their bases, the opinions of second-tier organizations tend to be taken into account by national leaders. Reaching out to the second-tier organizations created a more deeply rooted base of support for the project and reduced the risk of facing politically motivated decisions by a few indigenous leaders.

Targeting Ethnicity and Poverty

One of the first challenges of the project was to identify the indigenous peoples and Afro-Ecuadorians who were the intended beneficiaries. Two major questions that needed to be answered in terms of inclusion of groups were (1) whether the mestizo population living in the same areas would be part of the project's target population and (2) how to settle the politically contentious issue of defining who is indigenous.

To tackle these questions, the project adopted an approach that combined quantitative methods and geographic location with the notion of self-identification and community affiliation with second-tier organizations. Census information on indigenous and Afro-Ecuadorian population at the parroquia level was crossed with data on poverty (an index of unsatisfied basic needs) to obtain figures on level of poverty by ethnicity. Additional information was gathered in the field, particularly self-identification of communities as either indigenous or Afro-Ecuadorian and membership in a second-tier indigenous organization. This information was then represented in an indigenous poverty map.

The quantitative analysis gave an idea of which parroquias had a majority indigenous and Afro-Ecuadorian population and which ones had a significant minority presence of those groups. Once the parroquias were known, second-tier indigenous organizations could be identified that were operating in them. The project would then form an alliance with these organizations for implementation purposes and in so doing would accept the membership eligibility criteria of the organization as the basis for targeting the intended beneficiary population in that particular parroquia. Depending on these locally defined criteria, the project would include the mestizo population to the extent that they were members of the second-tier organizations. Through this analysis the project targeted about 815,000 people who were members of indigenous and Afro-Ecuadorian communities in rural areas and around 180 second-tier organizations operating in the 288 parroquias in which indigenous and Afro-Ecuadorian populations are concentrated.[9]

Ethnodevelopment and Social Capital

Social exclusion, economic deprivation, and political marginalization are sometimes perceived as the predominant characteristics of Ecuador's indigenous peoples. But as they often remind outsiders, indigenous peoples are also characterized by strong positive attributes, particularly their high level of social capital. Much of this type of social capital is manifest at the level of the traditional community through informal networks of reciprocity and is strongly survival-oriented. The challenge is to mobilize or build upon this type of relationship for development purposes as well as more formal organizations that often require different types of collective action and hierarchies.

Therefore, besides language and their own sense of ethnic identity, the distinctive features of indigenous peoples include solidarity and social unity (reflected in strong social organizations). Moreover, they are characterized by a well-defined geographical concentration and attachment to ancestral lands, a rich cultural patrimony, and other customs and practices distinct from those of Ecuador's national society (c.f. Salomon 1981), which bears a strong Western influence. There are also some negative traits embedded in indigenous culture such as political and religious factionalism and particular forms of gender inequality. Nevertheless, the project aimed to mobilize this social capital, based on these characteristics, as a platform for ethnodevelopment (Van Nieuwkoop and Uquillas 2000).

The ultimate aim of the project is to generate results and impacts that directly benefit indigenous and Afro-Ecuadorian communities in Ecuador. In order to achieve this, the project finances investments to improve the stock human capital, financial and physical capital, and environmental capital at the disposal of these communities. In the process, it expects to build social capital in at least three different ways. First, there is already considerable social capital; the other forms of capital can complement it effectively (i.e., strengthening preexisting water-users' associations). Second, when social capital is weak, these additional resources, which in most cases are not individual goods, promote collective management and solidarity among members.[10] Third, when the social capital preexistent in traditional indigenous communities is different from and not necessarily contiguous with the type needed in modern administrative/economic and even social infrastructure management, the project stimulates the gradual extension of the original social capital into new fields, levels, or types of cooperation (e.g., women's solidarity credit associations, which have no equivalent in traditional Andean communities).

To ensure relevant use of these various types of capital, the project relies on participatory planning as a mechanism to facilitate an effective demand-driven approach and self-management as a tool to retain a strong sense of project ownership on the part of indigenous and Afro-Ecuadorian organizations. The configuration of investments in various types of capital coupled with the focus on participatory planning and self-management as the basic principles for the project's operational procedures forms the conceptual framework of the project.

Despite the strong desire of most organizations for self-managed control of the development process, there is a very wide range of available institutional capacities in these organizations. Some of them have a long history of providing services to their member communities, while others lack even the basic knowledge of managing their own finances. In view of the large variation in institutional capacity, it became clear that the project could not use a blueprint approach to enter into partnerships with these organizations as project implementing agents. A standard level of supervision might be interpreted by one organization as the absolute minimum level of operational support they need, while others might consider it as excessive micromanagement.

Ethnodevelopment and Human Capital

To increase the available pool of indigenous professionals in both quantitative and qualitative terms in the long run, the project entered into agreements with 27 universities and colleges that provide formal education at the high school and college level to indigenous students supported by the project. The project also supported students in disciplines that are particularly relevant for the modus operandi of the second-tier organizations, including, for example, community development, anthropology, and communications. Potential candidates for project support are proposed by second-tier organizations and subsequently selected by the project based on previous educational achievements. In order to increase the probability that students, once they have completed their education, remain in their respective communities and organizations, the formal education program puts a heavy emphasis on distance learning.

In addition to the formal training programs, the project supports short courses for professionals working in executing agencies. Courses include a wide range of topics, most related to participatory planning, project administration and management, procurement, and technical issues. Learning by doing is a key element of these courses and for this reason they are organized in close relation with the program of small-scale investments financed by the project. The project also offers a limited number of internships in its regional offices. These internships provide an opportunity for young indigenous professionals to obtain exposure to the operational aspects of the project's rural investment program that could be of use for their work in the second-tier organizations. By the end of 2002, 1,080 high school (335 graduated) and 850 college students (67 graduated) had received fellowships from the project, 77 persons had received courses in irrigation, soil conservation, agroforestry, and other topics, and 496 young men and women had benefited from an internship program in agroecology (World Bank 2002).

Ethnodevelopment and Environmental Capital

The project supports a land titling and regularization program in collaboration with the INDA. Given the sensitivity surrounding land property rights, the execution of this program is not in the hands of government officials but locally trained paralegals of indigenous and Afro-Ecuadorian communities. In collaboration with CARE, the project has supported a training program aimed at the formation of about 100 paralegals and the establishment of a professional network for these individuals. Given their local background and knowledge of participating communities and organizations, paralegals are in a much better position than outside government officials to effectively facilitate the resolution of land conflicts. The cooperation agreement between the project and INDA explicitly recognizes the integration of paralegals in INDA's operational procedures for land titling and regularization. By the end of 2002, about 122,685 hectares of land had been titled to 71 grassroots organizations. Currently 97,312 hectares of land are being processed for titling. In addition, 160 paralegals have finished their training program. Furthermore, 458 community irrigation systems have been studied, corresponding to 2,647 km and 37,194 users (World Bank 2002).

Ethnodevelopment and Financial/Physical Capital

The project finances a substantive program of small-scale rural investments identified through a participatory planning process at the community level. Investments with a public-goods character are financed through matching grants. Investments with a private-goods character are financed on a credit basis. The use of traditional collective labor (*minga*) is accepted as the counterpart contribution of the communities for financing particular rural investments. Community enterprises are also financed under the project. These enterprises are typically some sort of small-scale agro-business venture owned by the community and operated by community members. After covering all relevant costs, including salaries of personnel, eventual profits are plowed back into the communities and invested in social infrastructure (e.g., school, health clinic). While these agri-business ventures might be seen as private firms that should be financed with credit, indigenous communities view them as public ventures, since the communities own them and profits are used to finance public goods. The project accepts the latter definition, and so community enterprises are financed on a matching grant basis.

After about four years of implementation, PRODEPINE has supported the preparation of 210 local development plans, 1,918 subproject proposals, and 830 preinvestment studies. It has also financed 654 small investment operations at over $12 million, plus an estimated $4.5 million in community contribution. As a special activity targeting indigenous women, 547 community banks have been created, benefiting 14,022 members (World Bank 2002).

Self-Management, Participation, and Cultural Identity

Project beneficiaries and their organizations are involved in the strategic management of the project through a Consultative Committee (*Comité Consultivo*) formed within CODENPE. The Consultative Committee includes representatives from CODENPE and delegates from the main indigenous and Afro-Ecuadorian organizations. The committee reviews and approves the project's Annual Operational Plans and discusses progress reports submitted by the Project Technical Unit.

Because the project's success largely is measured in terms of concrete results at the community level, the vast majority of professionals in the Technical Unit work in regional offices. This enables them to be closer to the second-tier indigenous organizations through which most project activities are implemented. Over time, the project has worked in close partnership with about 250 of these indigenous and Afro-Ecuadorian membership organizations. As a first step, second-tier organizations agree with their member communities on a local development plan that provides an overall perspective and tool to prioritize project activities in a particular area. Once defined, they prepare and implement small-scale investments, not exceeding $90,000 per subproject, that benefit their member communities. Second-tier organizations also provide input in the elaboration of the Annual Operational Plan of the project in a particular region, thereby further contributing to the demand-driven nature of the project.[11]

Recognizing self-management as a crucial element of community development implies that project activities by definition should be demand-driven. The project relies on participatory planning to foster this. The process is designed to facilitate community and grassroots organizations to be effective players in their own development. More specifically, participatory planning as used in the context of the project (1) contributes to the decentralization of decision making, (2) stimulates grassroots participation in local planning and demand generation, (3) helps rural communities formulate development strategies and investment plans, and (4) increases investment sustainability by intensifying stakeholders' commitment in the execution and supervision of rural investments. The participatory planning process used by the project draws heavily on the experience of the Inter-American Foundation (and Comunidec, a national NGO) in Andean countries, particularly on its methodology for participatory community planning.[12]

The project also includes features that aim to sustain and strengthen indigenous and Afro-Ecuadorian cultures. For instance, as part of the institutional strengthening efforts that are geared toward the CODENPE, the project supports a team of professionals who, among other things, review and assess the potential impact of new legislation on the indigenous and Afro-Ecuadorian population and propose changes in case of expected adverse impacts. As part of the land tenure regularization efforts supported by the project, an attempt is made to clarify the concept of ancestral rights in more concrete terms with the aim of strengthening land rights of indigenous and Afro-Ecuadorian communities in forestry and protected areas.

CONCLUSION

Although the trajectory of applied anthropology is short, in the case of Ecuador there are substantive evidences that show us that it is leading as the main activity for professional anthropologists. Applied anthropology in Ecuador is showing results in terms of (1) systematizing existing knowledge and developing scientific explanations of the process of socioeconomic change; (2) developing social research methodologies, in an effort to use the scientific method of the natural sciences, with a wide range of techniques for data gathering and analysis (formal surveys based on probabilistic sampling, informal surveys, systematic observation, ethnography); and (3) contributing to development practice as researchers, cultural brokers, change agents, evaluation analysts, planners, or policy makers. Thus applied anthropology has had a prominent role when methods and instruments for development are designed and implemented according to local needs and demands, exploring and defining new paths for the construction of a multicultural society. Through civil society organizations and governmental institutions, anthropologists have accompanied and radically influenced the development practices and discourses of both local and global agendas.

The case of PRODEPINE is an example of a major development project where anthropologists are playing an important role. They are involved in every phase of the project. PRODEPINE is part of a new breed of poverty-targeted interventions of the World Bank. It is also part of an experimental initiative, started in 1993 in Latin America, designed to build pro-poor forms of social capital and promote ethnodevelopment. The project represents an effort to operationalize new and old concepts in social science (ethnodevelopment, social and human capital, community-driven development, participatory methodologies) to address old realities. It is an effort to mobilize local resources and direct new ones to the poorest segment of the population and to have indigenous peoples manage them in accordance with their own vision of their problems and how to solve them.

NOTES

Acknowledgments. Emilia Ferraro, Anthropologist, University of Kent, provided substantial contributions to the first section of this chapter.

1. For a critical assessment and analysis of its work, see Breton 2001.

2. See Marzal 1993 for a thorough and detailed analysis of the different types of *indigenisms* developed in different L.A. countries, as well as Mires 1995 for a historical overview of how Latin Americans have dealt with the "Indian problem."

3. It was the successful results of Abya Yala on creating debate, exchange, and support for the indigenous people leadership which endorsed the creation of the School of Applied Anthropology. Abya Yala is currently the major ethnographic Latin American publisher, with more than 2,000 titles and constituting nearly 80 percent of total published titles in social science in Ecuador (Juncosa, personal communication, January 2004).

4. Indigenous organizations often give higher estimates (about 40 percent of the total population), while Ecuador's Integrated Social Development Indicators (SIISE 2003) puts the figure closer to 10 percent on the basis of census data.

5. Indigenous peoples in Ecuador prefer to be designated as "nationalities" or "peoples" rather than "ethnic groups." The first two terms imply having standing as a nation and a broad range of rights established in United Nations instruments and the International Labor Organization's Convention 169. Non-Hispanic nationalities in Ecuador are Runa or Quichua, Shuar, Huao, Siona, Secoya, Cofán, Huancavilcas, Manteños, Punaes, Chachi, Epera, Tsáchilas, Awa, and Ecuador's black population.

6. The 1998 financial crisis and its aftermath, however, have aggravated poverty. By 1999, 55 percent of the population lived in poverty (40 percent of the urban population and 76 percent of the rural population).

7. For discussions of federations, see CONAIE 1994, Bebbington et al. 1992, and Carroll 2002.

8. The total project budget was $50 million: $25 million from the World Bank, $15 million from the international fund for agricultural development, and $10 million from the Ecuadorian Government and from beneficiary communities and organizations. The project was prepared beginning in early 1995, was approved in early 1998, and became effective in September 1998. Implementation was completed in April 2003. A second phase, prepared during 2003 and 2004, was canceled by the Ecuadorian Government at CONAIE's request.

9. The target population exhibits great cultural diversity, especially among indigenous peoples. The most numerous of the indigenous people are the Quichua speakers (or Runa) in the Sierra. They may be further

subdivided by area of ethnic predominance, including the Otavalo, Carangui, Cayambi, and Quito in the northern region, and the Panzaleo, Puruha, Cañari, Salasaca, and Saraguro in the south-central region. The next largest groups are the peoples of the Amazon region, including the Shuar, Achuar, and Runa or Quichua speakers of the lowlands, and the Huaorani, Cofán, and Siona-Secoya. In the coastal region are found the Awá, Emberá, Tsachila, and Chachi, and other peoples such as the Huancavilca, Manteño, and Puna who have lost their language but retain strong indigenous cultural features. Afro-Ecuadorians live in both coastal and highland areas, though there is not as much diversity between subgroups as there is between the indigenous subgroups.

10. John Durston, in his work in Guatemala, argues that native communities have latent social capital, disrupted and repressed during the civil strife in that country, but now, with a combination of physical and financial investments and organizational assistance, can be resuscitated and built up in an atmosphere of trust (see Durston 1998).

11. An additional benefit of operating in a decentralized fashion in which most of the operational decision-making authority is shifted to the regional level is that, once the Annual Operational Plan is approved, the project operates relatively independently from the political arena. This relatively independent mode of operation of the project is further enhanced by the fact that small-scale investments are financed with loan funds and counterpart contributions from the communities only, thus avoiding dependence on government counterpart funds.

12. The methodology consists of the organization of community and district workshops over the course of several weeks. At the workshops, project field promoters and second-tier organizations help the communities to carry out a participatory diagnostic and to formulate a development strategy, by applying methods of group dynamics. Workshop participants are community delegates, representatives from development organizations, and interested individuals. After each workshop, time is allotted for the community delegates to return and inform the community of the workshop's proceedings and to receive community feedback. As some communities' decisions are taken by consensus, this process can be lengthy.

REFERENCES

Albó, X.
  1994   And from Kataristas to Mnristas? The Surprising and Bold Alliance between Aymaras and Neoliberals in Bolivia. *In* Indigenous Peoples and Democracy in Latin America. D. L. Van Cott, ed. Pp. 55–83. London: Macmillan. Press.
Arce, A., and N. Long, eds.
  2000   Anthropology, Development and Modernities. London & New York: Rutledge.
Bebbington, A., and T. Perreault
  1999   Social Capital, Development and Access to Resources in Highland Ecuador. Economic Geography 75(4):395–418.
Bebbington, A., H. Carrasco, L. Peralvo, G. Ramón, V. H. Torres, and J. y Trujillo
  1992   Los Actores de una Decada Ganada: tribus, comunidades y campesinos en la modernidad. Quito: Abya Yala.
Botasso, J.
  1982   Los Shuar y las Misiones: entre las Hostilidad y el diálogo. Mundo Shuar. Quito: UNESCO.
Breton, A.
  2001   Cooperación al Desarrollo y Demandas Etnicas en los Andes Ecuatorianos Quito: Flacso Ecuador.
Brysk, A.
  1994   Acting Globally: Indigenous Rights and International Politics in Latin America. *In* Indigenous People and Democracy in Latin America. D. L. Van Cott, ed. Pp. 29–55. London: Macmillan Press.
Cameron, J.
  2001   Local Democracy in Rural Latin America: Lessons from Ecuador. Paper prepared for the Latin American Studies Association Meetings, Washington, DC, September 6–8.
Carroll, T., ed.
  2002   Construyendo Capacidades Colectivas: Fortalecimiento Organizativo de las Federaciones Campesinas-Indígenas en la Sierra Ecuatoriana. Quito: Fundaccón Heiffer/PRODEPINE.

CONAIE

1994   Proyecto Político de la CONAIE. Quito: CONAIE.

Diskin, S.

1991   Ethnic Discourse and the Challenge to Anthropology: The Nicaraguan Case. *In* Nation-States and the Indian in Latin America. G. Urban and J. Sherzer, eds. Pp. 156–180. Austin: University of Texas Press.

Durston, J.

1998   Building Social Capital in Rural Communities—Where It Does Not Exist. Paper prepared for the Conference of the Latin American Studies Association.

Escobar, A.

1995a   Imagining a Post-Development Era. *In* Power of Development. J. Cruz, ed. Pp. 221–227. London & New York: Routledge.

1995b   Development Planning. *In* Development Studies: A Reader. S. Corbridge, ed. Pp. 64–77. London: Edward Arnold.

Hendricks, J.

1988   Power and Knowledge: Discourse and Ideological Transformation among the Shuar. American Ethnologist 15(2):216–238.

Larreamendy, P.

2003   Indigenous Networks: Politics and Development Interconnectivity among the Shuar in Ecuador. Ph.D. thesis, University of Cambridge.

Lehman, A.

1990   Democracy and Development in Latin American Economics, Politics and Religion in the Post-War Period. Cambridge: Polity Press.

Martínez, L., comp.

2000   Estudios Rurales, Quito: Flacso Ecuador/Ildis.

Marzal, M.

1993   Historia de la Antropología Indigenista; México y Perú Espana/México. Antrophos/Universidad Autónoma Metropolitana 29.

Mires, F.

1995   El Discurso de la Indianidad. Quito: Abya Yala.

Muratorio B.

1981   Protestantism, Ethnicity and Class in Chimborazo. *In* Cultural Transformations and Ethnicity in Modern Ecuador. N. Whitten, ed. Urbana: University of Illinois Press.

Radcliffe, S.

1998   Frontiers and Popular Nationhood: Geographies of Identity in the 1995 Ecuador-Peru Border Dispute. Political Geography 17(3):273–293.

Ramón, G.

2001   El índice de Capacidad Institucional de las OSGs en el Ecuador. *In* El capital social en los Andes. A. Bebbington and H. Torres, eds. Quito: Abya Yala.

Salomon, F.

1981   The Weavers of Otavalo. *In* Ethnicity in Modern Ecuador. N. Whitten, ed. Pp. 420–449. Urbana: University of Illinois Press.

Selverston-Scher, M.

2001   Ethnopolitics in Ecuador. Indigenous Rights and the Strengthening of Democracy. Miami: North-South Center Press.

SIISE (Sistema Integrado de Indicadores Sociales)

2003   Electronic document, www.ssise.gov.ec

Torres, V. H.

1999   Guamote el Proceso Indígena del Gobierno Municipal Participativo. *In* Ciudadanias Emergentes. Experiencias Democráticas de Desarrollo Local. M. Hidalgo et al., eds. Pp. 87–112. Grupo Democracia y Desarrollo Local/RIAD/Abya-Yala/Comunidec: Quito.

2000   Ampliación del Componente seguimiento y evaluación del SISDEL. *In* Seguimiento y Evaluación del Manejo de Recursos Naturales. Julio A. Berdegué and Germán Escobar, eds. Santiago de Chile: IDRC.

2001   Los municipios son agentes del cambio social? Reflexiones en torno al capital social y desarrollo local en Ecuador. *In* El capital social en los Andes. A. Bebbington and V. H. Torres, eds. Quito: Abya Yala.

Uquillas, J.

1993   Research and Extension Practice and Rural People's Agroforestry Knowledge in Ecuadorian Amazonia. Rural People's Knowledge, Agricultural Research and Extension Practice. Latin American Papers. IIED Research Series 1:4.

Uquillas, J., and B. DeWalt

1989   Aporte de las ciencias sociales al desarrollo rural. Paper presented at the II Seminar on Agricultural Development and Human Nutrition, Escuela Politécnica del Chimborazo, Ecuador.

Uquillas, J., and M. Van Nieuwkoop

2003   Social Capital as a Factor of Indigenous Development in Ecuador. World Bank: Latin American and Caribbean Region Sustainable Development Working Paper No. 13.

Van Nieuwkoop, M., and J. Uquillas

2000   Defining Ethnodevelopment in Operational Terms: Lessons from the Ecuador Indigenous and Afro-Ecuadorian Peoples Development Project. World Bank: Latin American and Caribbean Region Sustainable Development Working Paper No. 6.

World Bank

1995   Ecuador Poverty Assessment. Washington, DC: World Bank.

2002   Implementation Completion Report: Ecuador's Indigenous and Afro-Ecuadoran Peoples Development Project. Washington, DC: World Bank.

APPLIED ANTHROPOLOGY IN EGYPT: PRACTICING ANTHROPOLOGY WITHIN LOCAL AND GLOBAL CONTEXTS

EL-SAYED EL-ASWAD
University of Bahrain

This chapter discusses the locally and globally oriented domains of applied anthropology in Egypt. It examines the micro and macro factors that have both positive and negative impact on the progress of applied anthropology in Egypt, including extensive bureaucracy, inadequate education, insufficient funding, global violence, terrorism, security, civil society, and NGOs. Despite the challenging conditions of academic and applied research in Egypt, applied anthropology, as locally practiced but globally oriented, has developed new trends concerning the key theme of the local/global and related topics of such as development, environment, poverty, education, migration, violence, tourism, and media. A case study will examine some of these issues. Key Words: Egypt, localism/globalism, policy, government, academic/applied

The focal objective of this chapter is to address and assess the practice of applied anthropology in Egypt within a global context. This objective meets a need among scholars, students, and practitioners especially when one recognizes that there exists no study that exclusively discusses applied anthropology in Egypt or, more extensively, the Arab world. Factors that have weakened the practice of applied anthropology and hindered its progress in Egypt are also discussed. With the exception of the University of Alexandria, which established an independent department of anthropology in 1974, anthropology in Egyptian universities is primarily affiliated with departments of social sciences, especially sociology. There are 20 universities in Egypt (14 national or public and 6 private) that incorporate departments of sociology, in addition to the National Center for Social and Criminological Research, established in 1956.[1] These departments offer both undergrad and graduate students courses mostly in social or cultural anthropology within which applied anthropology is taught. Though the theoretical frameworks of functionalism and structuralism introduced by Radcliff-Brown, Evans-Pritchard, and pioneer Egyptian anthropologists in the 1940s have continued to influence anthropological teaching in Egypt, the practical dimension of anthropology has been emphasized not only to implement modernization and development plans but also to help build an Egyptian nation liberated from British colonialism.[2] "Anthropology in Egypt today is dominated by efforts to come to grips with contemporary patterns of change, often under the heading

NAPA Bulletin 25, pp. 35–51, ISBN 1-931303-28-2. © 2006 by the American Anthropological Association. All rights reserved.
Permissions to photocopy or reproduce article content via www.ucpress.edu/journals/rights.htm.

of development. Thus it has implicitly or explicitly a practical dimension. Many of the anthropologists who have published on Egypt have worked for the various national, voluntary, bilateral and multilateral development agencies, as either direct employees or consultants. The result is that the main thrust of anthropology in Egypt is not to improve cross-cultural understanding but instead to generate interpretations of Egypt relevant to Egyptian development" (Hopkins 1998:50).[3]

Despite limitations in theory and ethnography, both undergraduate and graduate students of social science are trained in methods of applied anthropology to examine locally oriented domains of concern including such issues as health, homelessness, unemployment, family problems, violence, education, and environment in rural and urban communities. Anthropologists are employed in both academic and nonacademic fields. In the latter field, however, they work in both public and private sectors especially in education, development programs, social or cultural institutes, the tourist industry, and rehabilitation centers. It is worthy to note that a substantive number of anthropologists working in nonacademic fields pursue graduate studies. This growing phenomenon strengthens the link between academic and nonacademic zones generating or supporting new research agendas that give priority to qualitatively analyzable projects, a neglected field compared to the quantitative research dominant in sociology.[4]

Unlike First World countries, however, there is not a formal association in Egypt that regulates membership and conferences or sponsors publications in anthropology or sociology.[5] In the past, however, there was a serious attempt to institute an association that would proliferate the activities of Egyptian scholars. To be more specific, in the early 1970s a group of Egyptian anthropologists and sociologists succeeded in establishing the first Egyptian Sociological Society (al-jam'iyya al-misriyya li 'ilm al-ijtima'). However, because of internal rivalry between its members, lack of funding and government complications, the society did not thrive. This setback has severely hindered the progress of social sciences especially in the field of collaborative work as well as in the domain of securing sufficient funding resources from the government.[6]

Although research in anthropology and the social sciences in Egypt depends on various funding sources including the national government, funding by foreign agencies and organizations, such as USAID, UNICEF, the Ford Foundation, Fulbright, the National Endowment for Democracy (NED), and the National Democratic Institution for International Affairs (NDI) among others, forms a dominant factor in sustaining research activities carried out by both university research centers and private research centers.[7] However, because of bureaucratic procedures, rigid regulations, or specific conditions demanded by the donors, many of these funding sources are not efficiently or completely exploited.

Despite the deteriorating quality of research in the social sciences in Egypt, due to such factors as an inadequate educational system, the heavy teaching loads of professors,[8] poorly trained graduates, and insufficient funding, researchers in applied anthropology strive to maintain their focus on addressing critical contemporary social and developmental issues. Put differently, in the face of these difficulties and challenges, social sciences including anthropology have gained recognition as being social engineering disciplines, showing great interest in problem-solving practices akin to natural or applied sciences (el-Aswad 1997:96).[9] There has never been a clear-cut distinction between academic and applied anthropologists in Egypt. Also, as members or consultants affiliated to influential national centers and government institutes such as the National Center for Social and Criminological Research and the Supreme Council of Culture among others, many Egyptian anthropologists, still holding positions in universities, are involved in development projects dealing with local and global issues.

It is worth stressing that the core role of anthropologists or social scientists here is not confined to the diagnosis of problems threatening the society so as to suggest solutions to them, but it encompasses conceptualization of future practical plans based on ethnographic accounts. For example, through the National Center for Social and Criminological Research, social scientists initiated an ambitious program entitled "the Assessment of Social Policies" that has been under way since 1988. The program comprises three major circles. The first circle, dealing with the basic cultural structure of society, includes two research foci: (1) budget of time and (2) worldviews of Egyptian society. The second circle, surveying cultural policies, encompasses three research foci: (1) cultural environment, (2) cultural needs, and (3) quality-of-life indicators. The third circle, utilizing the findings of previous research, concerns the planning for future cultural policies (Yassin 1998).

GLOBALIZATION AND ANTHROPOLOGY

Though globalization is defined as a multifaceted phenomenon typified by time–space compression, its primary feature resides in "the consciousness of the global, that is, individual consciousness of the global situation, specifically that the world is an arena in which we all participate" (Friedman 1995:70). The practice of anthropology in Egypt has been affected by globalization and the world events that have occurred during the past two decades. These events include expansion of the global market economy, privatization, labor migration, the use of multiple media and the Internet (trans-communication portrayed as symbols of globalization), worldwide religious extremism, and global violence including wars and terrorist attacks. These global factors, notwithstanding their potential positive features, have not only aggravated social problems such as poverty, unemployment, consumption, homelessness, and violence but also generated serious questions concerning indigenous culture and national identity. The conflict between the global and the local in contemporary Egyptian experience is but one instance of what is increasingly a common phenomenon not just in Egypt or the Arab world, but worldwide.

Within this context, applied anthropologists have addressed some crucial social issues caused by globalization processes in Egypt. Economically, the swift change from the socialist or state-led development model (from the 1950s to the early 1970s) to the more recent one based on privately oriented market mechanisms integrated into the global economy has had a profound influence on Egyptian society. For example, agricultural or peasant modes of production have been rapidly changing in Egypt as globalization and the free market have been attracting agricultural laborers to work in nonagricultural domains, such as privately owned factories, building construction, and road maintenance. Also, the free market has widened the gap between the rich and the poor as shown by the increasing class stratification and polarization exceeding that which prevailed during the monarchic regime prior to 1952. Moreover, inflation, corruption, and the declining value of the national currency have perpetuated the ongoing distrust of the government. Privatization and the free market have generated or encouraged excessive consumption of consumer goods that were not known or even available during the socialist regime (Amin 2000; el-Aswad 2004a). These goods have become signs of globalization as well as indicators of the change in people's attitudes toward new lifestyles. The irony of this unique global feature exists in the competitive spirit of consumerism where Asian products (from China, India, Japan, or Southeast Asia) compete with Western products for attracting the bewildered and impoverished Egyptian consumer.

As being linked to globalization, the privatization policy that gives the private sector unprecedented priority to the public sector has had grievous impact on the educational, social, and health services offered to poor Egyptians in general and rural Egyptians, especially women and children, in particular (el-Aswad 2003c).[10] In her case studies Morsy argues that the problem of maternal mortality, a major public-health issue in Egypt, coincided with the implementation of the state's open-door economic policies in which health care had been privatized. The real problem is that women had been blamed for the deterioration of health service, while actual experience proved differently. For instance, traditional midwives were blamed by government authorities for the high rate of maternal mortality, but the fact is that most of the deaths occurred as a result of complications from cesarean operations done in hospitals (Morsy 1993, 1995).[11]

Privatization of education especially in the domain of universities has become a means of profit making. Students who have failed to find a place in public or national universities are admitted and pay tuitions and related fees to such universities. Instead of solving the problem, these privatized universities or institutions have aggravated the entire educational process by producing unskilled and unemployable graduates. In addition, the lack of employment security within the private sector indicates that employees have been discouraged from pursuing their rights or resisting poor working conditions and wages for fear of dismissal, an actual and frequent occurrence. Rates of unemployment are increasing and the GNP growth during the 1990s has not been effective in solving the problem of job creation, while 500,000 are prepared to enter the workforce on an annual basis.[12] To be more specific, a recent study made by the World Bank (1997:1) declared Egypt's long-term challenges to be that "official estimates of unemployment stand at about 10 percent. Over the next 10 years, there will be yearly increases of more than one million in the working-age population. The numbers of those entering the labor force (assuming a constant participation rate) will expand at 2.8 percent a year. This will amount to, about 560,000 new job-seekers, more than one-fourth of whom will be of the 15–24 age group—a most politically vocal and active segment of society. Thus, it is essential for Egypt to create jobs and income opportunities to meet the rising expectations of the younger generation."

Various global events and forces, especially since September 11, 2001, have influenced anthropologists' activities in Egypt. For instance, global violence and terrorism triggered by regional and international conflicts (in the Middle East: Israel/Palestine and Gulf wars [Iraq/Iran, Iraq/Kuwait, and the U.S. occupation of Iraq]) has had negative impact not only on the economic, social, and political lives in Egypt but also on the practice of social science in general and anthropology in particular. However, one maintains that despite the negative impact of global terrorism on local settings, anthropologists and social scientists have painstakingly investigated the ideological and pragmatic causes of such phenomenon so as to reach practical solutions. Anthropologists have been seriously interested in studying forms of violence generated by such factors as religious extremism, socioeconomic injustice, and others. Some authors view the rise of global terrorism as a tool of resistance against Western capitalism and consumerist domination resulting in a countervailing increase in repressive state power aimed at curbing it.[13]

One of the consequences of globalization, for instance, is the revival of Islamic extremist movements in Middle Eastern countries including Egypt. These movements, however, have historical roots in the society waiting for a chance to exercise violent acts. In his sociological and comparative study of Egypt's militant Islamic groups,[14] sponsored by the National Center for Social and Criminological Research, Ibrahim (1980:427, emphasis in the original) defines 'Islamic militancy' as "actual violent group behavior committed collectively against the state or other actors in the name of Islam." In addition to their feelings of alienation in a society plagued by a national crisis that has to do with foreign encroachment, these groups share fundamental common features and similarities with regard to age (17 to 26 at the time of joining), education (secondary school/university students, university graduates), occupation (government employees and the self-employed), motivation (strong achievement motivation with little economic and political opportunity), leadership (followers are 14–16 years younger than their leaders, implying an age-reverence code), class (lower and middle sectors of the middle class), and rural and small-town background. They are motivated to change the society using violence if necessary. In such a study the social scientist urges the leaders, authorities, and decision makers to reconsider practical actions to alleviate the miserable conditions of people, especially the young. It is worth mentioning that in "the absence of a credible, secular national vision and lacking effective means to repel external encroachment, to enhance the present and future socio-economic prospects of the middle and lower classes, and to galvanize the imagination of the educated youth and give them a sense of being essential parts of a grand design, Islamic militancy becomes the alternative" (Ibrahim 1980:448).

Though the Egyptian government managed to crack down on Muslim extremists, it is still highly reactive to any unexpected events that might be triggered by them. In response to the irrational acts of extremists that have fostered negative stereotypes of Islam, public lectures, sermons, conferences, and media programs have recently and abundantly been made to present Muslims positively at both national and global levels (el-Aswad 2003a). All in all, through their research and writings, Egyptian social scientists, indicating that socioeconomic injustice and lack of democratic practices are major causes of violence, send direct and indirect messages to the government advising it to relieve people from economic burden and allow for democratic dialogue. However, facing the problems of funding in addition to the threat of multiple forms of domestic and global violence that have necessitated the tightening of the government's security regulations, the activities of anthropologists in doing fieldwork have been restricted. One must indicate that if the shortage of government funding can be solved by seeking other alternatives such as the sponsoring by international and local private funding agencies, the issue of security or intervention of the state as in the case of martial law, for example, still hinders the conduct of significant field research especially in its practical and applied aspects. Also, the government has developed a sort of research phobia related to the "hidden motive" or "hidden agenda" of some foreign agencies that might use research data along with other sensitive information for nondevelopmental or nonacademic purposes.

Another form of violence has been depicted as economic violence against women (Halim 2002), not just physical or domestic violence. Some recent studies have attempted to explicate the impact of globalization on women's role in social and developmental activities. Though Egyptian women gained significant benefits by entering the capitalist market as well as by competing with men for jobs, they are economically impoverished and still far behind educationally and politically. The deteriorating economic position of Egyptian women especially those living in rural communities is caused by multiple and complicated factors. One of these factors is the privatization policy, reflecting global agendas, generating unprecedented problems of social and health services offered to poor women in Egypt in general and in Upper Egypt in particular (Sa'adat 2001). Also, this problem is caused by the blind and hasty adoption of Western capitalism and technology (incompatible with the traditional economy) that, with overwhelming demands, negatively affect the role of women in public life.

Serious studies of applied anthropology have revealed that Egyptian women are not motivated toward the private sector because of the lack of sufficient financial resources, the fluctuating and unsettled market conditions, and the imbalance between the demands of private jobs that require long periods of time and of family demands of domestic and household activities. However, women have a better chance to work in the government than in the private sector. In 1994 women working in the government reached 33.7 percent, while those working in private sectors reached 12 percent. Nevertheless, men enjoyed the lion's share in the private sector where they increased in 1988 from 52 percent to 56 percent while women decreased in the same year from 47 percent to 35 percent. In addition, 75 percent of females working in the private sector are holding temporary or part-time jobs that can be easily terminated when necessary. Moreover, wages of working women are less than those of men. In 1994 the average weekly wage of men was 54 Egyptian pounds while that of women was 37 Egyptian pounds.[15] Though social banks (sanadiq ijtima'iyyah), which are national projects aimed at helping people economically, created 360,681 job opportunities, they solved only 10 percent of the unemployment problem in Egypt. Women who benefited from these banks constituted 12 percent of the total number of the beneficiaries. In short, women are torn between their traditional roles as wives and mothers and the new social or civil role as active members in the society. The poverty of women has hindered them from having the modern equipment necessary for maintaining the house. Furthermore, women are marginalized or discouraged to be fully involved in political activities such as the right to elect or to run for political position or office, rendering them vulnerable and ineffective in fighting for their economic and social rights (Halim 2002:31–35). The point here is that through revealing the harsh conditions women face, social scientists, recognizing that the process of improvement might take a long time, have managed to stimulate the government to rethink women's rights to be treated equally.

RECENT TRENDS IN APPLIED ANTHROPOLOGY

It is extremely difficult if not impossible to understand the local without considering the global and vice versa. The "world investigated by anthropologists is a world already transformed structurally by its integration into the global system" (Friedman 1995:74). Anthropologists in Egypt as everywhere strive to investigate the practical aspects of the dialectical relationship between localism and globalism without severing the local culture from its roots. The impact of globalization on the local culture has required holistic understanding of development and has necessitated conducting certain research projects to demonstrate the changes in local worldviews and patterns of behavior. For example, the National Center for Social and Criminological Research, founded in Cairo, as afore-mentioned, initiated timely projects including that of the "Worldviews of Egyptian Society" undertaken by anthropologists in the late 1980s and early 1990s. Although some theoretical outlines of this project have been discussed (el-Aswad 1990), the final analysis of the collected data whose objective is to explicate the inside and outside factors, includ-ing global culture, influencing the structuring of Egyptian worldviews continues to be under investigation and analysis.

In addition to academic research projects, anthropologists in collaboration with soci-ologists and other social scientists have held conferences, workshops, and public lectures discussing the practical aspects of their research and possible solutions to the problems facing Egyptian society. For the last five years in Egypt, the newly constructed dominant theme of the local/global (and related topics of globalization/development, globaliza-tion/environment, globalization/migration, globalization/worldviews, globalization/identity, globalization/family, globalization/education, globalization/poverty, globalization/violence, globalization/youth, among others) has been the major focus of the anthropologists and social scientists in Egypt. The main point here is that the government that used to be indifferent to social research has unprecedentedly implemented some recommendations and advisory statements made by social scientists. Most recently (October 2003) and in the field of human rights Egyptian citizenship has been granted to children of Egyptian women married to foreign or non-Egyptian husbands.

As a rule, migration provides firsthand experience, the impact of which goes beyond the individual to include those who have never gone beyond the borders of their home-land. This movement between local and global zones has played a major role in generating a particular sense of identity attached to both local and global communities. Egyptian migrants have become aware that instead of altering their outside environment or exterior conditions that seem beyond their control, it is more suitable for them to work on their inner views or attitudes to be more flexible and open to all possibilities, whether positive or negative. It must be stressed that historically and prior to the 1970s it was nearly impossible, for political-economic reasons, for Egyptians to go abroad or work overseas (el-Aswad 1988). However, since then, migration or working abroad, tied to the global market, has proven to be a practical solution to domestic and economic problems. This is palpably demonstrated in remittances sent to families or brought home with workers. These remittances are invested in projects related to the operation of farms, factories, or businesses connected to global corporations, or they are applied to the purchase of land, trucks, and machines such as tractors and pumps to help with the development agricultural endeavors (el-Aswad 2004a).

Although workers are concerned with investing their money, they spend a considerable amount on purchasing consumer goods, such as television sets, satellite dishes, mobile phones, computers, and video recorders, reflecting global orientations. In addition, the proximity of Arab Gulf countries to the birthplace of Islam bestows meaning to this migration as being motivated not just by material interest but also by the Islamic concept of hijra, or migration to sacred places. What is new here is the economic open-door policy (al-infitah)[16] that offered exceptional and unprecedented opportunity for Egyptians to migrate and move beyond national borders enacting their worldviews that, when liberated from political and economic constraints, worked to promote material gains as well as to accentuate social connections (el-Aswad 2002).

As aforementioned, in the 1980s and 1990s Egypt experienced rapid social and economic change due to the impact of globalization that has had a profound effect on many Egyptian institutions. Attention has been paid to private, professional development organizations and the voluntary sector of development agencies. The influence of non-governmental organizations (NGOs) is increasing as privatization policy decreases the role of the state in providing necessary services to people. NGOs work directly with the grassroots rather than working from the top downward. Unlike many government or donor projects, criticized for being away from individuals' immediate needs, many of the successful NGOs have effectively served local communities in multiple social and economic domains.[17] For instance, there have been active movements of civil society organized by Muslim associations (jam'iyyat Islamiyya), charitable associations (jam'iyyat khayriyya), and private voluntary organizations to serve different local communities in both urban and rural settings (Sullivan 1994).

Another new trend in applied anthropology in Egypt concerns the adequacy of traditional and modern systems in dealing with problems of the social care for the elderly. For instance, globalization has influenced some practices of the social care for the elderly in urban settings in Egypt. People were promised that privatization and the global market would create new and effective care systems especially for the retired, but nothing has been accomplished. In addition to meager benefits and insignificant retirement income the elderly acquire from public or private sectors, they and the other needy suffer from an insufficient social security system and inadequate policy of medical insurance. Economic aid is subject to contradictory policies. Locally as well as nationally, economic aid offered by the government to the needy is tied to certain political leaders giving the false impression of the aid as if it were a personal donation. For instance, during Sadat's regime there was the "Sadat retirement" (ma'ash al-Sadat) which was used to help the needy, especially those who were unable to work and had no other financial resources. This "Sadat retirement," however, was replaced by what is known as the "social welfare of Mubarak" (mashru' Mubarak lil-takaful al-ijtima'i) (Hegazy 2001:5–6).

Although Egypt does not have the lengthy experience in the social care of the elderly as the developing countries have had, it has to face the social problems resulting from this new phenomenon. New research has initiated a change from concentrating on traditional-informal social care based on kinship relationships (el-Aswad 1987) to focusing on institutional care centers such as "elderly clubs" and "care homes" similar to nursing homes in the Western societies.

According to a recent study, Egypt has experienced a rapid increase in the number of elderly (60 years old and above). In 1986, for example, the total number of elderly was 2.7 million (5.7 percent of the total population) while in 1996 it reached 3.4 million (5.8 percent). The number is expected to reach 7.3 million (6.5 percent) in 2006, 8.4 million in 2016, and 9.4 million (11.3 percent) in 2026. The history of care homes, started very slowly in numbers, goes back to 1896.[18] Presently, the total number of care homes is 82. They are distributed into 18 governorates; however, Cairo, Alexandria, and Tanta have the largest numbers. Though private cooperatives as well as other civil society institutes play a major role in care homes, their overall conditions need further attention. Some negative aspects of care homes include inappropriate housing (small and crowded apartments), lack of privacy, bad habits of some of the elderly (smoking, sleeping late, etc.), noise, administrative laxity, and incompetent parishioners (Hegazy 2001:40).

The interplay between local and global scenarios, as a fresh field of applied anthropology, is distinctively reflected in the mass media and the Internet or World Wide Web. Anthropological and sociological studies have been conducted to assess the influence of global media and trans-communication on local culture, the household or family, and youth. The global mass media and Internet, influenced by Western worldviews and role models, play a tremendous role in changing patterns of behavior of young Egyptians especially. In the present-day public space there are new or modern coffee shops, designed to offer Internet and trans-communication services, side by side with the traditional coffee shops. A new form of phone globalization, presented in owning or using cell (mobile) phones that drain the modest income of both people and the nation, has become a fashionable and urgent trend among the young generation (el-Aswad 2004a). Also, global satellite channels broadcast live news that go beyond local news or national government propaganda or presidential talks. Though Arab transnational media or Arab satellites are globally oriented, Egyptians view them as representing the local concerns of their culture. The effectiveness of the transnational media, especially in the absence of effective mechanisms of democracy, forms another important concern of anthropologists seeking to understand the audiences' views about world events that occur inside and outside of Egyptian society (el-Aswad 2004b). From an Egyptian's point of view these channels have developed different perspectives and conflicting views even in dealing with the very same event. These different and conflicting views, however, attract the Arab viewers. They offer different perspectives than those of Western or American channels, such as CNN and the BBC. In addition, Arab satellite stations present critical programs and talk shows inviting eminent Arab thinkers, as well as Western and American intellectuals, to discuss issues related to liberty, democracy, peace, violence, civil society, civil rights, and regional conflicts (el-Aswad 2003a, 2003b).

DEVELOPMENT IN SINAI: A CASE STUDY

The rest of this chapter is designed to discuss in detail one of the new types of research in practiced anthropology that seeks to assess mega development projects such as those undertaken in Sinai.[19] In his study of desert societies in Egypt, with special focus on Northern Sinai, Abou-Zeid (1991), aided by a team of 23 anthropologists and social practitioners with applied focus, discussed projects related to holistic development as processes through which a better life can be achieved. The team was directed by the "Fieldwork Guide" (or a set of guidelines) authored by the head of the team covering ecological, economic, social, political, and practical aspects of the project. The Guide emphasizes the participatory methods and close interaction with the community members. The objectives of the study are (1) to assess projects of development implemented in Northern Sinai so as to know their positive and negative aspects and whether they meet people's needs and (2) to capture the residents' points of view regarding the significance of these projects and to determine to what extent the government, foreign or global agencies, and the locals interact and participate in carrying out these development projects.

Sinai has been selected as having the natural potential to ease the problems of overpopulation, stagnant economy, and shortage of agricultural products, and focal attention has been paid to such projects as land reclamation, irrigation, fishing, tourism, and industry.[20] These projects have been viewed by locals as essential for supporting the Egyptian economic system, especially when they recognize that the traditional economic activity of herding sheep and goat is deteriorating. Through using the natural resources and arable land of Sinai in building new communities to attract people to live there instead of concentrating on the Delta, problems of overpopulation and unemployment can be addressed. The size of the arable land in Sinai is approximately 5 million feddans;[21] however, water resources are not enough to irrigate the land nor are they good enough to be used for development projects. In addition, a great amount of water is lost because of flooding. Dams have been built to control the flooding and manage the water supply necessary for irrigation. Some of the chief dams in which people have actively participated are, for example, al-qusayma and al-qudayrat ('ain al-qudayrat). These particular projects are considered a prime example of comprehending the relationship between the local or social needs of people, natural resources found in the immediate environment, and the demands of global market especially in the domain of exporting agricultural products. Also, the research team shows that people participated in the process of decision making while conducting the project. It also shows how the foreign-aid agencies cooperated with the folk while the government and local authorities played the role of mediation (Abou-Zeid 1991:441–446). This statement implies that local governments and administrators are careful to respond to both local and global forces.

The Sinai project at first was seeking to reclaim about 80 feddans irrigated by a dam established in al-qusaymah and supplied by water coming from the well of al-judayrat with the purpose of increasing the land to 200 feddans irrigated perennially. The project was supposed to be done by a Japanese company; however, because of the high cost (200 million Egyptian pounds), people decided to undertake it using their local knowledge and skills. They decided to choose a flat area of land (about 6 kilometers from al-qusaymah reservoir) to build the reservoir (khazzan) of al-judayrat. Members of the al-judayrat tribe, as well as members belonging to 'araishiyya roots (from 'Areesh region or city) who own land on which the dam was established, participated in building the judayrat reservoir. The project helped the cultivation of olive trees, palm trees, and vegetables used for both domestic consumption and export (Abou-Zeid 1991:447). In a word, the locals or Bedouins began to respond to the needs of both local and global markets.

Also, as a fundamental economic resource in Northern Sinai, fishing has been incorporated in the global market through the export of high-quality fish to Western or European market. Part of the hard currency gained from exporting excellent fish is utilized to import massive amounts of inexpensive or "folk fish" used in domestic consumption compensating for the food (or protein) shortage in Egypt. The improvement of the fishing condition has created more jobs for fishermen and traders. For example, the number of fishermen in the al-Bardaweel Lake[22] as well as in the Mediterranean numbered 1,615 in 1979 and reached 3,850 in 1989. The amount of fish production tripled from 1,107 tons in 1979 to 3,023 tons in 1989.

The global economic orientation is clearly reflected in the tourist industry in Sinai. Tourist activities have positive economic results at both local and national levels. Indicators referring to rapid tourism development include the increase of the number of hotels and of privately owned tourist villages. For instance, the number of tourist nights tripled in six years from 60,001 in 1983 to 182,991 in 1989. Tourism development is not confined to the economy; it also encompasses social and cultural activities. Sinai has the necessary elements for global or transnational tourism such as cultural artifacts, Bedouin heritage, monuments, and religious and archeological sites (temples, churches, castles, and forts), not to mention the fact that the desert has its own charm attracting tourists from different parts of the world. For example, the old road that extends from Rafah to al-Qantara Sharq, known as the "Horus road," witnessed historical military operations and political campaigns. Also, there is the "Holy Family road," used by the Holy Family when they migrated from Palestine to Egypt and then went back to Palestine, extending along the ocean coast north of the Horus road. In addition, there is the "pilgrimage road" (tariq al-Hajj) that crosses the middle of Sinai connecting Egypt with al-Hijaz or

Mecca (the location of the Ka'ba) and Medina (the city of the Prophet) in Saudi Arabia (Abou-Zeid 1991:450–454).

The research, conducted by the team of applied anthropologists, concludes that people are the fundamental factors in these development projects, and that they are participating in them and not just benefiting from them. Nevertheless, there is a discrepancy between the view of the government and that of the people, which has caused a lack of confidence between them both. From the people's point of view there is a bias in the government's decision as related to the development of cities along the north coast at the expense of the interior communities living in the middle of the desert or Sinai. The reason for that interest, as people suggest, is that the north coast is very close to the government headquarters where the authorities reside.

Water resources and roads are top priorities for the people in Sinai. They appreciate the effort of the government to establish and pave roads connecting the various parts of Sinai. However, it seems that the government is insensitive to people's views of development. Development projects are decided or determined in advance without considering people's needs. For instance, the government attempted to prepare some deep-water wells in the region of Nekhel, but the authority did not consult the people and started digging in a place lacking water. The result was the failure of the project and the waste of a huge amount of money. Similarly, the government built garage and car shops for car maintenance costing 15,000 Egyptian pounds, but locals were asking: where were the cars that need such a car shop? Also, people recounted, to take another example, that the government paid more than 33,000 Egyptian pounds to build public lavatories that were never used. They indicated that it would have been much better to spend that money or less in repairing and renovating water wells (Abou-Zeid 1991:460–462).

The problem is not only between the government and people but also between the government and foreign (Western and non-Western) agencies. It is evident that the basic interest of the government is to secure the infrastructure of the society or to undertake big projects as building new houses and villages for the settlement of Bedouins or establishing industries that serve a large number of communities. Such projects are very expensive and require a large budget and long periods of time. Foreign agencies, on the other hand, are not interested in such big infrastructure projects but rather attempt to conduct small projects with specific objectives that help the local communities and, in the long run, might help the infrastructure. Also, foreign agencies give great attention to people's participation in implementing the projects by donating money or work. This interest should not be understood as related to a shortage of funding but as related mainly to the philosophy of the agencies that the folk or local people should be actively involved in the development projects. For example, the Canadian project of supplying the farmers with agricultural tractors and providing fishermen with small boats is a good example. These means of production projects necessitate that people participate in the development projects since the means of production is their direct and immediate responsibility. Therefore, the development projects are not (and should not be) confined to food aid or food programs that prolong dependency, but they should involve people's participation and involvement (Abou-Zeid 1991:463–465).

This study has argued that trans-communication, global flows of culture, capital, and political power have recently changed certain patterns of social life in Egypt and, in turn, necessitated that anthropologists give considerable attention to the applied aspects of anthropology. Despite its positive outcomes, globalization or global modernity, as in other Third World countries, has had dramatic consequences on Egypt. The problem here is that Egyptians need to cope with the growing demands of modernity and globalization as well as with their demands to maintain their national identity and local heritage.

Applied anthropology in Egypt is locally practiced but globally oriented. Anthropologists have moved away from the classical view of development (dependence theory and related issues of bilateral and multilateral aid) to discuss the interrelationship between local and global forces and development processes. Put differently, the interplay between localization and globalization has required holistic procedures and perspectives of development and has necessitated conducting certain research projects to explicate the changes in terms of local orientations and modes of behavior. Migration, media, agriculture, industry, family, and women's conditions among other issues have been addressed by applied anthropology within local/global contexts. Some studies have concentrated on women's views of the most negative factors that hinder their participation in the development processes in Egypt in general and in rural Egypt in particular. There is a relationship between the global market as represented in the open-door policy that accentuates privatization and the deprivation of women in social and developmental activities. In addition, as I have shown, applied anthropology is currently addressing the role of civil society and nongovernmental organizations (NGOs) in development.

NOTES

Acknowledgments. I would like to thank Ahmad Abou-Zeid, Donald Cole, Said Farah, Ezzat Hegazy, Nicholas Hopkins, and Ula Mustafa for their valuable and insightful information as well as for the time spent with them discussing the major issues of applied anthropology and sociology in Egypt.

1. For further information on education and particularly higher education in Egypt, within both present and future perspectives, see Mina 2001.

2. For the impact of colonialism on practicing anthropology, see Talal Asad 1973 and Escobar 1991.

3. It is worthy to note that during the 1960s and 1970s anthropologists, affiliated to the AUC and national (Egyptian) universities, worked collaboratively in various development projects including the project of resettlement of Nubian communities initiated by Laila el-Hamamsy and Robert Fernea (Hopkins 1998). For more information on the Nubian Project, see Fernea 1966, Fernea and Kennedy 1966, Kennedy 1977 and 1978, and Jennings 1995.

4. Though anthropologists do not have any problem in interacting with other social scientists or practitioners within sociological circles, they are very often faced with misunderstanding from the public, especially when it comes to job marketing. One reason is that though the term *anthropology* is translated into Arabic as *'ilm al-insan* (the science of man), it is still used in both academic and nonacademic circles in its transliterated (Arabic) form of *anthrobolojiya*, generating a sort of confusion among ordinary people and most educated persons as well.

5. Contribution to social sciences is published through either universities' and research centers' periodicals and bulletins or private publishing companies.

6. Though the link between research institutes or universities and decision-making centers including the Information and Decision Support Center (*markaz al-ma'lumat wa da'm al-qarar*), associated with the government cabinet, is not as ideal as expected, there is mutual cooperation between them especially in the domains of development projects, crime, drugs, terrorism, and family problems, especially those related to women and children. Also, to advocate and protect the rights of social practitioners, a syndicate of social professions was founded in 1973. The syndicate, nonacademic in nature, has been active in the domain of social and legal concerns of its members. Also, there is the Arab Society of Sociology, a broader organization at the level of the Arab world, that strives to revitalize the intellectual contribution of Arab social scientists, including anthropologists, through organizing annual meetings and public lectures.

7. Private or nongovernment research centers, though relatively new, are increasing in Egypt. Some of these centers, for example, include ICDS or Ibn Khaldun Center for Development Studies, founded in 1988 and directed by Saad Eddin Ibrahim (http://www.ibnkhaldun.org), and Al-Mishkat (http://www.almishkat.org), established and directed by Nader Fergany. Such private research centers, however, are out of the scope of this study.

8. The insufficient income of professors as well as university regulations that demand providing a textbook for each course drive professors to produce costly unpublished manuscripts, books, or manuals to be assigned to students. These manuals are instrumental and designed for the purposes of teaching, not for the applied aspects of training students to conduct research or to think critically. The consequence is that generations of graduates are rendered incompetent in conducting research. The main concern of the graduates is to seek job opportunities even in areas that are not related to their field or specialization. Unfortunately, some top university leaders are involved in private practices that might have a negative impact on their performance. For example, a president of a regional university, who works afternoons as a physician in his private clinic, devotes his time to gain personal benefits charging patients who might be staff or faculty members of the same university. One day a professor offered him a copy of an academic book in social sciences published in the U.S. Instead of thanking or encouraging the professor, the president asked him how he managed to write the book amid the heavy teaching load and other responsibilities. A deputy chancellor of the same university, a social scientist, rationalized his habitual behavior of assigning students costly books by claiming that he did not have other private revenues as do instructors in the schools of medicine, commerce, or law.

9. See also Shami 1989 and Ammar 1992.

10. In her study of the conditions of children in some slum areas (al-sharabiyya and al-hutiyya) in Cairo, Anwar (1998) indicates that though slums have a long history in Cairo, their number has increased, reaching most terrible and devastating conditions because of the greed and consumptive behavior that has visibly coincided with the spread of globalization. Although education is free (especially basic or elementary, middle, and high school), families complain of enrollment fees and other costs related to private tutoring. Schoolgirls told that their teachers asked them to buy them sandwiches or lunches or asked them to clean dishes or do laundry for free. Some teachers beat the students or asked them to clean the classroom or collect garbage. Teachers force students to take private tutoring or pay them money. Sometimes when teachers treat students in inhuman ways, the students retaliate. A male student, using a knife, slew a teacher who had mistreated him (Anwar 1998:208–236).

11. For further discussion of the deteriorating conditions of the government health units, see Mehanna and Winch 1998.

12. For more on poverty and unemployment in rural Egypt, see Bach 2002 and Fergany 2002.

13. For further discussion of terrorism, globalization, and state, see Chomsky 2002 and Baba and Hill 2003.

14. Relying on extensive interviews, Ibrahim (1980) studied two militant Islamic groups—the Technical Military Academy group (*Jama'at al-Fanniyya a-'askaryya*) and the Repentance and Holy Flight (*al-Takfir w'al-Hijra*)—comparing them with other militant movements such as the Muslim Brotherhood (Egypt) and the Wahhabis (Saudi Arabia).

15. In that year one U.S. dollar was approximately equivalent to 3.35 Egyptian pounds. Presently (January 2004), one U.S. dollar is officially equivalent to 6.18 Egyptian pounds.

16. The phrase *al-infitah al-iqtisady*, or "the open-door economic policy," appeared "for the first time on April 21, 1973, in a government statement. Initially, it referred to the role of Arab and foreign capital in the

housing and construction sectors. In 1974 it acquired a high political sanction when the October Paper, issued by the president and approved in a referendum, adopted it" (Dessouki 1982:75).

17. For further discussion of the importance of the NGOs, see Gardner and Lewis 1996 and Sullivan 1994.

18. The first care home was established in 1896 by members of foreign communities including Armenians, Greeks, and Italians. From the beginning of the 20th century until 1950 there were 11 homes. Twenty-one additional homes were established between 1951 and 1980. Over the subsequent decade the number increased and an additional 21 homes were established between 1980 and 1990 (Hegazy 2001).

19. Another mega development project is Toshka. However, this project, which is a long-term plan of development aiming at reclaiming some 540,000 feddans west of Lake Nasser (behind the High Dam) at Aswan, is out of the scope of this study. For an assessment of development projects in other desert societies such as those of the Northwest Coast (in Egypt), see Cole and Altorki 1998.

20. Although it is a dry desert with a hot climate, Sinai has the privilege of being surrounded by the Red and Mediterranean Seas. In addition to mineral resources and underground water, it has the al-Bardaweel Lake, which is one of largest lakes in Egypt (Abou-Zeid 1991:441–445).

21. One *feddan* = 1.038 acres.

22. The Lake of al-Bardaweel is considered by Egyptian authorities as an important fish resource because it exports 65 percent of the nationally exported fish abroad. It is a clean and pollution-free lake where no waste materials have been deposited. To settle the fishermen, a village named al-Tulul was built.

REFERENCES

Abou-Zeid, Ahmad
  1991   Al-mujtama'at as-sahrawiyya fi misr: shamal Saina', dirasah ethnografiyya lil-nuzum wa al-ansaq (Desert Societies in Egypt: Northern Sinai, an Ethnographic Study of Institutions and Social Systems). Cairo: The National Center for Social and Criminological Research.
Amin, Galal
  2000   Whatever Happened to the Egyptians: Changes in Egyptian Society From 1950 to the Present. Cairo: American University in Cairo Press.
Ammar, Hamid
  1992   Al-tanmiyah al-bashariyyah fi al-watan al- 'Arabi (Human Development in the Arab World). Cairo: Dar Sina'.
Anwar, 'Ula Mustafa
  1998   Zuruf al-atfal wa awda'ahum fi ba'd al-manatiq al-'ashwa'iyyah (The Conditions of Children in Some Slums). In al-tifl fi al-manatiq al-'ashwa'iyyah (The Child in the Slums), 'Ula Mustafa Anwar, 'Azzah Kurayyim, Hiba al-Nayyal, and Suhair Sanad, eds. Pp. 191–238. Cairo: The National Center for Social and Criminological Research.
Asad, Talal
  1973   Anthropology and Colonial Encounter. New York: Humanities Press.
Baba, Marietta, and Carole Hill
  2003   As the World Turns: The Evolution of Global Practice in Anthropology. Paper presented at 102nd Annual Meeting of the American Anthropological Association, Chicago, IL, November 19–23.
Bach, Kirsten H.
  2002   Rural Egypt under Stress. In Counter-Revolution in Egypt's Countryside: Land and Farmers in the Era of Economic Reform. Ray Bush, ed. London & New York: Zed Books.
Chomsky, Noam
  2002   Who Are the Global Terrorists? In Worlds in Collision: Terror and the Future of Global Order. Ken Booth and Tim Dunne eds. Pp. 128–140. Palgrave/Macmillan.
Cole, Donald P., and Soraya Altorki
  1998   Bedouin, Settlers, and Holiday Markers: Egypt's Changing Northwest Coast. Cairo: American University in Cairo Press.
Dessouki, Ali E. Hillal
  1982   The Politics of Income Distribution in Egypt. In The Political Economy of Income Distribution in Egypt. Gouda Abdel-Khalek and Robert Tignor, eds. Pp. 55–87. New York: Holmes & Meier Publishers, Inc.

el-Aswad, el-Sayed

1987   Death Rituals in Rural Egyptian Society: A Symbolic Study. Urban Anthropology and Studies of Cultural Systems and World Economic Development 16(2):205–241.

1988   Patterns of Thought: An Anthropological Study of World Views of Rural Egyptian Society. Ph.D. dissertation, University of Michigan, Ann Arbor.

1990   The Concept of "World View" in Anthropological Writings (in Arabic with English abstract). The National Review of Social Sciences (published by the National Center for Social and Criminological Research, Cairo) 27(1):9–54.

1997   Social Engineering: A Critical Study of the Contribution of the Social Sciences in the Field of Social Service (in Arabic). Proceedings of the First Conference of Social Service and Continuous Learning (UAEU, al-Ain, April 18–20) 2:89–108.

2002   Religion and Folk Cosmology: Scenarios of the Visible and Invisible in Rural Egypt. Westport, CT: Praeger.

2003a   Sanctified Cosmology: Maintaining Muslim Identity with Globalism. Journal of Social Affairs 24(80):65–94.

2003b   The Symbolic Significance of the Regional Culture: An Analytic View of the Process of Communication and Differentiation between North and South. Paper presented at the Conference of Regional Culture and the Problems of Local Society, Dept. of Sociology, Faculty of Arts, Tanta University, Egypt, March 17.

2003c   Peace Be upon the World: Voices of Women and Children from an Arab Society. Paper presented at 102nd Annual Meeting of the American Anthropological Association, Chicago, IL, November 19–23.

2004a   Viewing the World through Upper Egyptian Eyes: From Regional Crisis to Global Blessing. In Upper Egypt: Identity and Change. Nicholas Hopkins and Reem Saad, eds. Pp. 55–78. Cairo: The American University in Cairo Press.

2004b   Sacred Networks: Sainthood in Regional Sanctified Cults in the Egypt Delta. In Yearbook of the Sociology of Islam, vol. 5. Georg Stauth, ed. Pp. 124–141. Bielefeld: Universität Bielefeld.

Escobar, Arturo

1991   Anthropology and the Development Encounter: The Making and Marketing of Development Anthropology. American Anthropologist 18(4):658–682.

Fergany, Nader

2002   Poverty and Unemployment in Rural Egypt. In Counter-Revolution in Egypt's Countryside: Land and Farmers in the Era of Economic Reform. Ray Bush, ed. London & New York: Zed Books.

Fernea, Robert, ed.

1966   Contemporary Adaptations to Resettlement: A New Life for Egyptian Nubias. Current Anthropology 7:349–354.

Friedman, Jonathan

1995   Global System, Globalization and the Parameters of Modernity. In Global Identities. Mike Feathersone, Scott Lash, and Ronald Roberston, eds. Pp. 69–90. London: Sage Publications.

Gardner, Katy, and David Lewis

1996   Anthropology, Development, and the Post-modern Challenge. London: Pluto Press.

Halim, Nadia

2002   Al-mar'ah wa al-'unf al-iqtisady: zahirat (Women and Economic Violence). In the Proceedings of a Conference on the Egyptian Woman and Societal Challenges. Pp. 13–43. Cairo: The National Center for Social and Criminological Research.

Hegazy, Ezzat

2001   Al-ri'ayah al-mu'assasatiyya li-kibar as-sin: dur al-musnnin (Institutional Care for the Elderly: Care Homes). National Review of Social Sciences 38(2):1–44.

Hopkins, Nicholas S.

1998   Anthropology in Egypt. Anthropology Newsletter, February: 50–51.

Ibrahim, Saad Eddin

1980   Anatomy of Egyptian Militant Islamic Groups: Methodological Note and Preliminary Findings. International Journal of Middle East Studies 12(4):423–453.

Jennings, Anne M.
  1995   The Nubians of West Aswan: Village Women in the Midst of Change. Boulder: L. Rienner Publishers.
Kennedy, John G.
  1977   Struggle for Change in a Nubian Community: An Individual in Society and History. Palo Alto, CA: Mayfield Pub. Co.
  1978   Nubian Ceremonial Life: Studies in Islamic Syncretism and Cultural Change. Berkeley: University of California Press.
Mehanna, Sohair, and Peter Winch
  1998   Health Units in Rural Egypt: At the Forefront of Health Improvement or Anachronism? *In* Directions of Change in Rural Egypt. Nicholas S. Hopkins and Kirsten Westergaard, eds. Cairo: American University in Cairo Press.
Mina, Fayizz Murad
  2001   Al-ta'aleem fi Misr: al-waqi' wa al-mustaqbal hatta 'aam alfain wa itnain (Education in Egypt: Present and Future until 2020). Cairo: al-Anglo.
Morsy, Soheir
  1993   Gender, Sickness, and Healing in Rural Egypt: Ethnography in Historical Context. Boulder: Westview Press.
  1995   Deadly Reproduction among Egyptian Women: Maternal Mortality and the Medicalization of Population Control. *In* Conceiving the New World Order: The Global Politics of Reproduction. F. Ginsburg and R. Rapp, eds. Pp. 162–176. Berkeley: University of California Press.
Sa'adat, Anwar
  2001   Al-mar'ah wa at-tanmiyyah: dirasa sosiollojiyya a'n dawr al-mar'ah fi at-tanmiyya bijanub as- sa'eed (Women and Development: A Sociological Study of the Role of the Woman in the Development in Upper Egypt). Ph.D. dissertation, Dept. of Sociology, Faculty of Arts, Janub al-Wady University, Egypt.
  Shami, Seteney
  1989   Socio-cultural Anthropology in Arab Universities. Current Anthropology 30(5):649–654.
Sullivan, Denis Joseph
  1994   Private Voluntary Organizations in Egypt: Islamic Development, Private Initiative, and State Control. Gainesville, FL: University Press of Florida.
World Bank
  1997   Egypt in the Global Economy: Strategic Choices for Savings, Investments, and Long-Term Growth. World Bank Middle East and North Africa Economic Studies, 0253-7494. Washington, DC: World Bank.
Yassin, El-Sayed, ed.
  1998   Takhsis al-waqt (Time Budget). Cairo: The National Center for Social and Criminological Research.

ANTHROPOLOGY IN POLICY AND PRACTICE IN INDIA

L. K. MAHAPATRA

Utkal and Sambalpur Universities

Anthropology was introduced into India as an early colonial concern. In these early years, controversy surrounded the development of anthropology because of its application in the colonial/nationalist juxtaposition. Later theoretical and applied studies in anthropology were framed in nationalist terms not based on a value-neutral approach. This chapter examines the work of applied anthropologists from these early times to the present with an emphasis how global issues are increasing anthropological work. It will also discuss the structure of applied anthropology in the country and present examples of anthropologists working for government and international agencies, Universities, NGOs, and for tribal and vulnerable sections of India. Key Words: India, colonialism, tribal groups, applied anthropology, values

Anthropology is a European discipline of study, which was introduced to India as a practical aid to administration by the British colonial power in the 19th century. Antiquarian interest, however, not distinguished from the anthropological concern, was at the base of the foundation of the Asiatic Society of Bengal toward the latter part of the 18th century. As early as 1807, the Court of Directors of The East India Company made a formal decision to acquire anthropological information on India, as "such knowledge would be of great use in the future administration of the country" (Roy 1921). Francis Buchanan was appointed by the Governor-General in Council to undertake an ethnographic survey to inquire into the conditions of the inhabitants of Bengal and their religion (Buchanan 1820). In pursuit of this policy of The East India Company, the British government of India sponsored many anthropological/ethnographic regional studies. They include E. T. Dalton (1872), Sir H. H. Risley (1892), W. Crooke (1896), R. E. Enthoven (1922), Edgar Thurston (1909), R. V. Russell (1914–16), and others who undertook regional studies in eastern and northeastern India. The area included the Bengal Presidency, Northwest and Oudh, the Bombay Presidency, the Madras Presidency (which covered the major part of South India), and the Central Provinces of India.

The Imperial Gazetteers of India, based on districts of India, were compiled by British civil servants and were brought up to date from time to time for administrative purposes. Other British civil servants, either anthropologically oriented or trained, wrote books and monographs on individual tribes and castes and on village communities (Sir Henry Maine, 1871; H. Baden Powell, 1896). British civilians like Sir H. H. Risley, J. H. Hutton,

NAPA Bulletin 25, pp. 52–69, ISBN 1-931303-28-2. © 2006 by the American Anthropological Association. All rights reserved. Permissions to photocopy or reproduce article content via www.ucpress.edu/journals/rights.htm.

and a few others who were responsible for conducting the Census of India, beginning with 1872 (later on, decennially, from 1881 onward), wrote some analytical general studies on the caste system of India and on the transformation of some tribes into castes. J. H. Hutton had engaged a trained anthropologist, Guha, who was Harvard-trained, to bring out a systematic racial classification of the Indian population for the first time, without bringing in cultural and linguistic parameters to confuse the biological and biometrical indices. In the first two decades of the present century, some princely states like Cochin State constituted their own ethnological survey to compile reports on tribes and castes (Anantha Krishna Iyer, 1909).

At the university level, there were some Indologists and anthropologists, such as R. P. Chanda, S. C. Mitra, B. C. Majumdar, H. C. Chakladar, and from the Bar (Roy 1912), who were carrying on anthropological studies on India's past, Aryanization of India, folklore, ethnology, racial affinities, and monographs on tribal groups during the second and third decades of the 20th century. These early anthropologists, centered at Calcutta University, were trying to present the civilization of India, which is a significant achievement of mankind. The nationalistic upsurge of writings on continuities of India's past since prehistoric times is an example. Professional anthropological teaching was instituted for the first time at Calcutta University, which started the Department of Anthropology in 1920. Scientifically trained anthropologists with professional learning in social and cultural anthropology, physical anthropology, and prehistoric archaeology became more and more active on the scene toward the end of the 1920s. Mitra was the first Indian scholar to have made a field study of other cultures (in Polynesia) after his anthropological training at Yale University. He was the head of the Department of Anthropology until 1936, after having succeeded the first head of the department in 1931–32. W. H. R. Rivers at Cambridge University became the guru of two scholars from India: G. S. Ghurye in sociology and K. P. Chattopadhyay in anthropology. These two scholars came to head the postgraduate departments of Bombay University and Calcutta University, respectively.

Defying the prevailing perception that contact with outsiders and neighbors would result in deleterious effects, some Indian anthropologists posed a contrary interpretation by pointing the accusing finger at the colonial anti-people policy of the British. For example, Roy (1912:375–377) stated, "With the opening up of the country by roads and railways under the British rule and the gradual deforestation of the country and even the increasing restrictions on the use of forest, these forest tribes (the Birhor and the Korwa) are slowly but surely dying out partly from famine and partly from loss of interest in life." We find that the controversy around anthropology was not around its panhuman concern or theory but rather around its application in colonial/nationalist juxtaposition.

Therefore, one is not surprised to come across the condemnation of anthropologists by the nationalists: "The anthropologist(s) . . . were labeled as 'isolationist', revivalist, and 'no changer' by the social workers and the members of the Indian National Congress party" (Vidyarthi 1984:103). This negative characterization of the anthropologists in general stuck to Indian anthropologists even after Independence with the further caustic comment that they wanted to keep the tribes as museum specimens for their study and romanticization. These charges were rather unfair to Indian anthropologists.

Anthropologists of Calcutta University studied and exposed the "man-made" nature of the terrible Bengal famine of the early 1940s during the Second World War, when hundreds of thousands died. As against the government claim that the destitute were professional beggars, a survey by the Anthropology Department revealed that they were mostly landless laborers and poor cultivators, fishermen, and artisans, who were hit by the famine and the denial policy of the colonial power. Prof. T. C. Das's "Bengal Famine 1943" was published, in spite of the threat of government action against the alleged alarmist reports. The report was discussed in the British Parliament, which assessed the study's methodology and findings. The Government of India was then forced to take corrective steps on the basis of a complete survey (now sponsored by the colonial Government) of the famine-affected areas (Basu 1974).

VALUES AND POST-INDEPENDENCE APPLIED ANTHROPOLOGY

After Independence, anthropology was still considered as the discipline appropriate for the study of tribal folk. Departments of anthropology at Delhi, Lucknow, Gauhati, Osmania, and Madras Universities were established in the late 1940s. In the 1950s, departments of anthropology were started at universities in other states with large tribal populations (e.g., Ranchi in Bihar, Sagar in Madhya Pradesh, and Utkal in Orissa). Slowly and steadily, more and more university departments of anthropology contributed to the production of a huge manpower trained in anthropology. Anthropologists were also active in the Social Science Research Institutes and Funding Agencies, Institutes of Management and Advanced Studies, Indian Institute of Technology, and Institutes of Mass Communication. They also were heavily present in the Anthropological Survey of India, in the Census of India organization, and, somewhat marginally, in the Archaeological Survey of India.

We may also note that since the 1950s, the scope, concerns, and clientele of both anthropology and sociology as teaching and research disciplines have overlapped to such an extent that these two have often become indistinguishable in the areas and methodology of their applications. If tribes and castes, as well as the cultures of ethnic groups and village society, were the traditional fields of anthropology since the colonial times, the sociologists of today are contributing to these studies in a substantial measure. Similarly, if the study of classes and elite, factions, interest groups, associations, society, social institutions and social change, mass organizations, and urban and industrial society was the traditionally exclusive preserve of the sociologist, it is no longer so. Especially in the field of applications, a research worker tends to be eclectic in approach and methodology, combining a good mix of case studies and informal interviews as are characteristic of anthropology, with social survey, formal interviews, and mailed questionnaires, as befitting the traditional sociological method.

Bose, who dominated the horizon of anthropology for well over four decades, was a great thinker and nationalist fighter for freedom of India. He wore the mantle of the Director of the Anthropological Survey of India (the foremost anthropological research organization) and that of the Commissioner for Scheduled Castes and Scheduled Tribes (the constitutional authority for the welfare of the weaker sections). Bose gave forceful expression to the interdependence of theoretical and applied studies in anthropology in India. He stated:

> There are two sides of our science; one is theoretical, the other practical. In theoretical social anthropology, we try to discover correctly: (1) how power is distributed between different classes in a society, and through what institutions; (2) how one part of culture is related to other parts—whether they rise and fall together or separately; (3) how individuals interact with one another under different situations, or through institutions, and so on.

> Anthropology does not merely play the part of an observer in a game of chess. He has a greater and deeper commitment, namely, that in India he has to draw a lesson from what he observes, so that he can utilize his knowledge in the attainment of the egalitarian ideal that our nation has set before itself as its goal. If he also accepts this ideal, then, with his superior analytical apparatus, and the use of comparisons and synthetic thinking, he can suggest many modifications in the ways in which the government or leaders of society are trying to bring about justice where injustice prevails today. And this is where anthropology has a very significant role to play and a heavy responsibility to bear.

> Let me place the view that there can be no applied anthropology without the right kind of theoretical anthropology. Just as there have been great advances in physics and chemistry before a hundred doors were opened up for their application in agriculture and medicine, in peace and war, so also there should be adequate advance in theoretical anthropology before the knowledge can be applied to the achievement of desired social ends. [Bose 1974]

In his conceptualization, an Indian anthropologist should not be value-neutral if he is to apply scientifically acquired anthropological knowledge. It showed deep humanism, especially that which is located in, and bounded by, India.

Anthropological leadership and holistic approach took root and shaped policy only when the political leadership has felt itself to be unsure and ignorant and when it has come face-to-face with explosive, volatile, and unpredictable situations. For example, the Government of India grappled with the pacification and administration of the frontier region, called North Eastern Frontier Agency (NEFA), in the 1950s. V. Elwin, an anthropologist, was made the tribal adviser to the governor of Assam, who administered the territory under guidelines emanating from a receptive and understanding prime minister, Jawaharlal Nehru. Nehru has acknowledged Elwin's inspiration in forging the five basic principles of policy toward the tribal peoples of India (Foreword in Elwin 1960). Elwin established a large institute for research on the cultures and languages of the tribal communities of NEFA, which employed anthropologists and a few linguists. Without the all-sided understanding of the phenomena of blood feud and slavery through the research of anthropologists, including that of the author in the initial phase of the institute, it would have been impossible for the administration to cope with the problems of eradication of both of the deep-rooted institutions.

No less significant than the constitutional provisions was the formulation of policy toward the tribal peoples of India by the first prime minister of India, Jawaharlal Nehru.

He drew upon the basic approach toward the tribal peoples of India evolved by the Indian nationalists in the planning documents of the All-India Congress Committee. His policy was also influenced by the great experiment in pacification and welfare of the tribal peoples of the northeastern frontier region that was undertaken by Elwin, who was informally called a philanthropologist. Nehru acknowledged, "I agree not only with the broad philosophy and approach of Elwin, but with his specific proposals as to how we should deal with these fellow-countrymen of ours" (Elwin 1957). Nehru formulated his famous five basic principles of India's policy toward tribal peoples in his foreword to the second edition of Elwin's book, *A Philosophy for NEFA* (1960):

1. People should develop along the lines of their own genius and we should avoid imposing anything on them. We should try to encourage in every way their own traditional arts and culture.

2. Tribal rights in land and forests should be respected.

3. We should try to train and build up a team of their own people to do the work of administration and development. Some technical personnel from outside will, no doubt, be needed, especially in the beginning, but we should avoid introducing too many outsiders into tribal territory.

4. We should not over-administer these areas or overwhelm them with a multiplicity of schemes. We should rather work through, and not in rivalry to, their own social and cultural institutions.

5. We should judge results, not by statistics or the amount of money spent, but by the quality of human character that is evolved.

SUBSTANTIVE FOCI OF APPLIED/PRACTICING ANTHROPOLOGY

A great opportunity to involve anthropologists in fields other than tribal studies, in fact, in the economic growth and development of India as a whole appeared in India after 1950 through the U.S.-inspired Community Development Project. Because many of the experts were from the U.S., individuals recruited for jobs in the areas of personnel training and extension programs for community development in India were required to be anthropologists. New roles for anthropologists were created in analysis and evaluation of development processes, diffusion of innovations, leadership, and communication, and other subjects came to be accepted by the political leadership and bureaucracy of India. Their role was extended to the levels of policy formulation, implementation, and evaluation at the Planning Commission of India. Thus, we find today anthropologists active in government or government-sponsored statutory institutions and corporations in the following fields:

Population; Health and Nutrition; Agriculture, Wasteland Development, and Swidden Cultivation; Land Alienation and Indebtedness; Handicrafts; Rural Entrepreneurship; Rural Empowerment; Forest and Environment; Impact of Nuclear Units; Rural Electrification; Rural and Tribal Development; Mass and Tribal Education with Use of Tribal Mother Tongue; Institutional Finance; Child and Women Development; Rural

Energy Alternatives; Rehabilitation of Development Project–Affected People; Sports; Space Applications for Development; Personnel Training and Orientation; National Planning & Policy Reformulation, and Futurological Studies. Other more recent topics include Human Rights in all aspects; Social Protest Movements; Urban Renewal; Group Discrimination on the level of ethnic groups; and Discrimination and Atrocities against women.

Soon after Independence state-sponsored studies of many diverse subjects were supported. The thrust of India's planned development imperatives reflected the shifting focus of global anthropology from the study of tribes to the study of complex societies. Many studies, therefore, focused on village communities, group formation, factions and leadership, problems of urban communities, handicrafts, land alienation and distribution, forest utilization and deprivation, ecological balance, and conservation of the biosphere. In addition, studies were conducted on poverty alleviation, proper rehabilitation of people displaced due to large and medium projects of industrial, power, and water resource development, and health and family planning. Many of these studies were undertaken by nongovernmental organizations (NGOs) and by nonacademic anthropologists. Other studies undertaken by practicing anthropologists included issues of exploitation of the organized and unorganized labor and studies of weaker sections of society such as children, women, backward classes, scheduled castes, and tribes. These studies required the services of anthropologists for their painstaking, in-depth, holistic studies of the issues and the social phenomena for identifying the interplay of forces and factors at the grassroots level.

The development of the "emic" approach, along with the induction of the insiders' view and the participants' and beneficiaries' perspectives, became very important, as the focus of planning, implementation, and evaluation of state-sponsored projects shifted from "top-down" bureaucratic regimented centralization to decentralized, grassroots participation of the project-affected. Not a little of the above shift is due to the insistence of foreign aid givers, with their enlightened humane interest, that their aid reach the ultimate users—the downtrodden, weaker sections. This insistence sometimes specified the employment of social anthropologists in the stipulation of their aid package. The NORAD (Norwegian Agency for Development), the DANIDA (Danish International Development Agency), the SIDA (Swedish International Development Agency), the CIDA (Canadian International Development Agency), the IMF (International Monetary Fund), the World Bank, the USAID (U.S. Agency for International Development), the IFAD (International Fund for Agricultural Development), and the Asian Development Bank, among others, set the tone by placing anthropologists on their supervisory and evaluation staff for projects in India.

Apart from these preoccupations of anthropologists, NGOs are more and more requisitioning the services of anthropologists, whether as field research personnel or as consultants in their projects for working with, on, or for the local people, whether tribal or nontribal. Some anthropologists are themselves operating as heads of NGOs active in various fields. Anthropologists of India within the academic parameters had participated as chairmen or members of various IUAES commissions, viz. on Anthropology of Development, on Futurology, on Nomadic Peoples, on Global Change, on Folk Law and

Legal Pluralism, on Urban Anthropology, and on Anthropology in Policy and Practice. Recently an Indian anthropologist has become chairman of the newly constituted IUAES Commission on Human Rights. Anthropologists have also participated in international arenas on human rights and impact of globalization on the tribal and indigenous peoples.

LINKAGES BETWEEN ACADEMIC AND APPLIED ANTHROPOLOGY

More and more anthropologists, and also other social scientists of India, are assuming the role of social activists and organizers of social movements, not merely as "students" of social movements but as champions of the cause of the socially and economically weaker sections for socioeconomic and even political justice and equity. Some anthropologists have become forthright in their views on the inadequacy of their value-free academic approach to social problems. This perspective can be traced to classical anthropologists like Radcliffe-Brown, who, in 1950, stated: "A wise anthropologist will not try to tell an administrator what he ought to do; it is his special task to provide the scientifically collected and analysed knowledge that the administrator can use if he likes" (Radcliffe-Brown 1950). In contrast, Mahapatra candidly asserted, in 1990, that "however humanistic, analytical and futuristic, the approaches of the social scientists are by nature and circumstances incomplete instruments for action. Anthropologists and other social scientists have studied the problems of tribal people for about two centuries, but they have not been able to contribute significantly to the regeneration of the inherent capacities of the tribal people to fight for their interests and to claim their legitimate share in the polity and economy. Political parties and social workers have taken up where social scientists have left off" (Mahapatra 1990:97). He ruefully reminisced further by stating: "I have realized bitterly through this life that only research does not solve the problems, as policy makers and administrators in our country do not attach much weight to the findings and recommendations of the social scientists, including anthropologists, even when the same administrators and policy makers have sponsored relevant research or supported social science research institutes. Therefore, I have also come to realize that we have to fight for the right causes and against the wrong programmes and decisions with the added role of a social activist. Social science researchers are just not enough by themselves" (Mahapatra 1992b:328).

Some anthropologists in the field of sustainable development of poorer sections in India have come to be employed by social science research institutes, sponsored by the premier social science research organization: Indian Council of Social Science Research under the federal Government of India. State-based or research-area-based research institutes in different parts of the country are multidisciplinary institutions that seek to promote research on poverty and its eradication, and recently on its reproduction through generations. This latter perspective approaches poverty in cyclical and not linear progression.

Another field of application of anthropological knowledge, interpretations, and, above all, skills concerns the persuasive community rapport buildup, which has been used now and again by the government for finding workable compromise toward solution of tribal movements (often violent) to assert their tribal identity and autonomy from the majority community. This has become somewhat frequent in the last two decades, when the tribal peoples of east-central India agitated for carving out a tribal state, named Jharkhand (forest-based state), or of northeastern India, which struggled violently to have their tribal state, such as Bodo land. Administrators who had anthropological training and who were professionally active as anthropologists were asked officially by the government to soothe the ruffled feelings and bring about a compromise solution, acceptable to both the majority community of the state concerned and the agitating tribal peoples. At an informal level, some senior anthropologists were involved in evolving a compromise solution to these complex interethnic problems of the tribes and also the problems of estrangement of the majority people of a state in northeastern India from the federal government of India—a classic case of center–periphery relations. Here, anthropologists assumed the roles of cultural and political opinion-makers and motivators, and not merely the role of political go-between. This was, indeed, a value-laden task and a far cry from Radcliffe-Brown's prescription.

In an overwhelming number of cases, political compulsions outweigh anthropological insight in policy-making bodies. I recount one case. The government of India and the government of each state with sizable tribal populations are constitutionally enabled to evolve new state policy or laws, or to amend or even repeal existing state policy or laws, toward the tribal peoples. This constitutional provision may be enacted by instituting a Central Tribal Advisory Council at the federal level and a Tribes Advisory Council at the state level in the states of Andhra Pradesh, Bihar, Gujarat, Himachal Pradesh, Kerala, Madhya Pradesh, Maharashtra, Orissa, Tamilnadu, Tripura, and Uttar Pradesh. This institutional arrangement is not necessary in tribal-majority states. It was by some consideration of appropriateness that two anthropologists, myself included, were made members of the Central Tribal Advisory Board. But in the states, no such consideration is usually shown.

In the early 1970s, however, this author happened to be a member of the Central Tribal Advisory Council and, because of that position, was also nominated to the Tribes Advisory Council of Orissa State. At his initiative, the question of prohibition of trade in distilled liquor in tribal areas was taken up and he recounted how the tribal women of Sundargarh district had repeatedly and spontaneously agitated against this evil (i.e., for prohibition). However, as the tribal representatives of the district did not press for prohibition and as the policy of the ruling Swatantra Party was to allow liquor trade as private enterprise, no change in liquor policy was entertained. There was no interest in asking for any study to be made on the impact of liquor trade on the society, family organization, and economy of the tribal peoples and other poor sections.

Human rights is another field of interaction between theoretical studies and their application in day-to-day life problems of the people and civil society. Discrimination against vulnerable sections—tribes, depressed castes, women, the poor and illiterate, and so on—has been endemic in India. Atrocities have often accompanied such discrimination.

There are at least 12 tribal Research and Training Institutes in India, including two in tribal-majority states. These were established soon after Independence, beginning with those in Orissa, Bihar, and West Bengal in 1953. Anthropologists were most often directing these institutes and constituted the major scientific component of the personnel. The chief minister or the minister in charge of tribal welfare headed the Advisory Committee of the Institute. The research topics selected for study were related to the critical issues facing tribal peoples. The administration of tribal areas, as perceived by the public representatives and the bureaucrats, assumed that there was no sense of obligation on the part of the policy makers or the minister and members of the legislature or parliament, or even the administrators, to utilize the findings and recommendations so painstakingly brought out through the state-sponsored studies. A lot of evaluation studies have also been undertaken by these institutes. There is no evidence that the studies have made any dent in policy reformulation or in implementation with regard to the evaluated projects—their scope, objectives, or clientele.

Only one area or field of inquiry undertaken by the institutes has been directly relevant to the political process and hence of immediate concern to the political bosses. That is the area peculiar to the Indian situation: the determination of the eligibility of an ethnic group to be listed by the President of India as a scheduled tribe or scheduled caste or as a socially and educationally backward caste (SEBC). Monitoring of ongoing projects, wherever undertaken (most of the so-called evaluation studies are in the nature of monitoring studies), was possibly of direct use for correcting some minor imbalance or misdirection. For example, that there has been a disproportionate administration expenditure on micro-projects serving the more primitive tribal groups has never been acted upon and hence, in spite of policy to the contrary, development activities per se have been left financially high and dry (i.e., insufficient funds to support them).

The Anthropological Survey of India employs the highest number of anthropologists as well as linguists, psychologists, sociologists, museum specialists, and ethno-prehistoric scholars, among others. It is a large research organization engaged in all-India surveys of culture, social structure, health and nutrition, economic organization, social and political movements, customary laws, languages, ethnography, and physical, serological, and genetic markers. These have formed the basic stock of knowledge on the people of India, especially of the weaker sections—namely, the scheduled tribes—and occasionally of the scheduled castes and minorities. Naturally, this information base is available to the government for utilization while formulating development plans and modules. Both the Tribal Research and Training Institutes and the Anthropological Survey of India, being governmental organizations, generate research output that is mostly out-of-bounds for nongovernment persons, unless this is published and marketed for sale. This Survey functioned also as training ground for anthropological departments or research institutes in various fields for the country. When it undertook all-India bio-anthropological or ethnographic People of India studies on a mass scale, it attracted wide attention to variations and, at the same time, to the basic continuities among different regions or peoples.

Anthropologists at the universities have mostly handled research projects of applied value, funded by the government and quasi-government agencies or planning authorities, sometimes also by international agencies. But their findings and recommendations to reorient or amend or replace the existing policies or program implementation strategy often gather dust. Even when the university teachers of anthropology attached to Social Science Research Institutes were made the chairs of special committees of the Planning Commission or the government at the state or federal levels, their impact on policy reformulation was at best more than marginal, but only rarely has it gone all the way to policy review or reversal. The university Departments of Anthropology at the University of Ranchi and Utkal University at Bhubaneswar have been in the forefront of development anthropology in this country. In contrast with the anthropologists, who were active in the academic field, the administrators, trained as anthropologists and involved in the government or quasi-government institutions at the level of policy making, were always more effective in seeing their findings and recommendations bear upon policy change. It does not bother the government to consider the fact that the administrator-anthropologists are less likely to be more objective and more comprehensive in their understanding and analysis of the evolving socioeconomic phenomena and are more likely to be hesitant or circumspect in adversely affecting the vested interests or power wielders. But the age-old stereotype of the academic social scientist as working in the ivory tower, away from the dust and din of the grassroots world, continues to haunt the perception of the political policy makers in India.

CASE STUDIES IN APPLIED AND ACTION ANTHROPOLOGY

Very rarely, anthropologists have been provided with governmental authority and resources for intervening in the implementation of a program in midstream to correct the course, as have action anthropologists, trying alternative modus operandi. Such an opportunity came to the anthropologists working in the Department of Space in its ISRO wing in reversing the rehabilitation policy toward the Yanadi on Sri Harikota Island. However, this is an exception to prove the rule (Agarwal et al. 1985).

A great experiment in action anthropology was undertaken by the senior academic anthropologist, Roy Burman, who was invited by the local tribal people of Manipur state to advise and guide them through an association, The Institute of People's Action, established in 1977. This institution was centered through the people's participation in the learning and documentation process, communication and decision- making process, and participatory action process. The scientists of Jawaharlal Nehru University Center in Manipur (which later became the nucleus of Manipur University) undertook a survey of resources and development potentials of the region, the findings of which were discussed with the people. From time to time the plan of action was scrutinized, reviewed, and improved upon by the people in consultation with the technical experts from government departments. The anthropologist did play a role similar to that of a coordinator or moderator. The land given to the institute was increased by the community from time to time and was utilized for cultural regeneration, model and demonstration cultivation, forestry, horticulture, development of handicrafts, institutional marketing, land improvement, and resource and finance management. "A remarkable achievement of the Institute which brought about tremendous change in the life of the village was the survey and distribution of terraceable lands to all families of the village [of swidden cultivators]" (Kabui 1988:234). "Through the experience of ten years a determined leadership has come up from within the village, which understands the wide implication of the meaning of the experiment and which is capable of taking autonomous decisions in the matters towards self-reliant development" (Kabui 1988:236).

As the initiative, resource input, and full participation came from the people themselves, this was a unique case of action anthropology. What Peattie was searching for when she commented, "Though I know of anthropologists who have informally put themselves at the service of the 'underdog,' I do not know of any clear case of the underdogs hiring themselves an anthropologist" (Peattie 1984:4) had at last arrived!

The late Professor L. P. Vidyarthi had taken up study and rehabilitation of the seminomadic Birhor (Vidyarthi 1984:276–278), but though he called it "Birhor Action Project" to evolve "a concrete and scientific model for the development of the marginal communities," it was in the nature of a case of applied anthropology rather than action anthropology (cf. Tax 1958). Similar is the case of Professor P. K. Bhowmick's rehabilitation project of the ex-criminal (officially called "de-notified") tribe, Lodha, who have not yet fully adapted themselves to agricultural life, away from criminal propensities.

Fortunately, the report of the Study Group on Land Holding Systems in Tribal Areas, set up by the Planning Commission (Roy Burman 1986), was placed in the Indian Parliament, and the recommendations of this anthropologist-headed study group were supported further by another interstate study on "Historical Ecology of Land Survey and Settlement in Tribal Areas and Challenges of Development," sponsored by the Ford Foundation of India (Roy Burman 1987). These were somewhat instrumental in motivating the Government of Orissa State to effect change in granting land and forest rights to the tribal people. To this was added the issue of intensive development (sponsored by the IFAD, International Fund for Agricultural Development from FAO) of the tribal-swiddener groups of Kashipur region of Rayagada district. They were hard to be convinced and motivated without their title to land (already terraced or otherwise cultivated above ten-degree slope) and rights of usufruct over the fruit trees to be planted and over the forest resources on the hills to be utilized. These rights were further extended and liberalized in 1992 by the state, conceding their land ownership rights up to 30-degree slope.

Anthropologists have put pressure on the Government to extend these rights to all the "more primitive tribes" in Orissa State, which may be emulated in other parts of India, ushering in a phase of equity and effective economic justice in favor of the scheduled tribes (Mahapatra 1994a). In 2000, at last under such pressures, in Orissa State all the hill regions with more primitive tribes practicing swidden cultivation have been brought under the same regime of land rights.

The Hill Bonda swiddeners had to be assured of the same land rights and usufructuary rights over trees and forest resources, if a project directed by the author was to be carried through in 1991–92. But though the chief minister had accepted his arguments and granted the same rights to the Hill Bonda, this was made possible because of the (already decided) government concession in another area for the swidden cultivators and because of the commitment and support of the sympathetic administrator attached to the chief minister. Even then, the chief minister's decision on the Bonda Hills is yet to be approved by the cabinet and codified, as already done in the IFAD-funded tribal development project.

Traditional rights of the tribal groups over common property resources in their habitat, on which they had exercised rights of control, utilization, and management for thousands of years, are yet to be conceded by the Government in India (only in the northeastern border regions are these rights still respected). Without such concessions, compensation for common property resources and usufructuary rights is always denied to the tribal people following their displacement due to development projects in their habitat (Mahapatra 1994a; Roy Burman 1988). Anthropologists have been in the forefront in decrying the predatory nature of the modern state in India, which denies the tribal people rights in land and forest on some specious pleas (Mahapatra 1991, 1994b).

Anthropologists employed as part-time consultants or whole-time experts in international agencies such as UNICEF, the World Bank, NORAD, DANIDA, and SIDA are taken more seriously and are given responsibility, however specific, to formulate new policy guidelines or suggest improvements upon the old ones. In the field of Resettlement and Rehabilitation (R&R), for example, Indian consultants to the World Bank, like this author, have had the opportunity to advise the World Bank to revise its own policy on R&R on the one hand and to formulate revised Compensation and Rehabilitation Policy to be adopted by the Indian governments on the other (Mahapatra 1994a, 1994b).

ANTHROPOLOGICAL PRACTICE AND GLOBAL DEVELOPMENTS

Globalization in tandem with liberalization processes have unleashed an unprecedented range of options for flexibility, mobility, and spread of men, resources, ideas, networking, relations, and linkages between the past roots, the present constellations, and the expanding horizon into the future. Comparisons and contrasts between nations, peoples, and their cultures, achievements, successes, and failures are now available at the click of the computer mouse for comprehension and further action. If there was cultural relativity as a major plank of anthropological perspectives, at present, there was a plethora of options and alternatives. These opportunities for rethinking about the past and the present across the time scale and about the existential institutions, structures, and models across the space scale have given rise to assessment of alternative development, alternative medicine, alternative industrialization, alternative agriculture, alternative housing, alternative fashions, alternative cuisines, and so on, in which the Western model, often raised to the pedestal of ideal model especially in ex-colonial countries, is no longer dominant or sacrosanct. Rather, more and more the homegrown, indigenous ones are preferred and acted upon, as these are more adaptive to the local environment, genetic makeup, and resource base and are least disruptive of the sociocultural and natural balance with foreseeable harmless consequences or less hazardous fallouts.

Consider one simple example of the depth of awareness and the sensitiveness of the so-called primitive closed societies of yesterday: the interior-placed Naga tribal people of India's northeastern frontier areas. The Naga villages in recent decades have resisted building all-weather roads in their hill regions, which they realize will expose their forest and bio-resources, including medicinal herbs, to exploitation by multinational companies and other corporations, leaving them to their doom as the deprived people. The people's "green movement" resistance to displacement for mega-projects in infrastructure, mining, or industrial sectors is part of the same process of mobilization of people at the grassroots level against globalization and liberalization of the economy. In this process of awareness and sensitization buildup, anthropologists and the NGOs have made major contributions.

Tribal groups and their elites are asserting their ethnic identity, searching for their roots and alliances and migration, which have often led them to identity expansion to include a number of allied groups under one ethnic umbrella. This is equivalent to the diaspora identification and consolidation in different parts of the world, as has happened in the case of Indians, Chinese, Africans, and others. In this, anthropologists and their methods have played a crucial role in the context of globalization processes.

As already sensed by some anthropologists—for example, by L. K. Mahapatra at the 1983 World Congress in the IUAES Commission on Futurology—the indigenous and tribal groups have developed a new sense of their identity and of their worth and they feel they are better interpreters of their life and of their past for the rest of the world. The outsiders, the white, middle-class people in developed nations and their counterparts of the nontribal class in the colonial countries writing on the tribal or peasants, have become suspect in the eyes of the newly educated and emancipated among the erstwhile "subjects" for anthropologists, archaeologists, linguists, political scientists, and so on. In an extreme situation, the local church priests have been penalized by the Naga villagers if they decried or viewed their past culture as obnoxious, which the white missionaries had usually done in 20th-century India. In this context, participatory research with the direct participation by some of those who are being "studied" or investigated/surveyed was already practiced by Roy Burman and a few others since the 1970s.

It may be of interest to note that of late the concern of Indian anthropologists for safeguarding human rights and spreading awareness about them through education and activism has become institutionalized. Chowdhuri has become the organizer and chairman of the IUAES Commission on Human Rights, and a postgraduate degree in human rights has been instituted in the Department of Anthropology at Calcutta University. Roy Burman, a very senior anthropologist-activist of India in the field of human rights, was involved in drawing up a course of teaching on them in Indian universities under the aegis of the University Grants Commission Panel on Human Rights (1995–99). He has also tried, as a champion of human rights awareness in all sections of the people, to apprize the judiciary about the nonlegalistic approach on human rights.

Globalization and liberalization processes have made the anthropologists in India aware of, and sensitive to, various facets of transgression of human rights in India. One dimension of these human rights may be called "third-generation" rights, which include rights belonging to peoples, communities, and ethnic groups rather than to individuals. At one end these may expand to self-determination and even to sovereignty over natural wealth and resources of the country or region that they have occupied for centuries. The rights of disadvantaged groups to special protection and the right to equitable development are also subsumed in this vision.

He, like other anthropologists, has highlighted the complex impact of globalization in developing countries and especially on the marginalized, vulnerable sections, such as indigenous tribal people and women. The UN General Assembly passed the Resolution on New International Economic Order in 1974 in the face of abstention by highly industrialized countries. In the New World Order, the WTO concentration of wealth in the hands of a small number of transnational corporate bodies of richer countries creates an unequal world order in which even in highly industrialized countries large numbers of people are becoming jobless and insecure. This has led to social tension, conflicts, ethnic strife, and further marginalization of the vulnerable groups, who lose their land and other resources to corporations. It is no wonder that many social scientists including anthropologists visualize the withering away of the national welfare state, usurped by the transnational companies (Gosden 1999). When the authority of the UN bodies is challenged and when even new regulatory bodies are not recognized by the powerful countries in the world, very ironically, the indigenous groups and minorities look up to international agencies ranging from the UN organs to Amnesty International to help them out.

However, anthropologists have not specifically studied the impact of liberalization and privatization of resources on the middle class. In general terms, the economists have come to realize that the trend has been an increase in consumption in all areas of life and living among the rich and the middle class. The blaring of advertisements even in the villages on the radio—and, where available, in the television—has led to both higher consumption of nonessential items and consumption beyond means, as well as to a heightened sense of "relative deprivation." The latter is more apparent in the urban slums, which may cumulatively lead to increase in criminality. On the other hand, in an early study of liberalization in the economy, the real wage changes showed a significant decline and became negative for skilled labor. However, the silver lining in this rather bleak scenario is that a higher percentage of households in both rural and urban areas began getting two square meals a day in the progressive amelioration of food scarcity from 1983 to 1992. But it is not clear if this is directly related to liberalization of the economy. Though the Government is committed to the concept of reform with a human face, there emerged a new type of poverty, known as "new poors," those who were normally not in the lower income bracket but who suddenly became poor by losing their jobs because of retrenchment or being affected by closures of enterprises (Gupta 1995).

There has been another area of significant change. "Under the new economic policy, the agri-business sector has emerged as an important area for export, and government support with this segment of agriculture is becoming a sub-sector of industry in the agro-industrial chain of production" (Paul 2004). The small and marginal farmers are increasingly selling or leasing out land to the agribusiness corporations, as a sequel to the penetration of markets into the rural areas (cf. Acharya 1995). This is likely to lead to alienation of land from the owner-producers and convert them into wage workers (Singh 1997). Hence, class-wise the rural middle class may swell in numbers at the cost of the poor.

The anticolonial stance of pre-Independence days in Indian anthropology has been further sharpened in retrospective studies by younger anthropologists, and the neocolonial, hegemonic, and multinational ramifications of development aid from international financial and other agencies are being linked to micro-level programs and projects. The predatory nature of the colonial and modern welfare state (Mahapatra 1991) and the elitist hegemony (Roy Burman 1992), and the contradictions and constraints in the welfare state, have been taken more and more into consideration while evaluating macro-level and micro-level projects. The state and the global economic order, and also the sociopolitical hegemony of the neocolonial and multinational forces, are brought into perspective by the anthropologists in India, as they impinge on the situations of deprivation, exploitation, and loss of freedom, dignity, and autonomy in the tribal world in particular and in the country in general.

Other aspects of the impact of global scientific and cultural developments researched by Indian anthropologists in teaching, research, and government policy reorientation/ reformulation may be exemplified. Some of these are cultural dimensions of wild biodiversity; developing methodologies for people's biodiversity register; developing participatory approaches and models for the management of natural resources, especially in forest and water resources; developing social and health impact indicators; anthropological dimensions of HIV/AIDS; developing methodologies related to intellectual property rights (IPR) regarding biodiversity, food plants, and genetics; impact of tourism and pilgrimage on cultural conservation; balancing people's habitat and survival needs in natural parks and bio-reserves; and genetic mapping of normally endogamous caste groups and tribal communities for eventual discovery of group-specific genetic markers for curative, preventive, and population quality research. Mahapatra and others have been active in Indian and international forums on many of these fronts.

Roy Burman succinctly places the anthropologists on the world stage from the perspective of development anthropology in value conflict: "One problem the anthropologist faces is the problem of harmonizing his professional role with that of his role as a citizen. In India, many anthropologists gave higher priority to their professional role in defiance of their role as citizen of a subjugated country. After Independence, the situation changed. By and large, the professional skill of the anthropologists was placed at the disposal of the ruling establishment. But during the last decade or so, a realization is coming that the professional role can find its fulfillment only when harmonized within the role of a citizen of the world, or that of a child of humanity" (Roy Burman 1988:560–561).

CONCLUSION

Anthropology was introduced into India as an early colonial concern. That "such knowledge would be of great use in the future administration of the country" is very clear since the 1807 decision of the East India Company (British). There was controversy around anthropology, not around its panhuman scope and theory but rather around its application in a colonial/nationalist juxtaposition. Professional anthropologists at the universities, engaged since the 1920s, made waves with a study of Bengal famine as a man-made disaster, traced to colonial misgovernance.

Bose had provided the goals for theoretical and applied studies in anthropology, which were framed in nationalist terms. It was not a value-neutral formulation as against Radcliffe-Brown's dictum. However, the nationalists had always looked askance at the anthropologists, who were misunderstood as apologists for colonialism. Prime Minister Nehru restored their respect by relying on anthropologists' role in the administration of tribal areas.

After Independence senior anthropologists were engaged in utilization of anthropological knowledge in planning and advice on tribal administration and policy formulation. Later anthropologists were engaged in the Anthropological Survey of India, the employer of perhaps the highest number of all specializations in anthropology in any country in the world. Through fieldwork for ethnographic studies or through laboratory and fieldwork in biological anthropological markers, linguistic and psychological studies, filming, prehistoric or museum displays, and conservation, the survey had contributed to the development of anthropology as a professional science.

Apart from working for government agencies or in universities, anthropologists have been engaged also by the NGOs, as they worked among the tribal and vulnerable sections of our country. With numerous infrastructure development projects operating in the country's interior, many anthropologists were engaged by international funding agencies and, later on, also by the government for proper and adequate rehabilitation of the displaced and deprived people. Anthropologists have also sometimes been approached for bringing about rapprochement between estranged tribal people and the regional majority.

The complex impact of globalization and liberalization has not yet been properly studied by anthropologists in India. Senior anthropologists have questioned the role of the state and the multinational corporations, as well as that of the WTO and other world bodies for bending the policies in India to serve the ends of neocolonialism and hegemonic power play.

REFERENCES

Acharya, Shankar
   1995   The Economic Consequences of Economic Reforms. Sir Purushotamdas Thakurdas Memorial Lecture. Pune: The Indian Institute of Bankers.
Agarwal, B. C. et al.
   1985   Yanadi Response to Change: An Attempt in Action Anthropology. New Delhi: Concept Publishing Co.
Anantha Krishna Iyer, L. K.
   1909   The Tribes and Castes of Cochin. 3 vols. Reprinted. New Delhi: Cosmo Publications.
Baden Powell, B. H.
   1957   The Indian Village Community. New Haven: HRAF Press. (Original Work published 1896, London: Longmans, Green)
Basu, M. N.
   1974   Fifty Years of the Department of Anthropology, Calcutta University. Indian Anthropology Today. Dharani Sen, ed. Dept. of Anthropology, Calcutta University.

Bose, N. K.

1974   Anthropology after Fifty Years. Indian Anthropology Today. Dharani Sen, ed. Calcutta University, Department of Anthropology.

Buchanan, F.

1820   History, Antiquity, Topography and Statistics of Eastern India. London.

Crooke, W.

1896   Tribes and Castes of Northwest and Oudh. 4 vols. London.

Dalton, E. T.

1872   Descriptive Ethnology of Bengal. Calcutta: Government of Bengal Press.

Elwin, Verrier

1939   The Baiga. London: John Murray.

1959   A Philosophy for NEFA. Shillong. North East Frontier Agency.

1960   A Philosophy for NEFA. 2nd edition. Shillong. Government of Assam.

Enthoven, R. E.

1922   The Tribes and Castes of Bombay Presidency. Bombay.

Gosden, Chris

1999   Anthropology and Archaeology: A Changing Relationship. London: Routledge.

Gupta, S. P.

1995   Economic Reform and Its Impact on Poor. Economic and Political Weekly, June 3.

Hutton, J. H.

1931   Census Report of India. Vol. 1, Part III. New Delhi. Registrar General and Census Commission of India.

Kabui, Gangumei

1988   Experiment in Participatory Learning, Communication and Social Science, and Social Concern in Felicitation Volume in Honour of Professor B. K. Roy Burman. S. B. Chakrabarti, ed. Delhi: Mittal Publications.

Mahapatra, L. K.

1973–74 Ritual Kinship in Peasant Societies. Man in Society, Inaugural Volume. Bhubaneswar: Department of Anthropology, Utkal University.

1990   Rehabilitation of Tribal Affected by Major Dams and Other Projects in Orissa. In Report of Workshop on Rehabilitation of Persons Displaced by Development Projects. A. P. Fernandez, ed. Bangalore: Institute for Economic & Social Change.

1991   [1983] Development for Whom? Depriving the Dispossessed Tribal. Social Action 41(3) (originally, Presidential Address at 11th ICAES Symposium on Development and Population Displacement, Vancouver, 1983)

1992a   Report on Model Feasibility Survey in Bonda Hills, Koraput District, Orissa for Extensive Terracing and Alternate Land Use Modules for Rehabilitation of the Shifting Cultivators In Situ. Bhubaneswar: Nabakrushna Choudhury Centre for Development Studies (under publication).

1992b   Professional Reminiscences and Musings. In Science, Culture and Development: Prof. L. K. Mahapatra Felicitation Volume. N. K. Behura and K. C. Tripathy, eds. Bhubaneswar: Paragon Publishers.

1994a   Tribal Development in India: Myth and Reality. Parameter of Forest Policy for Tribal Development in Social Action (44)4: 91–104. New Delhi: Vikas Publishing House.

1999   Resettlement, Impoverishment and Reconstruction in India: Development for the Deprived. New Delhi: Vikas Publishing House.

2005   People and Cultural Traditions of Orissa: Civilization, Society and Worldview. Cuttack: New Age Publications.

Paul, M. Thomas

2004   Poverty and Economic Reforms: Social Concern. G. S., ed. Aurora: Academic Foundation.

Peattie, Lisa R.

1984   Interventionism and Applied Science in Anthropology. In Applied Anthropology in India. L. P. Vidyarthi, ed. Allahabad: Kitab Mahal.

Radcliffe-Brown, A. R.
    1950   Introduction. *In* African Systems of Kinship and Marriage. A. R. Radcliffe-Brown and C. Daryll Forde, eds. London Oxford University Press.
Risley, H. H.
    1892   The Tribes and Castes of Bengal. 2 vols. Calcutta: Bengal Secretariat Press.
Roy, S. C.
    1912   The Mundas and Their Country. Calcutta. (Reprinted by Man in India Office, Ranchi)
    1921   Anthropological Researches in India. Man in India I(1).
    1931   The Jungle Tribes of Bihar. Journal of Bihar and Orissa Research Society V(1).
Roy Burman, B. K.
    1972   Integrated Area Approach to the Problems of the Hill Tribes of Northeast India. *In* Tribal Situation in India. Shimla: Indian Institute of Advanced Study.
    1986   Report of the Study Group on Land Holding Systems in Tribal Areas. New Delhi: Planning Commission.
    1987   Historical Ecology of Land Survey and Settlement in Tribal Areas and Challenges of Development (with particular reference to the Central tribal belt of India). New Delhi: Council for Social Development.
    1988   Epilogue. *In* Social Science and Social Concern: Felicitation Volume in Honor of Professor B. K. Roy Burman. S. B. Chakrabarti, ed. New Delhi: Mittal Publications.
    1992   Limitations of Welfare State: Problem of Tribal Development and Role of Bureaucracy. *In* Tribal Transformation in India. Vol. II. B. Chaudhuri, ed. New Delhi: Inter India Publications.
Russell, R. V.
    1914:16 Tribes and Castes of Central Provinces of India. London: Macmillan and Co.
Singh, Sukhpal
    1997   Structural Adjustment Programme and Indian Agriculture. Economic and Political Weekly XXX(51).
Tax, Sol
    1958   Action Anthropology. Human Organization 17(1).
Thurston, Edgar
    1909   Castes and Tribes of Southern India. Madras: Government Press.
Vidyarthi, L. P., ed.
    1984   Applied Anthropology in India. Allahabad: Kitab Mahal.
Von Fuerer-Haimendorf, C.
    1985   Tribes of India: The Struggle for Survival. Oxford: University Press Delhi.

APPLIED ANTHROPOLOGY IN CHINA

WANG JIANMIN
Central University of Nationalities

JOHN A. YOUNG
Oregon State University

This chapter examines the development of applied anthropology in China through the political twists and turns of history and politics during the last eight decades. Chinese anthropology has always had a strong applied emphasis. It began with a mandate to study the political-economy of ethnic groups in frontier/border regions in the 1920's and 1930's for national security reasons, and it continues today with the objective of cultural preservation and comprehensive development to raise living standards and bring these groups more fully into the national economy. After taking over in 1949, the communist government sent anthropologists throughout the country to provide the ethnographic evidence for conferring official minority status, determining political representation and establishing autonomous regions, counties and districts for ethnic groups. Soon thereafter anthropologists began a nationwide investigation of the history and social organization of already identified ethnic groups as preparation for implementing massive social and economic transformations planned by the government. The Anti-Rightist Campaign in 1957 ended these investigations, pushed Marxian social philosophy to the forefront, and sidelined anthropology until its post-Cultural Revolution revival in 1978. In the 1980's and 1990's Chinese anthropologists began to interact with their Western counterparts, adopting multiple theoretical perspectives (not just Marxian), turning to a variety of empirical methods, conducting ethnographic research, and building anthropology as a policy science. Key Words: China, applied anthropology, ethnic groups, politics, development

Power and politics inevitably affect academic research. Some scholars like to claim that they are independent and neutral in their research, but this is merely an ideal that is difficult in practice, especially in China. Since the earliest time of anthropological development in China, applied research has been an important part of the discipline. Traditional Chinese intellectuals believe that learning is for use. In other words, if you study something, you have to apply it in practice; otherwise acquisition of knowledge is futile and unnecessary. This tradition of emphasizing the value of applied research produced a strong relationship between anthropology and national politics, sometimes even combining them in one common enterprise. Since the introduction of anthropology into China from the West, the entire country has been swept with several waves of

NAPA Bulletin 25, pp. 70-81, ISBN 1-931303-28-2. © 2006 by the American Anthropological Association. All rights reserved.
Permissions to photocopy or reproduce article content via www.ucpress.edu/journals/rights.htm.

political change. The story of applied anthropology in China is intimately connected to ideologies and programs brought by political change.

THE EARLY HISTORY OF ANTHROPOLOGY

In the 1920s and 1930s, Chinese students went to America, Europe, and Japan to study anthropology and sociology. During their stay abroad, they followed the advice of their mentors in China, paying particular attention to practical issues in society. Cai Yuanpei, the founder of anthropology in China, regarded ethnology (cultural anthropology) as not only a theoretical discipline but also an applied enterprise directly related to frontier politics and national cultural development. Chinese anthropologists were not satisfied with pure theoretical research; instead they wanted to know more about social facts and the panoramas of culture in their time. After the establishment of the nationalist government in Nanjing in 1928, an urgent need arose to obtain knowledge of different cultures and the social systems of ethnic groups inhabiting border areas for the purpose of political control. Chinese anthropologists believed that their academic training prepared them to make more important contributions to this task than scholars in other fields.

The research policy of the Institute of History and Language, Academia Sinica, in its early years was to try to collect systematically all materials pertaining to history, linguistics, and ethnology of ethnic groups for the sole purpose of pursuing knowledge. Although its research was not supposed to be related to application, in actuality some of its fieldwork and research also focused on practical issues. Officials used the results of this work to meet objectives that went beyond original intentions, such as setting up a biological classification of the Chinese population and demarcating the borders between China and Burma. Some anthropologists gave radio lectures and public speeches publicizing the cultures of ethnic groups and concerns about the security of the frontier. They tried to change the old prejudices against minorities in China and to improve ethnic relations. The investigation of customs and habits throughout the country in 1937 can be considered research for application, because the main purpose of this program was to offer advice to formulate social policies and government legislation. Some anthropologists took part in drafting outlines of policy documents and other planning activities.

Chinese anthropologists did fieldwork as part of their academic training. Some emphasized a combination of theory and practical investigations. They advocated doing studies of rural, urban, and frontier communities as a means of showing the value of sociocultural anthropology in China. Most spent years in various communities. Several series of monographs and books emerging from these efforts laid a solid foundation for further development of anthropology in China.

THE WAR YEARS AND ANTHROPOLOGY

During the Anti-Japanese War, the Chinese government had to establish a stable political and economic situation for the many ethnic groups living in western China, in order to supply the frontlines with enough soldiers and resources. Applied research became an urgent task. Some scholars proposed to establish a new discipline, named "frontier political science." According to the definition offered by anthropologist Professor Wu Wenzao, this discipline was to research political thoughts, facts, institutions, and administration among frontier ethnic groups. He suggested that China must apply anthropology not only to frontier politics and policies but also to education, welfare, and culture change in frontier areas. He sought to combine the theoretical framework of functionalism with the reality of practice. Furthermore, in order to put applied anthropology to its best use, Wu initiated the "sinification of anthropology" campaign, incorporating his focus on frontier anthropological studies during the Anti-Japanese War. Wu called the attention of intellectuals to "frontier political science" and advocated for the reform of frontier politics as well as frontier education. In the early 1940s, Wu and his colleagues were very active in founding and sponsoring the Association for Frontier Political Science and in taking charge of the publication of *Critiques on Frontier Politics*. The government and other groups of scholars organized additional frontier associations. Along with these scholars, anthropologists held training classes and established two departments of frontier studies in two national universities—National Central University and Northwest University. Some Chinese anthropologists participated in frontier research and also served in related government positions (Wang 1997:267–270). Professor Jiang Ying liang wrote a book called *Handbook for Frontier Political Officials*, in which he discussed the reform of frontier policies. He suggested that the government should take special measures in the management of frontier areas to develop production and education adapted to the local culture. He also outlined a policy of "interiorization," proposing that political, economic, and cultural development should integrate the frontier areas into the interior of China (Jiang 1944). Jiang wrote two development plans for frontier areas.

Students trained in the field of anthropology helped the government and several Christian churches to set up aid stations in southwest China. In addition to providing medical and educational services, they devoted themselves to the propaganda work among border peoples during the wartime years. Part of their time was devoted to investigating social conditions, building alliances with local elite, and collecting ethnic artifacts in border regions. In 1941 Professor Li Anche, a famous Chinese anthropologist, went to the border areas of Sichuan, Gansu, and Xinjiang provinces to survey educational institutions, including both public and monastic schools. He submitted a report to the central government education ministry and provincial education office, giving them many suggestions about the teachers' salaries, school administration, supplies for local schools, increasing the number of minority students, and protecting local literature. Many other scholars joined in trying to develop culture and education on the western frontiers of China (Wang 1997:263–276).

In the 1940s, anthropologists wrote articles about how to apply anthropological knowledge and theory in frontier politics and development. They thought that anthropology should focus on practical issues. Yang Cheng zhi argued that ethnic problems in Chinese frontier areas were a result of imbalance in the development of education, culture, and economy between frontier areas and central China. The rise of ethnic nationalism worldwide heightened problems that arose from the failure of the Nationalist government's policy to achieve ethnic equality and its lack of attention to development in frontier areas. This failure caused a frontier crisis of divisiveness and conflict (Yang 1947).

ANTHROPOLOGY AFTER LIBERATION

After the establishment of the People's Republic of China in 1949, Chinese anthropologists who came from different academic schools and training had done research more or less on their own terms and under their own initiative. Now they were asked to work under the direction of Marxist-Leninist theory in order to meet the requirements of jobs assigned to them. Anthropology, like other fields of scholarship, borrowed a Marxist framework from the Soviet Union. In the early 1950s the government required anthropologists to undertake intensive and systematic study of the classics of Marxism-Leninism and Soviet writings on ethnic theory and ethnic issues. Thus, anthropology as a discipline was replaced by ethnic studies and was called "ethnology," as anthropology was thought of "a bourgeoisie discipline." Within this political-ideological framework, anthropologists still tried their best to apply the theories they studied to practical investigations in the field.

China, as a multiethnic state, was confronted with many complex problems concerning the deep understanding of ethnic minority societies, cultures, social customs, and religions, as well as the interrelations between various ethnic groups. The new government of the Peoples Republic of China had urgent needs, especially in frontier areas, to establish a new regime, gain the support of minorities, and stabilize social conditions. Chinese anthropologists took part in the work of the government, conducting required ethnological investigations.

ETHNIC IDENTIFICATION

In the early 1950s the government dispatched anthropologists in universities and institutes as members of Central Visiting Goodwill Delegations to frontier areas, where they met with ethnic groups to propagandize communist policies. They also interviewed minorities to determine the status and social situation of each group. Four teams each went to different parts of the country—the Central South, Southwest, Northwest, and Northeast Regions. Some provincial governments also organized several teams. In the mid-1950s the national government organized large-scale investigations throughout the country. The urgent needs of the government set new tasks for anthropologists in close concert with the social and economic transformation of minority groups. The most important of these tasks was ethnic identification, which was followed by intensive social and historical investigations.

China established a people's congress system and the institution of ethnic regional autonomy for governance of minority areas, which included voting to select representatives of ethnic groups who would hold seats in central and local congresses. Ethnic identification became a high priority as many groups with diverse cultural characteristics asked to be certified as separate nationalities. Beginning in 1953, anthropologists and their colleagues in related disciplines carried out extensive field investigations to clarify ethnic identification. Two questions were held to be the key. First, is this group an ethnic minority, or is it part of the majority Han nationality? And second, if the group falls into the category of ethnic minority, is it a nationality by itself or a part of another nationality?

From the time of the first national census in 1953 to the first National People's Congress in 1954, 38 ethnic minorities, most of them fairly easily determined, became officially certified as separate ethnic groups. During this period, many of the original 400-plus registered groups applying for minority status were officially certified as belonging either to the majority Han or to other minority groups. Between 1954 and the second national census in 1964, another nationwide ethnic identification project attempted to solve the more difficult problems of identification still remaining. Fifteen of 183 remaining applicant groups were newly certified, while 74 other groups were merged into the already certified 53 ethnic groups. Only 56 groups remained for further study. Before the third national census in 1982, the Luoba (1965) and Jinuo (1979) were officially certified. During the interval between certifications, the Cultural Revolution interrupted identification work for about ten years. By 1979 the Chinese government had confirmed the separate identity of 55 minority groups. At present, there are still other groups that want separate minority status. The 1990 census listed almost 800,000 people as "still unidentified." In addition, several dispersed groups have recently filed claims for re-identification.

Many experts from various fields engaged in in-depth research to identify each distinct ethnic group (Fei 1981). They investigated the history, language, ethnogenesis, economic life, social customs, religion, psychological makeup, and ethnic relations of the various groups. Their ethnic identification work employed four criteria first proposed by Stalin: common territory, common economic life, common language, and common psychological makeup as reflected in a common culture. However, the researchers applied these criteria rather flexibly, and they added historical study as an important supplement to the "four commons." Repeated discussions and negotiations with the people being identified, and with their leaders, were of great importance to the identification process. The wishes of each ethnic group were to be taken into full consideration. In some cases, however, this principle was not properly followed, and in several other cases investigations were not sufficiently thorough or intensive (Chen 1998).

The process of ethnic identification was very complicated and sensitive, since it had relevance to the number of minority seats allotted to deputies from different nationalities in the National People's Congress, local People's Congresses, and various levels of Political Consultative Conferences. Even more significantly, it affected the establishment of politically autonomous units at different levels of the administrative hierarchy and created career opportunities for minority cadres. In recent years, some (postmodern) scholars have claimed that ethnic identification played an important role in the creation, not just identification, of Chinese ethnic groups. In reevaluating their identification work, Chinese anthropologists have realized that they not only had found some new ethnic groups but also had created new identities in the process of their investigations.

The process of ethnic identification was both a research project and a deliberate political task. Professor Chen Yong ling, one of the most respected senior anthropologists in China, thinks that the general policy of national regional autonomy could never have been carried out as smoothly if ethnic identification had not provided a solid foundation for the political transformations to follow (Chen 1998).

From this experience, anthropologists learned that they had to consider the close relationship between academic research and national policy and have deeper understanding of the implementation of policies and their scientific significance. Today anthropology in China continues to address important issues concerning local autonomy and national solidarity.

SOCIAL AND HISTORICAL INVESTIGATIONS

After ethnic identification, the second major task given to Chinese ethnologists in the 1950s was the social and historical investigation of ethnic minorities. After 1949, Chinese scholars adopted the Marxist doctrine of unilinear evolution, according to which all human societies had evolved from pre-class primitive society to slave, feudal, and capitalist societies with classes and then to classless communist society. China's leaders believed that China's social transformation to socialism and communism under the leadership of the Communist Party would be achieved in a short time. However, they realized that all policy making for democratic reform and socialist construction in minority areas had to be based on thorough sociohistorical investigations. Because of the uneven social development of ethnic groups, their situation had to be studied carefully. The pressing need for a thorough investigation of minority social structures and social morphologies became a driving force pushing anthropologists to organize into research teams and devote themselves for several years to intensive fieldwork around the country.

Sixteen social and historical investigation groups worked from 1956 until the early 1960s to carry out a comprehensive investigation of minority areas, emphasizing economic structure and class relations. In careful investigation and analysis of the characteristics of each social system and other aspects of culture, they collected a huge number of materials, wrote many monographs and books, and produced a dozen documentary films on the social morphology of precapitalist societies. According to the analytic paradigm of that time, researchers confirmed that these precapitalist groups belonged to different stages of social development, including the feudal landlord economy, the feudal serfdom, the slave-owning system, and the pre-class social formation of primitive communism. Mao Zedong said that the purpose of this investigation was to "rescue the backward ones." The research on social morphology was the main part of these investigations, and the research results served to prove and explain communist theory and to advance Maoist ideology.

When they were in the field, investigators lived the same life as the indigenous minority people, eating common meals, living in the same houses, joining in communal labor, and studying together with local people. Scholars considered their involvement with indigenous daily living as a necessity for doing complete scientific research. Thus, in practice, this investigation was both an academic project and a deliberate political task for scholars to receive education by living with indigenous people.

After one year of social and historical investigations, the government launched the Anti-Rightist Campaign. Some scholars who participated in the investigations were the targets of severe criticism for overemphasizing abstract structural analysis, purposely "seeking backwardness," "hunting for exotica," and promoting "bourgeois nationalism." The primary tactic of ultra-leftists in interfering with academic work was arbitrarily labeling certain academic viewpoints as "opposing socialism" or "opposing the Communist Party's policy."

After this period of severe criticism, the term "ethnology" (referring to scholars who study ethnic groups) disappeared from use by Chinese intellectuals. It was a forbidden area of inquiry. Being an ethnologist or showing interest in the field was in itself almost a political crime. Nobody dared to be known as an anthropologist or ethnologist anymore, and nobody dared to apply anthropological knowledge to address practical issues. During the ten years of the Cultural Revolution, the government abolished all research institutes and teaching institutes of ethnology and dismissed or transferred personnel to other fields (Wang et al. 1998).

REHABILITATION OF ANTHROPOLOGY

The government rehabilitated anthropology as a discipline in 1978. Anthropologists again established professional associations, such as the Chinese Ethnological Society, the Society for Anthropology in China, the Society for World Ethnic Studies, and the China Urban Anthropology Association. At the same time they established departments of anthropology or ethnology in institutes and universities offering a major in anthropology and ethnology for undergraduate students, along with M.A. and Ph.D. programs. Research institutes were set up under the umbrella of the Chinese Academy of Social Sciences and its regional branches, including the Institute for Nationality (Ethnic) Studies in Beijing and several provincial institutes located close to areas inhabited by ethnic minorities. University programs included the Central University for Nationalities in Beijing, Yunnan University, Zhongshan University in Guangzhou, and Xiamen University in Fujian. Recently Xiamen University closed its anthropology department, while Beijing University established an anthropology department. Thirteen regional colleges for nationalities have anthropologists/ethnologists on staff but do not offer majors or graduate programs in anthropology. In the 1980s professional associations, universities, and institutes began holding conferences and discussions, some related to applied anthropology. Anthropologists began to believe that their mission should be to serve the interests of ethnic minorities by raising the level of their material and intellectual life. They emphasized the unity of theory and practice, while recognizing both the theoretical value and the applied value of anthropological study.

Economic development and the construction of infrastructure have become the focus of many anthropologists during the last two decades. They have been able to find money and support from the government to achieve their goal of "learning for use." For example, beginning in 1982, the Association for Southwest Ethnic Studies carried out two major, comprehensive multidisciplinary studies emphasizing the practical aspects of modernization. The first of these was the study of the peoples along six rivers—Nu (Salween), Lancang (Mekong), Jinsha (Upper Yangtze), Yalong, Dadu, and Min. These investigations focused on the study of history, as well as the current situation of the minorities in southern and southwestern areas. Specific topics included migration, economic development, ethnic relations, and the international relations between minorities on either side of China's international borders. Another extensive series of studies targeted the minority peoples in the region of six mountains and six rivers in Guizhou. All located in the border regions of Guizhou and Yunnan or Guizhou and Hunan, the six mountains included Yueliang Mountain, Leigong Mountain, Yunwu Mountain, Wumeng Mountain, Big and Small Ma Mountains, and Biandan Mountain. The six rivers included the North Pan, the South Pan, the Duliu, Qinshui, Wuyang, and Wu. In the past the relationships among local ethnic groups living in these areas were rather complicated, and at present these groups are isolated, poor, and undeveloped, although their environment is rich in natural resources. In order to create favorable conditions for economic development, these cold highlands and narrow valleys needed to be investigated. The "Report on the Ethnic Groups at Yueliang Mountain" discussed problems in reaching the goals of modernization. These problems included the relationship between economic development and the economic base; the relationship between the development of minority education and ethnic characteristics; the relationship between the introduction of a modern worldview and traditional culture; and the relationship between ethnic friction and ethnic amalgamation. These investigations tended to be quite theoretical and were closely connected to the drive to modernize minority areas. They demonstrated the contribution of applied anthropology to successful development. A 1991 article by Ren Yifei, "Policy Against Poverty: The Uygur Case," in *Practicing Anthropology* illustrates the kinds of issues addressed by Chinese anthropologists in the 1980s.

In 1992 Chinese researchers began to employ the method of participatory rural appraisal. Researchers in Yunnan province established the first PRA network. They focused on empirical data gathering in using ethnography and participant-observation to address issues of resource protection, agriculture, village development, health and medical services, and the need for government assistance. A team headed by Dr. Wen Naiqun from the Anthropology Institute of the China Academy of Social Sciences studied the social and cultural impacts on minority communities of the construction of a railroad from Nanning to Kunming. They wrote a report of their fieldwork with the title "Nanning to Kunming Eight Villages." The report included three volumes, one each on

Guangxi, Guizhou, and Yunnan. A 2002 article by Dr. Bilik Naran, "The Nan-Kun Railway and Sociocultural Change among Minority Nationalities," in *Practicing Anthropology* provides an example of this work.

Bilik Naran spent a total of more than six months in a small mountain village, Geyan, located on wooded mountains in Tianlin County Guangxi Zhuang Autonomous Region. Geyan had a population of 311 living in 62 households, with 98 percent being of Yao ethnicity. Most villagers were content with subsistence farming, while a few grew cash crops or had other kinds of entrepreneurial aspirations. For example, one peasant "got rich" by selling pigs and homemade colored threads outside the village. He succeeded despite losing money the first year when his horse loaded with goods fell into the river. The construction of the Nan-Kun Railway brought more opportunities for small merchants, wage labor jobs, a factory to make wooden planks, a new bridge improving rainy season transportation to the market town, electricity, a loudspeaker in the center of the village, and the national Chinese television network. Despite the intrusion of national culture into the schools and workplaces of the village, the net effect of the railroad was to restore moral authority to traditional culture. Under collectivism and secularism, and in comparative isolation, the township government and local village governing committee (cadres) were once quite powerful. Now the previous power-holders have been marginalized by the economic gains made by peasants in a largely privatized, capitalist economy. The former leaders have forfeited a large share of authority to customary law as affirmed by most villagers. Even the party secretary himself has become a ritual specialist who offers his services in castrating piglets and performing religious ceremonies for villagers. In this case study, the author shows that local symbolic systems will inevitably mediate economic rationality and that for this reason the outcome of infrastructure development and globalizing influence is not always predictable.

Some Chinese anthropologists devote most of their attention to ethnic cultural protection and social development. The focus of their applied research is on preserving traditional culture, religious practices, and the environment in frontier areas. Anthropologists in the Department of Anthropology of the Central University for Nationalities are researching the question of protecting cultural heritage in Three Gorges where the world's largest hydroelectric dam is under construction. They also have investigated festivals and tourism in Guizhou and made recommendations to local governments and administrative offices. They now have under way a program of investigation focused on the traditional knowledge of Miao and Yi women in Yunnan. In 1997 Professor Yin Shaoting and his colleagues at Yunnan University initiated a program to establish "Ethnic Cultural and Ecological Villages." Their objective was to promote ethnic cultural preservation and ecologically, socially, and economically sustainable development in rural areas prone to the impact of globalization and modernization. This program emphasized the participation of local communities in the preservation and transmission of ethnic culture and in environmental conservation while seeking ways to promote economic development (Yin 2002).

Other anthropologists have undertaken research on ethnic relations in Xinjiang, the status of minority women in Guizhou and Yunnan, rural immigrants in cities, cultural conflict, and emerging ethnic issues of various kinds throughout China. In 2003 Tsinghua University established a new interdisciplinary program involving the humanities and social sciences to study the SARS and AIDS epidemics and held an international SARS and AIDS summit on its campus in Beijing. Anthropologists have participated in both of these initiatives. The Department of Anthropology at the Central University for Nationalities presently is conducting a multiyear study of cultural factors in the spread of AIDS among ethnic minority populations in Southwest China. In recent years, international development agencies such as the World Bank, the Asian Development Bank, the United Nations Development Program, and the Ford Foundation have funded the applied research of Chinese anthropologists.

Since 1983, Chinese anthropologists have attended many international conferences such as those sponsored by the International Congress of Anthropological and Ethnological Sciences, the Society for Applied Anthropology, and the Society of Urban Anthropology. In the summer of 2000, the Inter-Congress of the International Union of Anthropological and Ethnological Sciences (IUAES) was hosted successfully by the China Urban Anthropology Association in Beijing. The theme of this conference was "Metropolitan Ethnic Cultures: Maintenance and Interaction." The 16th Congress of IUAES will convene in Kunming, Yunnan province, China, in the summer of 2008. A delegation from universities, institutes, and the State Ethnic Affairs Commission jointly developed the successful proposal to host the conference. Anthropologists in the Department of Anthropology of the Central University for Nationalities are planning to organize a number of sessions on various topics in applied anthropology for this 2008 conference. Chinese anthropologists also have attended numerous international meetings on Chinese and Asian Studies, have served as visiting professors and visiting scholars, and have engaged in research and scholarly cooperation with a number of universities and research institutes abroad. In addition, many foreign anthropologists have visited Chinese institutes and universities to give lectures on applied anthropological topics, including two presentations by John A. Young at Beijing University in March 2004. Academic exchanges and translated works in applied anthropology have influenced the development of empirical approaches and new theoretical paradigms. Chinese anthropologists are taking part in the debates on current issues in world anthropology, such as the shaping of the ethnic identity and globalization versus indigenization.

Despite the substantial gains made by applied anthropology in post-Mao China, it still lacks popular recognition for contributions to solving problems related to economic development, environmental protection, public health, and business and organizational effectiveness. Both as a cause and a consequence of the lack of public awareness of anthropology, Chinese anthropologists are not employed either in private sector companies or in nonprofit organizations. In addition, anthropology and its methods have had little involvement in studies of the mainstream culture of the majority Han, including its contemporary institutions, organizations, and subcultures. Students of anthropology still express concern over where they can find jobs and hear doubts from friends and relatives about the prospects of developing a successful career based on their interest in anthropology. It will be up to the next generation of young anthropologists to expand both topical interests and the niche for practice beyond government-sponsored institutes and universities, as their mentors continue to call greater public attention to anthropology through their studies of policy-related issues.

CONCLUSION

From the very beginning of the dissemination of anthropology into China, both its theoretical approach and its field investigations have emphasized applied value. Its service to the needs of the country accounts for the amazing vitality of Chinese anthropology, as it survived even through the period of the Cultural Revolution when it suffered severe academic and political setbacks. Because of its connection to China's ongoing agenda for social and cultural change, anthropology will find more opportunities to develop than ever before.

However, the relation between theory and practice is still an open question in the development of applied anthropology in China. Some scholars argue that if anthropologists merely comply with the demands of the government and do what the government needs, it will lead to the death of anthropology (He 1981). And if anthropologists remain satisfied to work on the tasks of the government, regarding this as their main work, they will ruin anthropology (Huang 1981). An increasing number of anthropologists are convinced that they must maintain the academic integrity of anthropology as they apply the special perspective of anthropological thought—relativism, fieldwork, participant-observation, comparative method, and theories—in applied research. They believe anthropologists' identity must be clearly defined when doing research; otherwise politics and power will have too much influence on the academy.

Chinese anthropologists apply their knowledge, methods, and skills to help government agencies solve real problems. Most Chinese anthropologists are involved in studying policy issues in one way or another. A few have become involved directly in making national or regional policies, especially those related to ethnic development, though in recent years government offices have not offered many direct employment opportunities for anthropologists. Chinese anthropologists realize that their analysis and insights must be well supported and judged superior to the casual observations of local party secretaries to be taken seriously by those who set policy.

Darby C. Stapp argues that if anthropology is to increase its influences among policy makers we must get better at playing the policy game. Just as anthropology students must learn the basics of anthropological theories and methods, so too they should learn the basics of policy making and implementation. They need to understand the role of anthropological research in policy planning and how its methods are critical for assessing policy effectiveness (Stapp 1999). The task for Chinese applied anthropology is to strengthen its academic foundation in theory and method in order to have a stronger and broader impact as a policy science.

REFERENCES

Bilik, Naran
    2002 The Nan-Kun Railway and Sociocultural Change among Minority Nationalities. Practicing Anthropology 24(1):21–24.

Chen, Yongling
    1998 History of Ethnology in China. *In* A Collection of Chinese Ethnological Studies: A Dream of Ethnic Unity, Equality and Prosperity. Yong-ling Chen, ed. Taipei: Hong-Yih Publishing Co.

Fei, Xiao Tung
    1981 Toward a People's Anthropology. Beijing: New World Press.

He, Yaohua
    1981 Comment in Seminar in Kunming. Newsletter of Ethnology 10.

Huang, Hui-kun
    1981 Comment in Seminar in Kunming. Newsletter of Ethnology 10.

Jiang, Yingliang
    1944 Handbook for Frontier Administrative Officers. Yunnan Province: The Committee of Frontier Administrative Design.

Ren, Yifei
    1991 Policy against Poverty: The Uygur Case. Practicing Anthropology 13(1):15–18.

Stapp, Darby C.
    1999 The Real World: Operationalizing Anthropology. Practicing Anthropology 21(1)50–52.

Wang, Jianmin
    1997 The History of Ethnology in China, Part 1 (1903–1949). Kunming: Yunnan Education Publishing House.

Wang, Jianmin, Zhang Haiyang, and Hu Hongbao
    1998 The History of Ethnology in China, Part 2 (1950–1997). Kunming: Yunnan Education Publishing House.

Yang, Chengzhi
    1947 Perspectives on the Ethnic Problems. Critiques of Frontier Politics 6:1.

Yin, Shaoting, ed.
    2002 Work Reports on the Project for the Construction of Ethnic Cultural and Ecological Villages in Yunnan Province, China. Kunming: Yunnan Minzu Publishing House.

PRACTICING ETHNOLOGY IN CONTEMPORARY RUSSIA

ANATOLY N. YAMSKOV
Russian Academy of Sciences

The chapter reviews changing priorities of applied studies in Soviet and post-Soviet Russia, presented on the background of institutional developments and changes in public status of ethnology in the country. Special emphasis is given to activities of the Institute of Ethnology and Anthropology (Moscow) in this field and to author's personal experience in practicing ethnology during the last 15 years. Key Words: Russia, applied ethnology, status, institutions, policy

If one looks at the history and present position of ethnology in Russia, one is certain to be puzzled by a paradox. This long-established discipline, which has accumulated an impressive compendium of data as a result of the efforts of many generations of top specialists, was little known to the general public until the late 1980s. Even now it enjoys limited influence in Russian society. Judging from the number of scholars or research and training centers, ethnology in Russia still falls far behind other social sciences and humanities, such as history, philology, economics, sociology, political science, philosophy, and social geography.

The discipline of ethnology was known as ethnography during the Imperial and Soviet periods. Thematically it more or less corresponds to cultural/social anthropology in English-speaking countries. Scholars, working in ethnology, have been receiving scientific degrees and academic statuses in "history," because in the middle 1930s ethnography was officially designated as its subdiscipline. In the Soviet tradition, physical anthropology, archaeology, and linguistics had been developing as separate disciplines, though close contacts between them and ethnography were always maintained. Nevertheless some scholars worked successfully in several of these disciplines, like late academician Valery Alekseev, who combined research in physical anthropology and archaeology with studies in ethnology and ethnic ecology. In Russia, only physical anthropology maintained rather close institutional contacts with ethnology, so that one can often choose to defend the same dissertation either in "history" (subdiscipline "ethnology, ethnography, anthropology") or in "biology" (subdiscipline "anthropology, human biology").

NAPA Bulletin 25, pp. 82–103, ISBN 1-931303-28-2. © 2006 by the American Anthropological Association. All rights reserved. Permissions to photocopy or reproduce article content via www.ucpress.edu/journals/rights.htm.

Generally speaking, there is no officially or unofficially institutionalized special subdiscipline of applied ethnology in Russia with its own professional organizations, departments or research groups, conferences or regularly held working meetings, uniform terms, research methods and goals, or even discussions of the latter in academic journals. The only exception is a collection of papers (Stepanov 1999), and the Institute of Ethnology and Anthropology in Moscow publishes the special series "Issledovania po prikladnoy i neotlozhnoy etnologii" ("Studies in Applied and Urgent Ethnology"), slightly more than 180 issues during 1990–2005, each one being a brochure of some 25–30 pp. long. On the other hand, Russian scholars have done great deal of work in this field.

A good illustration of this situation can be seen in the recent activities of the Association of Russian Ethnographers and (Physical) Anthropologists. It was formed in 1990 as a public professional organization on the initiative of Professor Valery Tishkov, convened six biannual congresses between 1995 and 2005, and became known to all professionals. Some 800 to 900 scholars have been sending their abstracts for the largest congresses, such as those held in Moscow (1999), Omsk (2003), and St. Petersburg (2005). Some 25–45 sections and symposia were working at every Congress, each attracting some 10–30 scholars or even more. Among these, there was only one special session on "Applied Ethnology" at the Moscow Congress in 1999, organized by Mr. A. Karpukhin, Dr. E. Miskova, and the author; the session was composed of only six papers, including three from the organizers themselves. At the same time, many sessions at these congresses were in fact dealing with applied ethnology, especially ethnopolitics, ethnolinguistics, land use practices, and land rights of aboriginal ethnic groups in Siberia and the Far North, with practically no attention to the methodological or ethical issues of the studies that have been done with the prime aim to prevent or induce considerable changes in the lives of many people.

In order to understand this situation better, one can compare "applied ethnology" with, for example, "ethnic ecology," a subdiscipline that is thematically rather close to American cultural ecology or ecological anthropology (Kozlov 1983). During the last decade, the Department of Ethnic Ecology in the Institute of Ethnology and Anthropology (Moscow) published several collections of papers and organized symposia at the biannual Congresses of the Association of Russian Ethnographers and Physical Anthropologists (a total of five in 1997–2005, each attracting 15 to 20 papers). There is also a series entitled "Studies in Ethnic Geography and Ethnic Ecology" (published in St. Petersburg), and several formally announced ethnoecological sections were held within other conferences. At the same time, numbers of all scholars, including those who work in ethnic ecology only occasionally, have been dozens of times less than those who have been engaged in applied projects.

Consequently, there are no special studies devoted to critical assessment of contemporary applied ethnology in the country. The only exception was a preliminary attempt to review the history of applying ethnological expertise in the USSR/Russia and the situation in this field as it was in the early to middle 1990s (Yamskov, Dubova, 1997). The latter review served as a basis for this chapter, but since this time my colleague and former coauthor, Professor Nadezhda Dubova, was unable to join in revising the paper, the issues of applying physical anthropology and human ecology were omitted from the following text.

HISTORY OF RUSSIAN ETHNOLOGICAL INSTITUTIONS:
A BRIEF OVERVIEW

The first ethnographic data recorded in Ancient Russia (Kievan Rus') in medieval chronicles began with Nestor's "Povest Vremennykh Let" (A Story about Old Years) in the early 12th century. This tradition survived for many centuries and, in Siberia, it stopped only in the late 17th century with the chronicle written by Semen Remisov.

During the time of Peter the Great, who transformed Russian Tzardom into an Empire and westernized the ruling elite in the beginning of the 18th century, the first scientific expeditions started to work in the country. Invited foreign scholars or Russians, trained in a Western manner, started to collect ethnographic data along with information about mineral resources, physical geography, and so on, mainly at the outskirts of the Empire. The tradition of government-organized expeditions in which both military personnel and civilian scholars took part lasted up to the start of the 20th century in the Far East (Pacific coast) or Central Asia, but the most productive period was in the 18th to 19th centuries.

Peter the Great established the first Museum, "Kunstkamera," in 1714, and the Academy of Sciences in 1724. Both of these were state institutions in St. Petersburg, organizing expeditions and studying and exhibiting the resulting collections, including ethnographic ones. In 1831 Peter's Kunstkamera was divided into seven separate museums, one of them being the Museum of Ethnography of the Academy of Sciences (Stanyukovich 1974). Having gone through many reorganizations, currently it is known as the Museum of Anthropology and Ethnography (Kunstkamera) of the Russian Academy of Sciences, being composed of museum and institute, and it comprises the oldest and second largest ethnological research center in Russia.

In the 19th and early 20th centuries, a great impetus to the development of ethnography was given by the state-sponsored or private activities of army officers or civilian administrators. They compiled descriptions, often very detailed and accurate, of certain newly acquired territories where they were stationed and of their new neighbors—the local peoples. Ethnographic and folkloristic research among ethnic Russians and other peoples of the European part of the Empire also started in the early 19th century, but mainly due to the efforts of unofficial, well-educated amateurs.

The Russian Emperor's Geographical Society was established in 1845 in St. Petersburg, and from the start, academician Karl Behr organized there the first official ethnographic research institution in the country, the Department of Ethnography. It became the major coordinating and consultative, publishing, and organizing center of ethnographic research, including state-sponsored expeditions, for the next 50 years.

The Russian Geographical Society and its Department of Ethnography also exists now, organizing symposia and occasionally publishing proceedings or collections of papers, which are presented at the regular monthly sessions. As in the last two centuries, branches of the Society still are formally surviving in major regional centers of Russia, but now, having virtually no funds and a staff of one or two clerks only, they do not act as real research and publishing centers.

In Moscow, the Society of Amateur Natural Scientists, Physical Anthropologists and Ethnographers was formed in 1863 in the form of a public organization, affiliated with the Moscow State University. It became a fund-raising, coordinating, and publishing center too, though less important than the Geographical Society, and unlike the latter, it ceased operating in 1931. Nevertheless, this Society started the first regular specialized journal in 1889—*Etnograficheskoe Obozrenie* (Ethnographic Review). In 1992 the journal *Sovetskaya etnografia* (Soviet Ethnography) was renamed after this predecessor.

Professor Dmitriy Anuchin, famous for his research in geography, ethnography, archaeology, and physical anthropology, established the first training centers in Russia. In 1880 the Chair of Anthropology was established with courses in physical anthropology and ethnography (Tokarev 1966), and in 1884 the Chair of Geography and Ethnography (Markov and Solovey 1990) was established. Both were located at Moscow State University.

The history of Russian ethnology before 1917 was studied in detail by Professor Sergey Tokarev, though he did not cover the problems and areas of applied research (Tokarev 1966). The same is true for many articles on the topic of Russian ethnology, appearing mostly in the continuing series of collections *Ocherki istorii russkoy etnografii, folkloristiki i antropologii* (Essays on the History of Russian Ethnography, Folklore Studies and Physical Anthropology), published by "Nauka" Press in Moscow and Leningrad/St. Petersburg.

During pre-Revolutionary times, Russian ethnology was forming as a discipline with a strongly applied character, as was typical for any colonial power of that time. It was even considered by the officials as a prime source of local-scale economic and geopolitical information. The major focus was on traditional economy and land use, settlement patterns, demography, folk law, beliefs (religion), and folklore of the populations under study. Social and military organization and political, economic, and marital links with neighboring groups also were studied in detail. Starting with the medieval chronicles, special attention was always paid to the folk knowledge of the origins, history, and past migrations of the surveyed populations.

SOVIET ETHNOLOGY: RESEARCH AND TRAINING CENTERS

After the October Revolution of 1917, the first departments of ethnography/ethnology were established in the country, showing the growing importance of the discipline. In 1919 the Department of Ethnography was organized in the newly established Institute of Geography in St. Petersburg (Tokarev 1974). The same year in Moscow, Professor Dm. Anuchin reestablished the Chair of Anthropology (with courses in ethnography) in the "old" university and the new "1st" university was organized with the Chair of Ethnology (from 1922), which transformed into the Department of Ethnology in 1925. Professor P. Preobrazhensky from that department produced the first Soviet textbook, *Ethnology*, published in 1929.

However, the methodological discussions of the late 1920s turned into ideological and finally into political ones in the 1930s. Professor P. Preobrazhensky, who advocated ethnology as a more "progressive" and nearly universal social science with strong links to sociology, strongly criticized the old "czarist" ethnography for its ties with geography. He later lost his case and was jailed and killed and his textbook was forbidden (for more details about those tragic events, see Slezkin 1993). For some time in the early 1930s, there was no training in either ethnography (not to speak about the banned ethnology) or history in the universities, and there were no classes in history in the schools of the USSR (except for the history of the Communist movement or October Revolution.)

In 1934 history courses were reestablished in the Soviet universities, the historical faculties and departments reopened, and ethnography was allowed again, but as nothing more than a specialized part of history. Chairs of Ethnography were organized from the middle 1930s at the Faculties of History in the Universities of Leningrad and Moscow, in the latter by professor Sergey Tolstov in 1939 (Markov and Solovey 1990). Due to ideological reasons, the "old" ethnography had been drastically transformed in its methodology and research priorities and compelled to avoid any methodological links or cooperation with geography (or ecology and environmental sciences, as was the case in the 1970s and early 1980s).

But some professionals continued their work in museums and some state research organizations even during the early 1930s. In Leningrad, in 1933, scholars from the former Department of Ethnography at the Institute of Geography were joined with the research staff of the Museum of Anthropology and Ethnology and of the former Institute for the Studies of the Peoples of the USSR (the latter was established in 1930 on the basis of the Commission on the Studies of Tribal Composition of Population in Russia and Adjacent Countries that functioned since 1917). Together they formed a new research institution that went through several reorganizations and in 1937 finally became the Institute of Ethnography of the USSR Academy of Sciences, while the Museum of Anthropology and Ethnology was merged into it as its part the same year.

The Moscow Branch of the Institute of Ethnography was formed and headed by Professor Sergey Tolstov in 1942. Soon it became the leading research center in the country, being renamed the Institute of Ethnology and Anthropology in 1990. In 1992 the Moscow and St. Petersburg branches became independent institutions of the Russian Academy of Sciences.

The postwar period saw the gradual spread of research and training institutions from Moscow and Leningrad to provincial centers, mainly during the 1960s and 1970s. Currently, every republic of the Russian Federation has a branch research institute, affiliated with the republican or regional branch of the Russian Academy of Sciences or the Republican Ministry of Education. In every one of 19 such institutes there are departments of linguistics and literature, history, ethnography, and archaeology. In some cases, such institutes have differentiated, but nowhere have independent ethnological research centers appeared.

Major regional centers, such as Vladivostok, Novosibirsk, Omsk, and Tyumen', have the same kind of research institutes as republics, but these regional institutions belong to the Russian Academy of Sciences. The research institutes usually have up to a dozen or slightly more ethnologists, with about one hundred in St. Petersburg and about two hundred in Moscow. Most of them have scientific degrees and are engaged in academic research. In Moscow and St. Petersburg they are training postgraduate students, and some scholars, purely by individual choice, have an extra job as lecturers in the universities or pedagogical universities. Professional ethnologists also work in many provincial museums that are devoted to local history and geography and usually have ethnographic sections. Often individuals combine work in the local university as a part-time lecturer and work in the museum as a researcher and lecturer, if both exist in the city.

Chairs of Ethnology are operating at the Faculties of History in the Universities of Moscow, St. Petersburg, Novosibirsk, Omsk, and Kazan' (Republic of Tatarstan) and in a few other places. The staff of these chairs rarely exceeds a dozen or two dozen trained scholars who combine lecturing in ethnology and academic research. Students, training in ethnology, do not have compulsory basic courses in applied ethnology or textbooks in this field.

It has been estimated that the leading training center in the country (Chair of Ethnology at the Faculty of History in the Moscow State University) prepared some 800 graduate and postgraduate students between 1945 and 1990 (Markov and Solovey 1990). This number includes some foreigners and persons from the previous Union Republics. It can be assumed that something like 500–600 of them were graduate students from the Russian Federation. We can add about 150–200 persons, trained during the 1990s to early 2000s, and some more 150–200 persons who got a five-year university education in geography, history, sociology, and other sciences but went for postgraduate studies in ethnography and thus became professionals too. The number of scholars, trained in ethnography/ethnology outside Moscow, is probably slightly less or at best the same. These figures give an idea of the general size of the ethnological community in Russia.

To better understand the very modest position of ethnology in contemporary Russia, it is worth mentioning that there were no faculties or departments of ethnology anywhere in the country before the 1990s. Most provincial and republican capitals had universities with faculties or departments of history and of geography (as a rule) and, often, departments of philosophy or sociology, and, in recent years, of political science. Numerous researchers and lecturers in such disciplines as the history of the Communist Party of the USSR, scientific communism, political economy of socialism, and so on, moved to the political sciences or sociology after the end of the USSR. They have organized many new or enlarged old departments and chairs of social sciences.

On the other hand, in the 1990s newly established non-state commercial universities in several cases started teaching ethnology, cultural studies, or social-cultural anthropology, forming such departments or faculties. It is still not clear what the actual standards of education there are. Practically the only one new center of ethnological education that has already gained good reputation has been organized within the State University for Humanities in Moscow, and mostly scholars from the Institute of Ethnology and Anthropology read lectures there.

THE SOVIET PERIOD: APPLYING RESULTS
OF ETHNOGRAPHIC RESEARCH

Though applied ethnology, as a distinct subdiscipline with its organizations, methods, and aims, had not formed during the Soviet period, the idea of translating research results into practice was always promoted by officials in both the Academy and universities. The section on application was, for instance, an important and unavoidable part of annual reports about one's work that every scholar or lecturer had to submit to the administration of his or her institution.

Generally speaking, Soviet ethnographers acted only as consultants to state officials, producing reports with information and recommendations on special requests, or on their own initiative, but with no influence on the process of policy formulation and decision making. Those few scholars who joined government organizations usually stopped their own research and publishing activities. There were two major exceptions to this rule that made it possible to speak about applied ethnography in a real sense—the work of ethnographers in the North in the 1920s and the Khoresm expedition to Aral basin in the 1950s to 1980s. In both cases, ethnographers were participating in the process of implementation of their recommendations.

In the 1920s the major focus of Soviet ethnography was on the Northern indigenous groups, and many ethnographers played crucial roles in developing alphabets and written (suited for future literature) languages of these groups, sometimes working as teachers themselves. This work was analyzed in a special article (Antropova 1972); a bibliography of some reports of practitioners that were published in the 1920s also is available (see Slezkin 1993). The ethnographers were successful too in such a delicate field as collectivization in the North. By constantly monitoring the actual subsistence economy and migrations, and being able to appeal to top state and party officials, ethnographers did the most to slow down the process, for more than a decade, and to minimize the losses that the people suffered. In the 1970s and 1980s, ethnographers produced many reports, criticizing the state economic and social policies in the North and their effects on indigenous populations. Judging from the role of ethnographers in changing or preserving traditional lifestyles of entire ethnic groups, the Soviet North and Siberia are the most important examples of applying results of ethnographic studies.

The other most important region of the USSR, from the point of view of economic and social consequences of applying results of ethnographic research, has been Central Asia. Here the founder and the first director of the Moscow Institute, Professor Sergey Tolstov, organized after World War II the Khoresm expedition for multidisciplinary research on ethnography, archaeology, and paleogeography of the Aral area. As a result, many formerly irrigated fields were found and some of them, after the information was given to local officials, were re-irrigated and settled again after centuries of being desert pastures. Two decades ago, the now late Professors Boris Andrianov and Alexander Vinogradov, and retired head of the department Professor Larisa Levina, took the lead in discussions and abortive planning (because of the split of the USSR) of measures to ameliorate the severe ecological crisis in the Aral area.

Ethnographers from the Commission on the Studies of Tribal Composition of Population in Russia and Adjacent Countries also played a crucial role in demarcating the boundaries of the republics and autonomous regions when they were formed in the USSR in the 1920s. Actually, the project to create ethnic maps, showing areas settled and used by all ethnic groups of the country, was launched just before the Revolution of 1917. The scholars, who survived and stayed in Russia, were recruited to finish the project and to consult on the new "national" boundaries. But in this politically sensitive field, the decision making remained in the hands of the party and state officials, and the scholars served as consultants only.

For almost the whole Soviet period there were repeated attempts to eradicate the folk or religious ceremonies, beliefs, and practices corresponding to major events of the life cycle and to introduce the new, socialist ones. Especially strenuous efforts were made in the 1930s and in the 1960s and early 1970s. However, no famous ethnographer took part in these actions despite heavy ideological pressure. But research in this field was organized and many scholars monitored the situation in different areas of the USSR and among different ethnic groups, informing the state and communist party institutions.

During the last years of the USSR, when ethnic conflicts started to spread over the country, ethnographers were very active in preparing reports to the Central Committee of the CPSU. Reports were also prepared for the government on the history, present situation, and possible future developments of ethnic contacts in all multiethnic areas, both conflict-ridden and still peaceful. Such reporting on interethnic relations was taking place in the earlier times too, but not on such a large scale.

By the middle 1980s, writing reports to official bodies on practical issues (i.e., interethnic relations, or social-economic, cultural-linguistic, and medical-demographical problems of certain ethnic groups) was considered one of the major components of professional ethnographic research. Others activities included fieldwork, publication of articles and monographs, or presentation of conference papers. Nevertheless, there is no mention of applied ethnography as a subdivision of the discipline and there are no reviews of the methods or goals of the application of ethnographic research in either of the two postwar Soviet-period textbooks. Both books, however, did refer to fields of applying results of ethnological studies and about their practical importance (Tokarev 1958; Bromley and Markov 1982).

PRACTICING ETHNOLOGY IN THE LATE 1980S AND EARLY 1990S

The period immediately before and after the split of the USSR should be reviewed separately for many reasons. Democratization made ethnologists far more active, not only in writing reports and providing information and recommendations but also in stressing the need for their active participation in all stages of activities organized by the state, and more likely to change the lives of the ethnic groups they study. The state officials themselves became more interested in joint work with specialists in cases where public opinion might turn out to be negative and generate opposition in the popular mass media. Ethnic tensions, pogroms, and open conflicts made ethnography/ethnology and ethnologists if not popular, at least known to the public, and the term *ethnicity* and its derivatives occupied newspapers for the first time.

Practicing ethnology in that period could be divided in two parts: (1) planned, but abortive, activities (usually very interesting methodologically) and (2) actions that were fully realized. Among the latter was a completely new development in which professional ethnologists emerged as key political figures or as state officials who continued (unlike in the past) to publish their scholarly works and political manifestos centered on ethnic issues.

Institute of Ethnology and Anthropology in Moscow also played an important role in the professional careers of well-known political figures. Some of these figures include (1) the late Dr. Galina Starovoitova, member of both the Supreme Soviet of the USSR (1989–91) and Supreme Soviet of Russia (1990–93), one of the leaders of democratic opposition, and chief advisor on ethnic affairs to President B. Yeltsin (1992); (2) Dr. Mikhail Chlenov, leader of the Zionist movement of Soviet (Russia and C.I.S.) Jews; (3) Dr. Evdokia Gaer, member of the Supreme Soviet of the USSR (1989–91) and Parliament of Russia (in the middle 1990s), deputy head of the State Committee on the North (1991–93), and one of the public leaders of indigenous minorities of the North, Siberia, and the Far East; (4) Professor Valery Tishkov, head of the State Committee on Nationalities' Affairs (1992); (5) late Dr. Arthur Mkrtchyan, first elected president of the self-proclaimed Nagorno-Karabakh Republic (1990); and (6) Dr. Eldar Namazov, advisor on ethnic affairs and the Nagorno-Karabakh conflict to the late former President of Azerbaijan Mr. Geidar Aliev during the 1990s.

Actually professional ethnologists were leading consultants on all sides in numerous ethnic conflicts all over the former USSR, thus splitting the professional community itself along ethnic lines. Many consultants finally moved into government to become officials. The Moscow Institute alone provided nearly a dozen officials who worked in various governmental institutions of the Russian Federation.

The consultative activities of academic or university ethnologists gained momentum and gradually turned into constant cooperation with government bodies or officials. It happened mostly because many scholars, who moved to government organizations in Moscow, were maintaining contacts with their former colleagues, including them in various teams of experts working on new prospective laws or concepts of federal policies that touch upon ethnic or cultural issues.

For the first time, ethnologists were able not only to criticize state actions or plans in their unpublished reports but also to play an important role in preventing some of the industrial projects they considered to be potentially harmful to the local ethnic groups. Though the main reasons to stop these projects were financial, articles in professional journals helped to postpone the construction of new electric power stations and water reservoirs in Siberia and Altay mountains (Savoskul and Karlov 1988; Stepanov 1993).

THE BAIKAL PROJECT: AN EXAMPLE OF ABORTED
APPLIED RESEARCH

The last years of the USSR witnessed many abortive projects based entirely, or to a large extent, on applied ethnology, which were terminated due to the political and economic crisis. The author and his colleagues were invited to the Baikal project in 1990 by its Buryat organizers. Originally the preparation of the special Law of the USSR on Lake Baikal, aimed at conservation of this largest reservoir of fresh water on Earth, was accompanied by a large-scale social and ecological development program in the basin of the lake. The idea was to restructure industry and agriculture in order to reduce the pollution. Local Buryat intellectuals seized the opportunity and put forward an idea to achieve both conservation of nature and preservation of the culture and language of the Buryats. Buryats are an indigenous minority ethnic group in the Buryat republic, located on the eastern shores of Lake Baikal. Former pastoral nomads and seminomads, Buryats had been forcefully settled in villages and predominantly Russian towns since the 1930s. Living and working among Russians, they were forgetting their Mongolian language and culture, which had been adapted for pastoralism but not for farming or an industrial lifestyle.

The basic proposition of the cultural-ecological approach to the Baikal project assumed that the Soviet system of collectivized agriculture caused sedentarization of previously unsettled groups. At the same time, local ethnic and culturally distinct components of the rural population were concentrated in and around the largest settlements. The human impact and its environmentally negative results were serious, causing soil erosion of large fields and overstocked pastures and contamination of river and runoff waters by refuse from large animal farms. In order to reduce erosion and pollution, technological innovations (often very expensive) are required, although simple decentralization of the rural population and its activities can help too since it can reduce the impact in crisis areas by removing part of it to presently unused territories. Decentralization of the rural population is simply a partial return to its traditional economic occupations and settlement patterns, including those that are seminomadic. Thus, it would not pose a problem, provided the population still remembers the former lifestyle and is ready to resume it. The portion of the rural population that would return to the traditional life and economy would also preserve its language (Buryats, Evenks) and unique culture (various Russian and Buryats groups) from linguistic Russification and cultural urbanization (Russians) or marginalization (non-Russians).

In the Baikal basin and in the Buryat Republic, the rural population (398,000 persons in 1989) is culturally heterogeneous. Ethnic Buryats (35 percent of the total) still remember well their "tribal" affiliation. The tribes, some of which moved from the steppes of Mongolia two to three centuries ago or from the Siberian woodlands on the western shore of Baikal, differed greatly with respect to the roles of pastoralism, hunting, and farming in their economies. They also differed in the frequency and distance of seasonal migrations and in the animals they were raising (for instance, all had sheep, but only

"Mongolian tribes" had camels). Those groups that formed Buryat Cossack regiments of border guards had a very specific economy and culture too. Evenks (0.3 percent), living in the northern areas, were once taiga hunters with reindeer used for transportation (Soviet Information Center 1990:145).

Ethnic Russians (62 percent of the total) in the area are comprised of the following groups: Old Believers (Semeiskie) engaged mainly in farming; Old Settlers (Sibiryaki) who combined farming with hunting; and Russian Cossacks who were engaged in farming and stock-breeding. All these Russian groups had the practice of using an individual seasonal household ("zaimki") in the forest or steppes for winter hunting or feeding and pasturing animals, or for summer plowing of supplementary lands and pasturing animals, in addition to a central home in the village. The other fraction of the rural Russian population—descendants of the migrant peasants of the 1900s to 1910s—had no such distant additional farms located 5 to 15–25 kilometers from the main village.

The traditions of most groups comprising the present rural population of the area make it possible to decentralize the rural population and its activities, revitalizing seminomadic pastoralism among Buryats and extensive private farming based on additional seasonal households among Russians. The problem was, first, to determine the exact nature of the economic, land use, and settlement patterns in certain villages, and among certain ethnic and cultural groups, some 60–70 years ago. The existing ethnographic data, being very rich in reconstructions of "typical" or more developed samples of traditional economic systems and seasonal migrations of Buryats or Old Believers, could not be used for this task. It was not designed to characterize every locality, not to mention specific villages and their major population groups. Second, it was necessary to find out what part of the present population from every ethnic and cultural group wants to, and has the knowledge and skills to, leave large rural settlements. Third, it was essential to work out some recommendations for possible problems related to schooling and medical services for those who would leave existing villages.

Unfortunately, financial problems in the early 1990s made our participation impossible. Colleagues from the Buryat Republic continued work for some time. By the middle 1990s fundamental economic and political changes in the country transformed both social priorities of regional authorities and public opinion. The planned project has been abandoned even in its research part, not to speak about attempts to implement the described social-ecological goals.

Essentially the same projects, though on a much lesser scale, also were launched in Northern Sakhalin among Nivkhs, in Western Siberia among Khanty and Mansi, and in a few other places in the North and Siberia. The idea was to use professional ethnographers, as specialists in the traditional cultures of these peoples, who could provide information about now abandoned hunting and fishing grounds of present indigenous populations, the present economy and culture of these groups, and their ability and desire to move from large modern settlements. The purpose of these projects was to allow populations to resume previous occupations and lifestyles in order to escape from linguistic Russification and cultural marginalization in predominantly Russian settlements.

KEY THEMES IN PRACTICING ETHNOLOGY
IN POST-SOVIET RUSSIA

Generally speaking, since the middle 1990s major areas for applied ethnological projects in Russia have been the following:

1. ethnopolitical studies, especially research in monitoring interethnic relations and tensions and managing ethnic conflicts;
2. studies of ethnic migrations and research in ethnic demography (demographic changes in multiethnic regions), closely related to the former;
3. studies of land use practices in the North and Siberia and of implementation of the rights of indigenous minorities, including social-ethnological assessments of development projects for international and Russian industrial companies or international organizations like the World Bank.

When speaking about major practical results, one should probably start with the works by Professor Valery Tishkov on the Chechen conflict with many critical remarks about what has been done wrong and many recommendations on what could be done and what options still exist (see, for example, Tishkov 2001). But from methodological and organizational points of view, it looks like much less known results of his activities in applied ethnopolitics are even more important. At his Center for the Study and Management of Ethnic Conflicts at the Institute of Ethnology and Anthropology, he formed a network of scholars from most multiethnic regions of Russia and many post-Soviet states, constantly monitoring and analyzing ethnopolitical information and sharing it via electronic mail with the Moscow office. To make different scholars work together and produce compatible analytical papers, the set of social, economic, demographic, environmental, and other sorts of criteria for measuring interethnic tensions and probability of ethnic conflicts has been prepared under his guidance. This "model of ethnological monitoring" has been described in Russian and in English in several publications (see, for example, Kisriev 1999). The results of the work have been published regularly as *Bulletins of the Network of Ethnological Monitoring* (usually six issues in a year) or as separate monographs, devoted to a particular republic or multiethnic province of the Russian Federation (like Kisriev 1999). The information has been provided to the governmental institutions on a regular basis. Many other Russian scholars work actively in this field of applied ethnopolitical studies too, making it by far the most popular type of practicing ethnology.

Studies of ethnic migrations and demographic trends make up another thematic area with really important results, achieved recently in applied ethnology. On the one hand, ethnic aspects of migrations and demography have become focal points of public discussions and political rhetoric, thus requiring scholarly analysis. The reasons are obvious—it is sufficient to say that in the 1990s Russia ranked third in the world (after the U.S. and Germany) in the total number of immigrants, coming mostly from the post-Soviet states. For more than a decade, ethnic Russians, Mordvins, Udmurts, and most other Christianized ethnic groups in the Volga basin and European North were diminishing in numbers due to low birth rates, while Muslim ethnic groups from the Northern Caucasus were demographically growing fast and migrating to the cities. This created widespread anti-migrant xenophobia, and to some extent ethnonationalistic and even racist sentiments, thus forming a strong demand to study the phenomena and to present advice for authorities on how to deal with such things. Practicing ethnology in this field means not only analyzing these issues and providing such advice but also sometimes taking part as experts in court hearings on alleged public manifestations of ethnic prejudice and ethnically or racially motivated public insults.

On the other hand, for several years Russian authorities were preparing the population census of 2002, and ethnologists played decisive role in working out the documentation. The problems solved, though not exactly in the way the interested scholars recommended, were the following: the form and sequence of questions and the list of ethnic groups, or "nationalities," of Russia. The most controversial was the latter—in fact, ethnologists were helping the authorities to decide what local communities with specific cultural identities should be considered separate ethnic groups ("peoples" or "nationalities"). They were concerned about which groups can register as such and what communities, despite their shared cultural identity and self-name, should be taken as parts of the larger ethnic groups.

For instance, especially heated debates have been taking place on the issue of Kryashens (from the distorted Russian word *Kreshchenyi*, meaning baptized) — a Tatar-speaking group belonging to the Russian Orthodox Church — for the last few centuries. Kryashens really have a strong identity, and their leaders started in the 1990s the public campaign to register from now on (and as it was in the 1926 census) as a separate ethnic group, but not as part of the Tatars. Most scholars from the Institute of Ethnology and Anthropology in Moscow recommended the federal authorities to accept these claims, while authorities and scholars from the Republic of Tatarstan maintained that most Kryashens have dual ethnic identity and perceive themselves as a culturally specific part of the Tatar people. The 2002 census registered Kryashens as in all the previous censuses, but the problem is how to calculate and publish data regarding whether Kryashens should be listed separately among peoples of the Russian Federation. Or should their number be added to that of the Tatars (as it was done in all previous censuses, except the one of 1926)? It looked as though political considerations would prevail again over ethnological assessment, and officially Kryashens would remain a part of the Tatars. There were many more such cases and other methodological and political problems in preparation of the population census of 2002 (for some details see Tishkov 2003).

Studies of the present position of aboriginal (indigenous minority) communities of the North, Siberia, and the Far East and consultative activities within regional and federal legislations conducted in order to safeguard their rights make up another major field of current work in applied ethnology. In this case we may probably speak about actual and rather important practical results in institutional development, achieved by professional ethnologists.

First of all, scholars took an active part on all stages of preparing new draft federal laws concerning these peoples. For instance, Professors Zoya Sokolova and Valery Tishkov from the Institute of Ethnology and Anthropology produced a first draft version of the basic Law on the Rights of Indigenous Ethnic Groups of the North, Siberia, and the Far East that would regulate their land rights, among other things. Later, they reviewed the draft version after its editing and transformation by other experts and officials, thus continuing the work on a permanent basis. Finally, with participation of many other scholars, a set of federal laws was prepared and passed: "On guarantees of the rights of the indigenous minority peoples of the Russian Federation" (April 30, 1999); "On general principles of organizing communities of the indigenous minority peoples of North, Siberia and the Far East of the Russian Federation" (June 20, 2000); and "On territories of traditional use of natural resources by the indigenous minority peoples of North, Siberia and the Far East of the Russian Federation" (May 7, 2001). In addition, ethnologists were quite successful in incorporating some indigenous rights for traditional use of biological resources into federal laws "On hunting" and "On fishing," while the law "On reindeer-breeding" was still under consideration in the State Duma at the start of the year 2006. General ideas and some information about the debates in this field can be found in some of my previous publications in English (Yamskov 1999, 2001). Unfortunately, adoption of these federal and more detailed regional laws, aimed at safeguarding rights of the indigenous minority peoples of the North and Siberia, failed to resolve the situation. The laws were either not fully implemented or were not covering all the social-economic or cultural problems that these ethnic groups were facing.

The potentially most important aspect of this legislation, judging from the point of view of further development of applied ethnology in Russia, was the federal law "On guarantees of the rights of the indigenous minority peoples." Article 1, part 6, and Article 8, part 6 of the law introduce the term "ethnological assessment" for the first time in Russia, stating that in certain cases it should be unavoidable and compulsory, like environmental impact assessment, and that representatives of indigenous communities have a right to participate in both of them. In 1999 activities started in the State Duma on preparing the draft law "On ethnological assessment," and the federal law "On environmental impact assessment in the Russian Federation" (November 23, 1995) is used as a model for it. Dr. Valery V. Stepanov from the Institute of Ethnology and Anthropology in Moscow prepared one draft version in 1998–99 (for details see Stepanov 2002), but during the last few years the work on the law stopped several times, leading to partial loss of documents. At the moment the work is postponed again, but it should be carried on, since one of federal laws now requires that the "ethnological assessment" should be defined in Russian federal legislation. Currently the collective monograph, compiled by Dr. Valery Stepanov (1999), is probably the only book in Russia devoted to methods of social-ethnological and ethnoecological assessments. The latter were developed by

V. Stepanov and the staff of the Department of Ethnic Ecology of the Institute of Ethnology and Anthropology during the late 1980s to middle 1990s.

Meanwhile, the World Bank's documents concerning the rights of indigenous groups in economic projects are often used as a model by Russian practicing ethnologists and indigenous activists. Many Russian scholars, especially those working in Siberia and the North, have personal experience of work for the World Bank as experts on indigenous communities and thus know about its procedures and internal documents on indigenous policies (see Yamskov 2002). It is hard to underestimate the positive role that this international agency played as a donor of modern concepts about indigenous rights to traditionally used lands and biological resources, as well as ways of organizing and methods of carrying out social-ethnological assessments of the planned economic projects.

In general, the impact of globalization on Russian applied ethnology in the 1990s was mainly manifested by two facts. First, some international agencies (like the World Bank) and transnational oil companies started operating in Russia. They organized social-ethnological assessments of their projects, affecting indigenous minority groups in the taiga and tundra natural zones and thus setting an example for the Russian private and state-owned companies and ministries to do the same. So ethnologists and sociologists found a new sphere of well-paid activities, and many scholars, especially residing in Siberia and the Far East, gained good experience in this field. Second, practically at the same time international aboriginal organizations, activists, and foreign anthropologists started working in the North and Siberia too, thus stimulating activities of the Russian scholars to defend aboriginal land rights through advising on or giving examples in organizing and financing such actions. Other influences of globalization could be hardly seen on the background of such fundamental changes as the end of the USSR (and of serious state support for academic institutions) amid rising ethnic conflicts and inter-ethnic tensions and inflow of migrants from southern republics and states.

It looks like another issue in applied ethnology, gaining momentum right now, in the late 1990s to early 2000s, represents a different case in a sense that methodological or organizational influences from abroad were of minor importance in its emergence and development. It is the study of Islamic fundamentalism (mostly in republics of the Northern Caucasus) in order to understand the social factors helping these Wahhabist communities to attract young people and to involve some of them in terrorist activities. These communities appeared in the early 1990s thanks to Islamic teachers from Saudi Arabia or Gulf states and their generous financial support, while ethnographic research within these communities and publication of its results started in the late 1990s. The research actually deals mainly with the question of why certain persons leave so-called traditional Islamic communities and join the new Wahhabist ones, despite inevitable open conflicts with the local traditional Mullah and their traditionally oriented parents, relatives, and neighbors. What could be done by the local authorities and leaders of traditional Muslim communities to prevent or minimize the number of such events (for example, see Yarlykapov 2000)? As yet, regularly voiced demands of traditional Muslim clergy and of some presidents of republics with Muslim population to ban Wahhabism in the Russian Federation have been ignored by the federal government. They are contradicting the constitutional rights for religious freedom, as well as freedoms of organizing public associations (including new religious communities), of meetings, and of speech. Nevertheless, the situation in many areas is quite tense, and there were many cases of open violence between "Traditionalist" and "Wahhabist" Muslims. However, in sharp contrast to speeches of some political or religious leaders, issues of preventing the spread of international radical Islamic terrorism do not prevail in such studies, and the problem is usually perceived as a socially and intellectually motivated split within the local Muslim community, though originally initiated by outsiders. Thus speculations about radical Islamic or terrorist dimensions of globalization are usually left outside ethnographic field studies of the phenomena, despite their applied character and strong demand for results from various public figures or institutions.

Speaking about major areas of applying ethnology, one can also use the series "Studies in Applied and Urgent Ethnology," published by the Institute of Ethnology and Anthropology in Moscow, as a source of quantitative information on research priorities in contemporary Russia. Between 1995 and 2006, 104 issues were published, each one being 20–30 pages. It is important to note that 35 papers were authored or coauthored by scholars from other institutions, including visiting researchers or persons who simply sent their manuscripts to the editors (V. A. Tishkov, M. Yu. Martynova, N. A. Lopulenko). So the themes covered in the series characterize academic interests and ideas of what is applied ethnological research of not only the Institute's staff but also a much wider group of researchers and practitioners.

In general, 70 papers from the field of ethnic conflicts and interethnic relations report current ethnopolitical situations in various republics or multiethnic regions of the Russian Federation. They also report on desired linguistic and cultural policies for certain ethnic minorities (except for the indigenous peoples of the North and Siberia) and the development of religions in multiethnic areas and relations between members of different confessions. There were also 16 publications about indigenous minorities of the North, their land use practices, and their social and economic position (Yamskov 1996; Klokov et al. 2001). One issue was devoted to the same problems of the Kazakh pastoralists and another one to social economic changes in several ethnic communities in Moldova. Papers on migrations and demographic trends of certain ethnic groups were published only 15 times, many of them being devoted to preparation or preliminary analysis of the Russian population census of 2002. One author wrote about the present role of folk law on the island of Sardinia.

In my personal experience in practicing ethnology during the same period of 1995–2005, I found that some 20 major unpublished works have been prepared by me, mostly becoming part of jointly authored papers. Among those there are 9 papers on the rights and land use of northern minorities in Siberia, six papers on ethnopolitics, and three on settlement patterns, migrations, and demographic trends in other areas of the country exist. It gives an idea of relative importance and financing of these fields of applied research in contemporary Russia.

Practically all requests for the works of the Russian governmental organizations came to me through the director or deputy directors of the Institute of Ethnology and

Anthropology. In most of those cases, I was paid small bonuses from the Institute's budget or had to perform the work for my basic salary only. For example, I prepared reports such as the following: (1) "Comments on the Analytical Report 'On Revising General Scheme of Population Distribution and Settlement Pattern of the Russian Federation and other Relevant Documentation in Order to Assess Regions' Capabilities to Receive Migrants' " (2002, 57 pp.), prepared in January 2003 for the State Committee of Construction Works; (2) "Proposals about Formulations in the Program of the Russian Population Census of 1999," written in August 1995 for the State Committee on Statistics (the census actually took place only in 2002); and (3) "Comments on 'The Concept of the State Policies towards Nationalities of the Russian Federation,' " prepared in April 2003 for the Minister, Mr. V. Zorin (former head of the Ministry of Nationalities' Affairs and Regional Policies). In all those and many other cases, I worked, for the most part, individually. However, at the same time, two to four of my colleagues were doing the same work, and at the end someone from the administration of the Institute was integrating the papers and preparing the final version of the document, thus formulating position(s) of the Institute on the issue under discussion.

After coauthoring several reports to the Security Council of Russia, in July 1996 I received a request directly from this organization to act as a scientific supervisor, organizing a research group. I would prepare the analytical document "Ethnopolitical and National-Cultural Aspects of the National Security of Russia"; the final text was 540 pages long (including 240 pages written by me personally), and the work was generously paid for by the Security Council itself, though the money was transferred through the Institute.

Works for international organizations were done after receiving personal requests from people whom I knew previously—either my colleagues, inviting me to join their projects, or members of the staff of those organizations. Here bonuses were many times higher and were paid directly in hard currency, while the works in some cases were prepared in English. For instance, I wrote "Commentaries on the Draft of the Revised World Bank Operational Directive No 4.20 'Indigenous Peoples' "(in November 1998, for Dr. Stan Peabody [The World Bank]) and "Commentaries on the Drafts of the World Bank Operational Policies and Procedures No 4.10 'Indigenous Peoples' "(in October 2001, for Dr. S. Artobolevsky [Russian coordinator of the Working Group] and Dr. Stan Peabody). The analytical paper "Social-Cultural Problems of the Aboriginal Peoples of the North and of the Local Populations in the Regions of the Pilot Project on Sustainable Use of Forests" was done in October 1997 (60 pp. long) for the World Bank too, and revised portions of the previous one ("Cultures and Social-Economic Problems of Ethnic Groups, Residing in the Forest Zone of Siberia and the Far East," March 1995, 145 pp.) have been published ("Russia: Forest Policy … ," 1997) in shortened form (see "Annex G. Poverty, Unemployment, and the Social Safety Net in Forest Communities" and pp. 52–54, 83–84; for the list of contributing authors, see p. X). Another work on possible ways to achieve sustainable development of indigenous northern minorities was prepared for the international Advisory Committee on Protection of the Sea (ACOPS) (see Krasovskaya et al. 2000).

These personal remarks, I hope, make it easier for the reader to understand what is considered to be the most accepted kinds of applied ethnological work in contemporary Russia.

APPLIED ETHNOLOGY IN MODERN RUSSIA: PROBLEMS AND PROSPECTS

The current situation is rather mixed and still uncertain. All the academic, university, and other research and training centers previously discussed continue to function. The end of state control over scientific activities made it possible to organize some new chairs or independent research centers or units, often having the term "ethno-" in their titles. However, in many cases, these new research institutions were created by former specialists in Marxism-Leninism and, as it turns out, they are now a serious competitor for applied projects (Tishkov 1992).

The tense competition between professional ethnologists and other social scientists for applied projects in interethnic relations and ethnopolitical studies has been accompanied by a prolonged financial crisis of the state-financed Academy of Sciences and universities. As a result, in 2005 in Moscow the regular fixed salary of a scholar with a Ph.D. and some 10–15 years of professional work was less than 50 percent of the mean salary in Russia and less than 20 percent of the actual mean salary in the city. Thus for those who decided to continue working in ethnology, the most common way to earn additional money is to apply for a research grant, to combine academic research with lecturing, and to join an applied project, specially financed by the state or international organizations, and thus to start practicing ethnology on a more or less regular basis. A majority of young and middle-aged scholars, at least in Moscow or St. Petersburg, have already gained the latter experience.

The typical characteristic of the present situation with applied ethnology in the country is the fact that in the process of reorganization of research activities in the Institute of Ethnology and Anthropology, started in 2002, there were fixed only 11 general research themes for the coming three years. So every department or laboratory of the Institute has to formulate its own research subtheme within those 11 generalized fields of studies. One of the latter was practicing ethnology, called "Ethnology on the Service of Social Development and Counteraction to Extremism." Ethnic ecology, for example, has been not included in the list. In addition, the project entitled "Social Potential of Historical Disciplines" was launched in the year 2003 by the Branch of Historical and Philological Disciplines of the Russian Academy of Sciences, and the Institute of Ethnology and Anthropology joined it, delegating several scholars with experience in applied ethnological studies.

So, from the first glance, it looks like applied ethnology has a bright future in contemporary Russia, simply as one of a few ways to survive as a professional scholar. Besides, for the first time in recent decades, ethnology has gained some prestige and publicity, and government officials have realized its importance and applied potential.

However, three major problems make the future of applied anthropology not so optimistic. First, in the early and middle 1990s the acute financial crisis in the country caused some applied projects to be canceled, even after some or most of the work had been done. The scholars who were once not paid for jobs they had already done are not very enthusiastic about launching or joining other applied projects. Besides, the number of applied state-sponsored projects is clearly diminishing, while certain reorganization in academic institutes is starting right now. The results are unpredictable, but it is already clear that the coming changes will mean that the scholars have less time for any other work apart from their own research projects, financed through the budget of the Russian Academy of Sciences.

Second, the unsatisfactory financial position of many scholars reduced the number of graduate and postgraduate students training in most sciences, including ethnology. The growing total number of graduate students since the late 1990s is due to those studying law, economics, and business management. The outflow of active scholars to private business or government agencies in the early 1990s, combined with the continuing retirement of many others, made the total number of ethnologists shrink. The Institute in Moscow, for instance, lost about 25 percent of its scholars in the middle 1990s.

Third, since 1999 when Mr. Vladimir Putin became president, a new political period has started in Russia, and governmental institutions' demand for applied ethnological studies is clearly declining. For example, a new Ministry of Nationalities' Affairs and Regional Policies in Russia was formed in early 1994 on the basis of the previous State Committee on Nationalities' Affairs that had been enlarged three or four times in 1993. This Committee, existing from the early years of Soviet power, was extremely uninfluential and weak in the 1970s and 1980s. In the early 1990s, however, it started to grow and absorb ethnologists. In the early 2000s this Ministry was closed down. The same was the fate of the Federal Migrations' Service, which was organized in the early 1990s and also closed down, becoming a small department in the Ministry of Interior Affairs. The former State Committee on the North was at first merged with the new Ministry of Nationalities' Affairs and Regional Policies and then disappeared with the latter. These governmental bodies worked in close contact with the Institute and the Chair in Moscow and with professionals in the provinces and republics, being major initiators and funding agencies for projects in applied ethnology.

A decade ago, two scholars from the institute and the university interviewed 13 of the most influential ethnologists in Moscow (ten from the Institute of Ethnology and Anthropology, three from the Chair of Ethnography) about their ideas on current methods and research priorities and on possible future developments in Russian ethnology. Most of them agreed that studies of interethnic relations and conflicts would remain the most important areas of research due to their applied character and, consequently, be the most probable projects for financial support from the Government (Filippov and Filippova 1993:8, 10). It is interesting to note that, even at this time, the leading scholars said nothing about the need to develop applied ethnology as a certain subdiscipline with its own methods, terms, and well-defined research areas and priorities. On the whole, the experts think that theory and methodology of ethnological research would not be studied in the immediate future at all, or at best would remain outside major discussions. Time proved they were right. There are practically no grounds to speculate about theory and methods in either academic ethnology or applied ethnology, since we simply lack public discussions, oral or published, on these issues, except for heated debates about the meaning of the term *ethnicity* and about the role that the Soviet theory of "ethnos" has played in helping to understand this phenomenon.

CONCLUSIONS

It is still hard to make judgments about the future of practicing ethnology in Russia. On the one hand, legislation states that the social-ethnological assessment is an integral part of any economic project that is likely to have an impact on indigenous minorities of the North and Siberia. The State Duma periodically initiates the work on the draft law about this type of assessment. Some publications are appearing regularly, but mainly as short brochures in the series "Studies in Applied and Urgent Ethnology" with a circulation of only 200 copies. Applied projects serve as a source of financial support to a large number of scholars, and both the public and government officials understand the importance of the subdiscipline.

On the other hand, though the financial and economic situation in the country is improving, both the number of projects and the number of scholars involved are diminishing due to institutional changes in the Russian government. There are also no attempts even to review research priorities, methods, and principles or the history of applied ethnology in Russia. Having gone through intensive ideological pressure in recent times, when it was compulsory to pay at least lip service to "Marxist methodology and theory" of the discipline, most Russian scholars are still not inclined to discuss any methodological issues for some time, except for some exotic and radical postmodernist ideas.

Finally, one can see that contacts with international organizations like the World Bank influence Russian scholars greatly at this particular moment, especially in drawing their attention to the methodological and ethical problems of applied ethnological research. Among very few reviews of methods, organization, and thematic composition of applied ethnological research published in Russia in recent years, there were papers about activities of the World Bank (Yamskov 1995, 2002).

Meanwhile the real influence of ethnologists on the lives of ethnic groups in Russia is substantial and rising. Thus practicing ethnology in Russia is steadily growing and it is bound to develop further. We have some ground to hope that after another decade or so one will be able to write about Russian applied ethnology as an institutionalized subdiscipline engaged in serious and regular discussions about both methods and ethics of its activities.

REFERENCES

Antropova, V. V.
   1972 The Role of Ethnographers in Implementation of Lenin's Nationalities' Policies in the Far North (1920–1930). Sovetskaya Etnografia (Soviet Ethnography) 6:19–27.

Bromley, Yu, and G. Markov, eds.

1982 Etnografia (Ethnography). Moscow: Vysshaya Shkola Press.

Filippov, V. R., and E. A. Filippova

1993 Ethnography in Our Country Today and Tomorrow. Etnograficheskoe Obozrenie (Ethnographic Review) 5:3–11.

Kisriev, E.

1999 Respublika Dagestan (Republic of Dagestan. Model of Ethnological Monitoring). Moscow: Institute of Ethnology and Anthropology.

Klokov, K. B., T. M. Krasovskaya, and A. N. Yamskov

2001 Problems of Transition to Sustainable Development in Areas, Inhabited by Indigenous Peoples of the Russian Arctic. Issledovaniya po prikladnoy i neotlozhnoy etnologii (Studies in Applied and Urgent Ethnology). Paper No. 141. Moscow: Institute of Ethnology and Anthropology.

Kozlov, V. I.

1983 Main Problems of Ethnic Ecology. Sovetskaya Etnografia (Soviet Ethnography) 6:3–16.

Krasovskaya, T. M., I. I. Abryutina, E. V. Agitaev, K. D. Arakchaa, B. Funston, K. B. Klokov, M. Y. Lyubimtsev, A. A. Mikhailov, O. M. Proskurkina, E. N. Sumina, M. A. Todyshev, T. K. Vlasova, A. N. Yamskov, and N. V. Zubarevich

2000 Indigenous Peoples of the Russian Arctic: Present Situation and the Transition to Sustainable Development. London-Moscow. Electronic document, http://www.acops.org/NPA_Arctic.htm

Markov, G. E., and T. D. Solovey

1990 Ethnographic Education in the Moscow State University. Sovetskaya Etnografia (Soviet Ethnography) 6:79–91.

Russia: Forest Policy during Transition

1997 Washington: World Bank.

Savoskul, S. S., and V.V. Karlov

1988 The Turukhansk Electric Power Station and the Fate (or Possible Future) of Evenkia. Sovetskaya Etnografia (Soviet Ethnography) 5:166–168.

Slezkin, Yu

1993 The Soviet Ethnography in Knock-dawn: 1928–1938. Etnograficheskoe Obozrenie (Ethnographic Review) 2:113–125.

Soviet Information Center

1990 Natsionalniy sostav naselenia RSFSR (Ethnic Composition of the Population of RSFSR). Moscow: Publication of the Information Center.

Stanyukovich, T. V.

1974 Museum of Anthropology and Ethnography in the System of the Academy of Sciences. Sovetskaya Etnografia (Soviet Ethnography) 2:3–11.

Stepanov, V. V.

1993 The Katun Electric Power Station Project: A Threat to Ethnic Culture. Vestnik RAN (The Herald of the Russian Academy of Sciences) 12.

2002 Ethnological Assessment. In Obychai i Zakon (Custom and Law. Studies in Legal Anthropology). N. I. Novikova and V. A. Tishkov, eds. Pp. 241–260. Moscow: "Strategy" Press.

Stepanov, V. V., ed.

1999 Metody etnoekologicheskoy ekspertizy (Methods of Ethnoecological Assessment). Moscow: Institute of Ethnology and Anthropology.

Tishkov, V. A.

1992 Soviet Ethnography: Overcoming the Crisis. Etnograficheskoe Obozrenie (Ethnographic Review) 1:28–36.

2001 Obshchestvo v vooruzhennom konflikte (Society in the Armed Conflict. Ethnography of the Chechen War). Moscow: Nauka Press.

2003 Historical-Anthropological Analysis of the Census-2002. Issledovaniya po prikladnoy i neotlozhnoy etnologii (Studies in Applied and Urgent Ethnology). Paper No. 161. Moscow: Institute of Ethnology and Anthropology.

Tishkov, V. A., and V. V. Stepanov

    2004 Izmerenie konflikta (Measuring the Conflict. Methods and Results of Ethno-Confessional Monitoring by the EAWARN Network in the Year 2003). Moscow.

Tokarev, S. A.

    1958 Etnografia narodov SSSR (Ethnography of the Peoples of the USSR). Moscow: Moscow State University Press.

    1966 Istoria russkoy etnografii (The History of the Russian Ethnography). Moscow: Nauka Press.

    1974 From the History of Ethnographic Studies in the Academy of Sciences. Sovetskaya Etnografia (Soviet Ethnography) 2:11–19.

Yamskov, A. N.

    1995 "Putting People First." Review of M. Cernea's Books on Applied Studies in Ethnology and Rural Sociology. Etnograficheskoe Obozrenie (Ethnographic Review) 2:164–167.

    1996 Territories for the Traditional Land Use in the Khabarovsk Region. Issledovaniya po prikladnoy i neotlozhnoy etnologii (Studies in Applied and Urgent Ethnology). Paper No. 134. Moscow: Institute of Ethnology and Anthropology.

    1999 Applied Ethnology and Ethnoecology in Combining Aboriginal Land Rights with the Preservation of Biodiversity in Russia. Practicing Anthropology, 1999, vol. 20, no. 2 (Spring), pp. 48–52.

    2001 The Rights of Small-Numbered Peoples of the Russian North in the Territories of Traditional Nature Use: Ownership or Use? Journal of Legal Pluralism and Unofficial Law, 2001, 46, pp. 121–134.

    2002 The World Bank Indigenous Policies. Obychai I zakon (Custom and Law. Studies in Legal Anthropology). N. I. Novikova and V. A. Tishkov, eds. pp. 261–283. Moscow: "Strategy" Press.

Yamskov, A. N. and N. A. Dubova

    1997 Practicing Ethnology in Russia: An Overview. The Global Practice of Anthropology. Eds: M. L. Baba, C. E. Hill. Williamsburg, VA: Collgge of William and Mary Press, pp. 263–281.

Yarlykapov, A. A.

    2000 The Wahhabism Problem in the Northern Caucasus. Issledovaniya po prikladnoy i neotlozhnoy etnologii (Studies in Applied and Urgent Ethnology), Paper No. 134. Moscow: Institute of Ethnology and Anthropology, 28pp.

APPLIED ANTHROPOLOGY IN ISRAEL:
BETWEEN INFANCY AND MATURITY

S. Zev Kalifon
Bar Ilan University

Malka Shabtay
Tel Aviv University and Emet Yezree, Academic College

At first glance, applied anthropology in Israel appears underdeveloped and underappreciated. There are no independent anthropology departments and the single attempt to create a training program in applied anthropology ceased to exit after four years. However, such a strict interpretation would not be fair to our applied and academic colleagues in Israel for much important applied anthropology has been and is being done in Israel. In fact, Israel has a long and impressive history of applied anthropological work, though not always labeled as such. In particular, important work has been done in the fields of immigrant integration and the medical problems of these new immigrants. This chapter will review the achivments of applied anthropology in Israel and its potential for the future. In particular, it will analyze the growing recognition of the need for applied anthropology within the departments of anthropology, the government and nongovernmental organizations. Finally, this chapter will critique the shortcomings of applied anthropology in Israel and examine the areas where more work needs to be done. Key Words: Israel, Applied Anthropology, immigration, integration

This collection is dedicated to applied anthropology around the world. If we were to take a narrow viewpoint, we could declare that applied anthropology in Israel is underdeveloped and underappreciated. There are no independent anthropology departments and the single attempt to create a training program in applied anthropology ceased to exist after four years. Applied anthropology even has had trouble gaining recognition by its colleagues; very few of the prominent anthropologists in academe identify themselves as applied anthropologists. Applied anthropologists working outside the universities struggled until 1990 before the Israel Anthropological Association granted them a session on applied anthropology at the annual meetings.

However, such a strict interpretation would not be fair to our applied and academic colleagues in Israel, for much important applied anthropology has been and is being done in Israel. In fact, Israel has a long and impressive history of applied anthropological

NAPA Bulletin 25, pp. 104–122, ISBN 1-931303-28-2. © 2006 by the American Anthropological Association. All rights reserved. Permissions to photocopy or reproduce article content via www.ucpress.edu/journals/rights.htm.

work, though it is not always labeled as such.[1] In particular, important work has been done in the fields of immigrant integration and the medical problems of new immigrants. In addition, anthropologists have worked in governmental ministries (such as Education and Health), in the army, in psychiatric hospitals, and even in marketing. Recognition of their efforts was given in the spring of 1993, when *Practicing Anthropology* dedicated a volume to Israeli anthropology (see Halper and Nudelman 1993).

The social structure and very geography of Israel also allow unique opportunities for the study of anthropology in all its forms, including applied. Within a few hours (sometimes even minutes) of all the major cities and the universities within them, one can find a wide variety of communities and ethnic groups. It is possible to involve students in projects in rural settlements, Bedouin encampments, ethnic neighborhoods, and development towns. In fact, it is quite difficult to finish undergraduate work in Israel without some such contact, even if no formal applied program exists.

Since the original paper appeared (Kalifon 1997), the term "applied anthropology" sounds less foreign in academic discourse. In addition to the one program in applied anthropology, several departments of anthropology have tried to introduce at least a basic course in applied anthropology (taught by the second author of this chapter). In spite of this progress, we would not go so far as to describe the status of applied anthropology in Israel as rosy. We would like to use the opportunity that this renewed chapter permits us to describe the achievements of applied anthropology in Israel.[2] More importantly, it is an opportunity to examine the interrelations of applied and academic anthropology in Israel.

A BRIEF HISTORY OF ISRAEL

The roots of the Jewish people in the land of Israel dates back, of course, to biblical days. Through the ages, this relation was religious and symbolic for most Jews. Occasionally, small numbers of Jews migrated to what was then called Syria or Palestine (the province and district in the Ottoman Empire). These Jews settled primarily in the holy cities (Jerusalem, Safed, Hebron, etc.) and lived on the donations of their coreligionists around the world. They did not have aspirations of political or economic independence; rather they saw themselves as guardians of the land until the coming of the Messiah.

The origin of the modern state dates to the 19th century with the establishment of political Zionism under Theodor Herzl. This was a secular movement that desired to create an independent Jewish state. This state was to be a shelter for oppressed Jews, especially the very poor Jews of eastern Europe. From the 1880s onward, Jews began migrating to Palestine in ever-growing numbers. Increasingly, the Zionist movement took on a Socialist political outlook. Not only was the proposed Jewish state to be a haven for oppressed Jews, but it also was to be a beacon of social advancement in the Levant.

Zionism would also change the very nature of the Jewish people; no longer would the Jew strive to be a merchant or an artisan but rather a farmer or a laborer. Talented middle-class European Jews abandoned the comforts of European cities to be farming *halutzim* (pioneers) in the deserts and swamps of their ancient homeland. In the early part of this century, these Socialist-Zionists established a variety of communal agricultural settlements for defensive and ideological reasons. These included the kibbutz, where all property (even clothing) was owned by the collective; the moshav shitufi, which permitted some private property; and the moshav ovdim (small-holders settlement), which only purchased goods and marketed collectively. Though only a small proportion of the Jewish population, these settlements were to play a central role in the creation of the Jewish state and in its institutions, ideology, and political elite.

The rise of Nazi Germany was to reinforce the purpose of the Zionist movement as a shelter for oppressed Jews. In the 1930s over 80,000 German and Austrian Jews migrated to Palestine. This sudden increase in the Jewish population disturbed the Arab population and led to violent demonstrations. The British (who ruled Palestine through a League of Nations mandate) decided to enforce a strict quota on Jewish immigration. During and after World War II, thousands of Holocaust survivors risked their lives to break the British blockade (established to enforce the quota) and enter Palestine. After much violence on both sides, the British returned the problem to the new United Nations, which decided to partition Palestine.

In May 1948 the state of Israel declared independence and immediately entered a long and costly war. Within ten years of independence, the population of the infant nation tripled. These new immigrants included survivors of the Nazi Holocaust and, in greater numbers, immigrants from the Muslim world. In general, these "Mizrachi" immigrants were not accustomed to the open, Western environment existent in Israel. In their countries of origin, they had been small shopkeepers, semiskilled laborers, and artisans. These skills were incompatible or inadequate in their new nation. Furthermore, there was little industry capable of absorbing the large numbers of unskilled workers.

When the region was placed under British rule after World War I, the British government tried to balance their commitment to create a Jewish homeland (not necessarily an independent state) with the Arab political aspirations in the region. To reduce friction, they planned a type of joint autonomy: The day-to-day affairs of the Jewish and Arab communities were to be managed through two parallel agencies, one Jewish and the other Arab. Only the Jews accepted the plan and created the Jewish Agency for Palestine. This agency served as an embryonic government until independence, when it became the temporary government of the State of Israel. After the first elections, the Jewish Agency was reorganized as a quasi-governmental agency in charge of immigrant absorption (the Israeli term for integration) and establishing new settlements. The Jewish Agency (through its Land Settlement and Youth Aliya Departments) has financed and supported most of the applied research on new immigrants by anthropologists and other social scientists.

The main endeavor of applied anthropological work (whether labeled as such or not) has been the study of the new immigrants who flooded into the country in the first years of statehood. The first generation of anthropologists in Israel studied these immigrant groups. They included local scholars (though not native-born Sabras) like Raphael Patai (1953), Phyllis Palgi (1993), and Naomi Nevo (1993) as well as visiting scholars like Dorothy Willner (1965 and 1969) and Alex Weingrod (1962a, 1962b, and 1966). Weingrod later returned to Israel as an immigrant and helped to establish academic anthropology in Israel. He was also, for a time, the director of social research for the Land Settlement Department of the Jewish Agency (certainly an applied position). The first (and only) training program in applied anthropology existed in the anthropology program that he headed.

In an effort to develop the country, defend the borders, and provide a livelihood to the thousands of immigrant families, new towns and communities were established along the frontiers. These included small-holder agricultural settlements and development towns (intended to be regional centers for the agricultural sector with some local industry). This policy did not always succeed; many families abandoned these new settlements and crowded into slum areas of the major cities. These poverty areas were to cause problems in the 1970s and 1980s, as we will see below.

The settlement of the land and the creation of new towns and communities was a unique opportunity for anthropologists, the chance to see the origin of villages and towns. Some examples of this settlement work are Weingrod's (1966) *Reluctant Pioneers: Village Development in Israel* and Willner's (1969) *Nation-Building and Community in Israel*. Both of these studies are ethnographies of new agricultural settlements created in the 1950s and reflect (as their titles suggest) the problems and difficulties of settling immigrants in these frontier areas when they lack the necessary ideological commitment.

From the beginning, it was understood that these new immigrants were not of the ideological mind-set to live in true collective settlements like the kibbutz. The "Oriental" immigrants were usually very religious and family-orientated. A new type of settlement, the moshav olim, was created on the model of the moshav ovdim (small-holder agricultural settlement). Social scientists (among them anthropologists) played a role in these decisions. As in the moshav ovdim, each family had its own piece of land on which they farmed or raised animals. There were some collective elements (bulk purchasing, marketing, and defense of the settlement), but basically each individual nuclear family was a unit of production.

It was hoped that such a model would be culturally acceptable to the new immigrants. Unfortunately, it was not. Many Jews from Muslim countries saw agricultural work as demeaning, something only Arabs do. They dreamed of owning shops and restaurants in large urban centers. These new settlements were very fragile and weak (Weingrod 1962a). They were "reluctant" pioneers at a time and in a place that demanded strong ideological commitment.

The development towns were also studied in these early years; particularly prominent is the work of Erik Cohen (see Cohen 1968, 1970 and Cohen et al. 1962). These larger settlements were also fragile and suffered from all the disadvantages of the moshavim (distance from the center, lack of cultural opportunities, etc.) with only marginal advantages. The economic base of these towns was even more precarious than that of the moshavim and their dependence on the central government even greater. In many cases, the mayors in these towns functioned like little dictators controlling almost all aspects of the citizens' lives, breeding additional bitterness and alienation.

A related area of social integration is the work on the Arab minority in Israel. The most prominent name in this field is Henry Rosenfeld (1958, 1970). Much of this work was done while Rosenfeld worked for the Ministry of Health and Hadassah Hospital. Rosenfeld's work centers on the use of traditional marriage/family practices to adjust to the new social and political environment that the Arabs in Israel found themselves in.

The second thrust of applied work in the early days of the state was medical. The name that stands out here is Phyllis Palgi, who returned to Israel from her doctoral studies in 1953 (Palgi 1993). Unable to obtain an academic position, she accepted a position in the Department of Mental Health. She received the impressive title of Chief Anthropologist; however, she was the *only* anthropologist in the Department of Mental Health. It is not a coincidence that the head of the department and the man who hired Palgi, Dr. Louis Miller, was the brother-in-law of British anthropologist Max Gluckman and sensitive to problems of culture.

Palgi's concerns were the psychiatric problems of immigrants and the relations between immigrant patients and Western psychiatrists (see Palgi et al. 1955 and Palgi 1963). She later moved into other fields of mental health, general health, and addiction (see Palgi 1975, 1993 and Snyder, Palgi, et al. 1982). Unfortunately, when Palgi left the Department of Mental Health, her position was never filled. Palgi, as opposed to most Israeli anthropologists, considers herself primarily an applied anthropologist and is by far the most consistent supporter of applied work.

THE OPENING OF ACADEMIC ANTHROPOLOGY

In the 1970s the Departments of Sociology across the country began to open Anthropology sections. The young professors who received positions included new immigrants (like Weingrod) and, more interestingly, the first generation of Israeli-raised anthropologists. This group of young Israelis was unified by another factor: They had all done their doctoral work under the guidance of Max Gluckman at the University of Manchester. Gluckman had directed the Rhodes-Livingstone Institute and had worked on problems of rapid urbanization and westernization. For example, Gluckman (1961) studied the changes in tribalism in the city (from a political system to a kind of mutual aid association). His students (though again *not* defining themselves as applied anthropologists) studied very pragmatic subjects concerning cultural change and adjustment. In Israel, Gluckman directed the Manchester Project (funded by the British Jewish Bernstein Family), which attempted to make an ethnographic portrait of Israel. This series of research projects helped to establish anthropology as an academic discipline in Israel (Shokeid 2002).

Most members of the Gluckman cadre did their work on communities in Israel like those mentioned above. For example, Shokeid (1968, 1971 and as Minkovitz 1967) and Deshen (1966, 1970) studied agricultural settlements of new immigrants; Marx studied the Bedouin of the Negev (1967). The work of Deshen and Shokeid was done under the auspices of the Land Settlement Department of the Jewish Agency, with practical goals in mind. Other members of this Gluckman-trained group were Africanists; however, when home in Israel, they began studying local communities in the pragmatic Rhodes-Livingstone style. A good example of this is Yitzhak Elam, who studied the Hima (Elam 1972) in Uganda and returned home to Israel to study the new wave of Georgian (Soviet Union) Jewish immigrants (Elam 1980).

The original research of scholars like Shokeid, Deshen, and Goldberg (one of the new immigrant anthropologists) took place in the 1960s. The emphasis had shifted from settlement of these new immigrants (which was a fait accompli) to adjustment, conflict resolution, and the acceptance of new cultural traits. For example, Shokeid (1968) studied conflict and how the traditional *hamula* (extended family) changed to rationally meet the new needs of life on a moshav olim. In the same period, Goldberg (1972) looked at a Libyan Jewish town that had been reestablished in Israel as a moshav olim. He examined adjustment of social organizations to the new environment and the ability of different generations to accept cultural change. Though not an applied work per se, Goldberg indicated ways to make the transition easier and less traumatic.

In the 1970s a new dimension to the problems of the 1950s mass immigration emerged: the problem of poverty. This problem represented the failure of the original integration but also new elements that developed in Israel. The nation was shocked to discover that the Israeli-born children of these immigrants were *not* integrated into the mainstream of the nation. Their educational achievements were on the average very low and they frequently were rejected for army service (it was and still is a stigma for a young man not to have served in the Israeli army).

Anthropologists began to examine these poor urban neighborhoods and development towns. Cohen (1972) studied the "Black Panthers," a group of young, urban, second-generation (mainly) Moroccan Jews who very cleverly chose their name in order to shock and embarrass the European establishment. The Panthers demanded entry into the mainstream of Israeli life and asked to be drafted into the army, claiming that their deferments for medical, social, or psychiatric reasons hindered their chances in civilian life. On the other hand, they tried to promote ethnic pride and occasionally played "Robin Hood" (stealing from the rich to give to the poor).

Don Handelman (another of the new immigrant anthropologists) in a very applied work evaluated the new "Miftan" (vocational training schools) intended to answer some of the shortcomings in education and training of these urban disadvantaged youth (Handelman et al. 1981). Similarly, Goldberg (1984a and 1984b) studied the impact of an innovative intervention program on a population of disadvantaged youth in a development town. In this very applied work, Goldberg found that the program creators had made incorrect assumptions about the problems of the disadvantaged young people in the development town. The program was in many ways inappropriate for the population it was meant to serve. Tal (1993) was to encounter a similar problem in a local program of neighborhood improvement under "Project Renewal" (the urban renewal project of the late 1970s and 1980s). The residents and the professional planners had very different notions as to the needs of the community.

This period saw a broadening of both general and applied anthropological interests. Elam (1978) studied the use of force by Georgian and Moroccan immigrants in bureaucratic situations, suggesting that the attitudes of officials can reduce or acerbate violent behavior. Handelman, who had studied bureaucracies in Canada (Handelman and Leyton 1978), continued this work in Israel (Handelman 1975). He has also studied a sheltered workshop for elderly welfare recipients in Jerusalem (Handelman 1977). These studies were an important change of pace for Israeli anthropology, looking at urban organizations rather than rural communities.

APPLIED ANTHROPOLOGY AT THE ACADEMY

Since 1995, there has been a slow and gradual progress in the development and establishment of applied anthropology at several universities in Israel. The first applied anthropology track was opened in the Department of Behavioral Sciences at Ben-Gurion University. The program was built from two specific courses: (1) an introduction to applied anthropology (in the first year) and (2) an internship in applied anthropology (in the second year). The track was initiated and conceived by the second author of this chapter, Malka Shabtay, an applied anthropologist with a mixed career both at the university and outside of it). She was trained (and prepared the program) at the veteran applied anthropology program at the University of South Florida.

This track existed for four years. Each student sought out his or her own "field site" and research topics where they felt that they could make a significant contribution. For example, one student examined drug usage ("trance" parties) among young people for the Drug Prevention Authority. Another student examined the development and use of anthropological perspectives in the diagnosis and treatment of psychiatric and psychological problems (in a psychiatric hospital under the supervision of a professional anthropologist). The problems of immigration were also evident here; for example, one student worked with immigrants from Syria training to be Arabic teachers.

After three years of intense work, Shabtay left the program at Ben-Gurion University. Veteran applied anthropologist Jeff Halper continued the program for one more year. Unfortunately, he too left the program and the applied anthropology track has ceased to exist.

At that time, the Department of Sociology and Anthropology at Tel-Aviv University invited Shabtay to teach a course on applied anthropology for their master's-level students. In the beginning, they were only willing to take "a small gamble" and agreed that the course would be a one-semester introduction. In spite of her belief that applied anthropology is doing and not passive learning, she agreed in order to start some training in applied anthropology at that department and increase student interest.

The students were enthusiastic and after that first semester they asked to continue the course and get some real-world experience. They approached the chair of the department and negotiated an additional second semester with practical experience. Shabtay agreed and organized this practicum within the limits of time and skills which the students could achieve in a one-year course. Even in this short period of practical work, the students made some meaningful contributions to their "clients." For example, one student studied the cultural awareness and sensitivity toward women in an emergency gynecological unit in a hospital. Another student prepared a new academic course for teachers during their on-the-job training. This course attempted to increase their awareness of cultural diversity in Israeli society and its impact on education.

After this one year of experience, Shabtay was invited to teach a similar course in the Department of Sociology and Anthropology at the Hebrew University in Jerusalem. This was a special moment, as this department is considered the leading department in Israel with the largest number of veteran and active anthropologists in the country. It was an important recognition of the existence and relevance of applied anthropology to the next generation of anthropology students.

During the 2002–2003 academic year, there were courses for master's-level students, in both Tel-Aviv and Jerusalem. Applied anthropology has gained a foothold in the academic center of Israeli anthropology. These courses were planned and taught as 12-month seminars with practical experiences (however, more limited than a full internship). The students had a wide variety of interests and experiences. One student worked with the police and helped to develop a course for police commanders to train them to be more effective and sensitive in a multicultural society. Another student studied the language and culture of criminals in prison (also for the police department). Another group of students focused on the problems of children. For example, one student developed and ran a special "children's space" at the Green movement's activism festival. Another student studied cross-cultural issues at centers for "children at risk" in order to increase the awareness and skills of the workers. Finally, in the field of medical anthropology, one student studied breast cancer among orthodox Jewish women (whose mortality rate is much higher than that of other groups) in order to develop ways to facilitate early diagnosis and treatment.

In addition to master's-level courses, Shabtay has taught applied anthropology workshops with small-scale practical experience to undergraduate students at Ben-Gurion University and for two years at the Ashkelon academic college. These experiences proved to be very empowering for the students, who discovered their ability to help various populations whom they care for and are committed to.

During the 2003–2004 academic year, the applied anthropology seminar was taught at Tel-Aviv University in the same year. Emek Yizrael College began a course in applied anthropology. Their intention was to open a new track in applied anthropology for undergraduate students. It is time to establish a full track or program in applied anthropology with internships and a wide spectrum of elective courses to train master's students for careers in the field. It is hoped that at least one of the two major universities mentioned above will take this next step and place applied anthropology alongside with other options for master's-level students.

It is important to bring more practicing anthropologist to teach in these programs and contribute their unique experiences and networks. We need to help students to develop their careers and to find their place in the real world. It is also important to develop and teach more courses for undergraduate students (at both the universities and the colleges). We also need to make a concerted effort to bring applied anthropology perspectives and skills to students in other departments such as social work, education, nursing, medicine, law, business, tourism, and so on.

Applied anthropologists themselves are making an effort to enrich our resources and networks. The Israel Anthropological Association has recently opened its website; the first interest group to open its forum was the applied anthropology interest group. In addition, Shabtay has published a booklet with a collection of interviews with prominent and active applied anthropologists. This booklet is a product of her seminars and will be distributed to anthropology teachers around the country. It will hopefully present a more organized picture of the people and fields of endeavor in applied anthropology in Israel.

RECENT TRENDS

Israel is a young country and so is our discipline here. Many of the "veterans" mentioned here are still active and productive, though several have retired in recent years. For example, a few of these "veterans" include Palgi (in the field of medical anthropology; see Snyder, Palgi, et al. 1982), Weingrod (in the field of immigrant integration; see Ashkenazi and Weingrod 1985), and Nevo (in the field of rural settlements; see Nevo 1986). The old themes of immigrant integration (or lack of such integration), poverty, and cross-cultural medical issues continue to be important subjects for Israeli anthropologists and other social scientists.

The raison d'être of Israel has been and will remain to establish a safe haven for oppressed Jews wherever they may be. Immigration of Jews to and from Israel is (in Israeli eyes) a special case. Linguistically, we use special terms *aliyah* (going up) and *yeridah* (going down) to refer to these population movements to and from Israel. *Hagira* is used for all other cases, and this is a "new" problem in Israeli eyes. Though global processes have often affected the flow of new immigrants (the breakup of the Soviet Union, the present economic hardships in Argentina, etc.), aliyah is still seen as something special and different. It is an ideological statement; the main purpose of the State of Israel is the physical protection of the Jewish people.

By any objective measure, the policy is expensive and often socially disruptive. However, it remains one of the central unifying themes of Israeli society. Even after 56 years of independence, immigrant integration remains a central public policy consideration in Israel. It is no surprise that the *Practicing Anthropology* (Spring 1993) issue mentioned above has three articles on immigrant integration. These include Georgian (former Soviet Union) immigrants (Tal 1993), Ethiopian immigrants (Shabtay 1993), and the medical problems of Ethiopian immigrants (Nudelman 1993).

A few years ago, the majority of the Ethiopian Jewish community immigrated to Israel. This community has had a difficult adjustment and in many ways reminds us of the great difficulties of the 1950s. In fact there is even a greater cultural difference between Israelis today and the Ethiopian immigrants than there was between European Jews and the "Oriental" Jews in the early 1950s. The Ethiopian community has become one of the most studied groups in Israel (see Ashkenazi 1985; Ashkenazi and Weingrod 1985; Rosen 1985; Shabtay 1993, 2003a, and 2003b; Nudelman 1993 and 1994; and Weil 1995). This is a reflection of both their very challenging integration into Israeli society and their "exotic" nature (which attracts anthropologists).

Halper (1985) asked if we have learned from the mistakes of the 1950s. Unfortunately, the answer is that Israeli society has not learned enough and has made some new errors. The bureaucracy is still insensitive to the cultural and religious needs of the Ethiopians as it was to the immigrants of the 1950s. Unfortunately, these very salient cultural differences are aggravated by a heavy-handed Orthodox Rabbinate which demands a partial conversion of Ethiopians before they can be married. The Ethiopian Jewish community, proud of its long traditions and religiosity, sees it as an insult to have to "convert" to a faith that they have practiced all their lives. Particularly grating is the fact that secular and irreligious Soviet Jews do not have to go through a similar procedure. The rabbis are not alone; other types of bureaucrats frequently (and unknowingly) insult Ethiopian immigrants. Applied anthropologists have been in the forefront of practical aid to the Ethiopian community (advocacy, cross-cultural training, organizational development, etc.).

New themes such as the problems of minorities and the territories have come to the forefront in recent years. For example, one of the ironies of the Israel–Egypt peace agreement is the displacement of Bedouin bands. Army bases removed from the Sinai into a smaller Israel have limited the pasture areas of Bedouin sheep and goats. There has also been an effort to create towns for the Bedouin. Much work is now being done by anthropologists to help the Bedouin protect their way of life and culture (see Kressel 1977 and Abu-Rabia 1993 and 1994).

Applied medical anthropology is growing in Israel both in the numbers of researchers and in the scope of their research. The needs of immigrant populations are also an element here, particularly the problems of this latest new wave of Ethiopian immigrants (see Nudelman 1993 and 1994). Following the pioneering work of Phyllis Palgi (1963) on the psychiatric problems of immigrants, Sara Minuchin-Itzigsohn worked for many years in a psychiatric day care center and has examined the implications of cultural explanatory models on psychiatric care (see Minuchin-Itzigsohn et al. 1984 and Durst et al. 1993). In a similar vein, Cooper (see Levy et al. 1986) has studied the degradation of psychiatric patients in a closed ward.

Other types of medical problems have been studied. Palgi later moved into the field of alcoholism and drug abuse (see Palgi 1975; Snyder, Palgi, et al. 1982). Henry Abramovitch, who replaced Phyllis Palgi at the medical school at Tel-Aviv University, continues to train future doctors in the cultural aspects of human health behavior. In his own clinical work as an anthropologist and Jungian analyst, he has studied and worked with Holocaust survivors (see Abramovitch 1986). AIDS has also arrived in Israel, and anthropologists (Kalka 1993 and Nudelman 2000) are involved in advocacy and in prevention programs.

Anita Nudelman has worked with immigrants (primarily from Ethiopia) and has developed health education programs (see Nudelman 2000 and 2002). She is also teaching in the School of Nursing at Soroka Hospital (Beer Sheba). Aref Abu Rabia, a member of the Bedouin community himself, has been studying and working on traditional Bedouin medicine (Abu Rabia 1999). He also teaches in the Department of Middle East Studies at Ben-Gurion University. Raya Gal, a nurse and anthropologist, is developing special services for the Bedouin community in the Negev (southern Israel) and teaching in the international medicine program (at the Soroka Medical School).

In the field of education, Shalva Weil combines applied research with training programs for specific populations, such as immigrants from Ethiopia, the Caucasus, and India. She has also headed a research team on violence in Arab and Jewish schools. Avigail Morris is teaching anthropology in elementary schools and has developed a curriculum and textbook for this age group. Hagit Peres has worked for many years with the Israelite community (a group of African Americans who immigrated to Israel 30 years ago; see Peres 1998) and was involved in the school that was opened for this group. She later studied and worked with Bedouin women; she has also taught social workers, focusing on social services for culturally different groups.

Finally, in the field of human rights, Jeff Halper is today engaged in political activism together with and on behalf of the Palestinian population (see Halper 1993 and 2003). Sharon Harel worked for several years with Amnesty International (see Amnesty International 2000a and 2000b) and is now working in the office of the High Commissioner for Refugees in Jerusalem. She has also studied and been working with the African foreign workers community in Tel-Aviv. This new community of migrants has raised many new and painful questions about social integration in Israel.

THE FUTURE POTENTIAL OF APPLIED WORK

The traditional areas of applied interest have suffered, I believe, from our fascination with the exotic and downtrodden. The poor, immigrant, exotic Bedouin and Ethiopians dominate our work. There is also a heavy rural bias; historically Israeli anthropologists have worked in moshavim and kibbutzim. There is a definite need to study "up" (Nader 1974, 1980). Applied anthropologists need to study the powerful, such as corporations, law firms, public bureaucracies, and so on. It is necessary to use the ethnographic methods and anthropological models "vertically rather than horizontally" (Nader 1980:38). Anthropologists must look at the links between the individual and the bureaucracy in which he or she must function. In a centralized economy like Israel's, this need is even more pressing. It is not possible to understand the behavior and attitudes of individuals, neighborhoods, moshavim, et cetera without looking at the wider economic and political system.

Though some work on bureaucracies in Israel has been done (see Handelman 1975 and Halper 2003), it has concentrated on the contact between bureaucrats and clients and has yet to reach the higher echelons of power. The time has come to study the economically powerful elements of Israeli society (like the Jewish Agency or the Ministry of Health) and not just the poor, the ill, or the immigrants who are in these agencies' care. The area where we see the greatest potential for applied anthropology in Israel is in the creation and examination of public policy. These policies need to respond to the cultural needs of those receiving public services and not merely reflect the cultural assumptions of the political elite. We would like to present four examples: the problems of organ transplants in Israel, the use of sign language in the instruction of the deaf, the ethnic identity of new immigrants, and violence.

Transplants

Israel has a very modern medical system in the Western mode. Over the last few years, Israeli physicians returning from advanced training in the United States and Europe have established transplant centers. They have had some success in transplanting kidneys and hearts and have made a few unsuccessful attempts in liver and heart/lung transplants. Transplants have been severely limited by a lack of donor organs. Though the shortage of donor organs is a problem throughout the world, it is particularly serious in Israel.

The traditional Jewish viewpoint concerning the body emphasizes wholeness. For example, it is considered a mitzvah (good deed) to bury amputated body parts with the deceased (should he or she not survive the surgery). There is a strong opposition to autopsies as being disrespectful to the dead. Frequently, families agree to donate, only to change their minds at the last moment due to pressure from more religious members of the family. Heart transplants are particularly problematic, as the Jewish definition of death is based on the heart; a transplant can be considered a double murder (removal of the heart from two people). There is also a problem of organ donations from Jews to Arabs (assuming organs are available), since the Jewish "heart" will be buried in a non-Jewish cemetery.

In recent years the modern Orthodox Rabbinate has accepted the notion of brain death; unfortunately the ultra-Orthodox have not. Giving up hope for an Israeli transplant, many Israeli patients now wait for organs in the United States, Britain, and other more developed transplant centers. This greatly increases the costs of treatment for the family and the nation. To increase the potential for transplants, Israel has joined the European organ bank. Unfortunately, we are now in a serious "overdraft"; we have taken too many organs and given too few.

At the same time, the Sick Funds (like HMOs) have increasingly encouraged kidney transplants as a cost-effective alternative to dialysis. Since cadaver organs remain scarce, dialysis patients must turn to their family and friends to find a tissue match or the means to find a match in a foreign country. Israelis now travel the world to find donor organs (even to very poor nations with underdeveloped medical systems), joining the new global black market in organ donors (see Scheper-Hughes 2003).

It seems to me that the physicians who advocated this method and the Ministry of Health that has supported it failed to examine the cultural determinants of the process. We could not find any study that examines the impact of donating a kidney on the health of the donor, nor could we find any study examining the cost-effectiveness of the transplant (is it really less expensive than dialysis?). It is important to have high-caliber surgeons capable of performing the operation and the necessary surgical theaters and equipment; however, they all mean nothing if no organs are available. Does not transplant technology need a cultural philosophy that sees the body as a machine with replaceable parts? Is it possible to create an effective transplant system without examining the cultural belief systems of those who are to supply the organs as well as those who need them?

Sign Language

Over the last ten to fifteen years, sign language has almost completely taken over the education of deaf children in Israel. This change in the educational method is several years behind our U.S. and European counterparts. That does not mean there was no use of signs prior to this change. There have always been some signers in Israel (living in small colonies in Tel-Aviv and Jerusalem); however, the schools were not committed to signing. This old sign language (which developed "naturally") is now slowly being altered and developed into a more effective language for use in education.

The system as it is constituted today still attempts oral training first. There is a selection process, and those children capable of oral communication are mainstreamed. However, from the first grade, those children who remain in the special education system are taught primarily in sign. The reasons given for switching to sign language are numerous; most prominent are the fear that children would get to be six or seven years old with no language at all and the fact that it is effective in teaching and certainly faster than oral programs. In addition, a social reason is often cited; the deaf need a language to converse with their peers.

In this latter reason, I suspect that the United States served as an important role model. Since most Israeli academics read English, the literature coming out of the States has a great effect on their methods. Deaf education in the United States has been committed to sign language for many years (it is nearly impossible to find non-signing programs today) and the cultural conception of a separate Deaf culture. However, the needs and resources of a small country are not the same as a large one. For example, how can a small country like Israel possibly emulate a major cultural and educational center for the deaf like Gallaudet University?

Israel has three schools for the deaf who go from first to eighth grade and two high school programs with a total population of less than 300 (including Arabic- and Hebrew-speaking communities). This means that the total peer group for any grade level is around 25. The ability of sign language to create a community is, therefore, limited. Considering that most parents never become fluent in sign language, sign language isolates the social world of most deaf children. Sign language hinders social adjustment and there is a great degree of frustration evident among the teenagers.

Here too one must question whether the system fits the cultural milieu. Oral communication may be difficult, but there may not be a choice given the small numbers of deaf people in Israel. What is good and efficient in the United States is not necessarily good for Israel. Is there not a need to examine the cultural implications of borrowing technology in a nation that imports so much technology? Applied anthropologists should be examining the cultural "fit" of imported cultural traits.

Israeli Ethnic Identity and Immigration Policy

Israel has had an open immigration policy for Jews since independence under the Law of the Return. This policy is not only open; it also includes generous grants and loans to new immigrants. As many Jews have intermarried in places like the former Soviet Union, this policy is extended to the spouses of Jews and people of Jewish extraction. The question for the religious establishment has always been defining "who is a Jew" and making that definition as close as possible to the Orthodox definitions (people born of a Jewish mother or converted by Orthodox Jewish courts). Secular Israelis have always had a more liberal viewpoint, seeing Israel as a shelter for anyone who has suffered because of his or her Judaism.

A few years ago, under pressure from the religious parties in the Parliament, the law was amended toward the Orthodox model. It was claimed that this correction would help to better scrutinize the background of new immigrants and prevent the immigration of non-Jews. There was probably another reason for the correction: limiting the influence of Reform and Conservative rabbis. In recent years, a group of practicing Muslims has arrived in Israel under the Law of the Return. They are the descendents of Jewish women who converted in order to marry Muslim men. They are therefore Jewish by Jewish law and Muslims by Muslim law.

The correction of the Law was a product of the refusal by rabbinical authorities to accept the notion of "Jews by ethnicity." By limiting the definition of Jews to Jewish law, they *opened* the gates to people who do not perceive themselves as Jews and are culturally Muslim or Christian but have the right ancestress. This is a cultural absurdity, an official sanction to bring practicing non-Jews to Israel. If immigration policy is seen as a method to integrate the Jewish people in Israel, greater consideration should be given to culture. Applied anthropology should be looking at that policy.

Violence Within and Violence Without

From the end of the 19th century, the renewed Jewish community in Palestine has faced violence from the surrounding Arab society. This violence grew in the 1920s and 1930s and only abated when the British authorities limited immigration. After World War II, when the survivors of the Holocaust tried to enter Palestine, this violence was renewed. When the United Nations decided in 1947 to partition Palestine into two states, open conflict began. In May 1948 the local Arabs were joined by the armies of seven neighboring nations and the costly War of Independence began.

For many years, Israel lived in a strange paradox: a tremendous amount of violence on the borders and peacefulness within the country. Lately, there is a growing feeling that the violence within is growing. Almost every day, there are reports of spousal violence, bar fights, road rage, and the like. It is time that anthropologists look at the connections between culture and violence. Some of the problems have ethnic roots where we have professional knowledge to contribute. For example, there is ethnographic data about the murder of Arab women who have "disgraced" their family's honor, the use of corporal punishment in some ethnic groups, or the drinking habits of certain communities.

Applied anthropologists need to look at the relations between cultural change and violent behavior, between migration and violence, and even between public policy and violence. Is there a relation between the violence without and within? What are the patterns of conflict resolution? More importantly, has the constant state of war created a culture of violence or have we developed the cultural means to dissipate these tensions? There are many open questions for research and involvement.

Finally, some changes in the self-perception of applied anthropologists themselves must be noted. First and foremost, applied anthropologists need to admit that their work is an important and vital part of Israeli anthropology. It is not possible to strengthen the status of applied anthropology among other social scientists, policy makers, and funding agencies when the scholars who do such work underrate it. We need to create a network of applied anthropologists (inside and outside of academia) in order to make an impact on our nonapplied anthropological colleagues and from there to our universities and the broader society.

We need to base ourselves on our known strengths and continue our work with minorities, immigrants, and disadvantaged neighborhoods. Medical and educational diversity has also been a recognized strength of anthropology and also should not be abandoned. More attention needs to be given to organizational culture, particularly the culture of bureaucracies in Israel. Neighborhoods exist within cities, immigrants are absorbed according to governmental decisions, and the ill are treated in government hospitals, and these links must be examined. Decision making is of particular importance here. Applied anthropologists need to examine decision making not only in the individual but also in the bureaucracy and in the community. Finally, we need to emphasize public policy and make the bureaucracies aware of our skills and the necessity to study the impact of culture on policy and of policy on culture.

It seems that our progress is slow and only partial. However, considering where we started, it is significant progress. Applied anthropology in Israel is finally out of its infancy, maturing and growing. There is an appreciation and an acceptance of our work in a wide variety of governmental and nongovernmental agencies. A PhD graduate from the Hebrew University (Orit Abuhav) wrote the history of anthropology in Israel; she dedicated a chapter of her thesis to the development of applied anthropology in Israel. So, we are both a formal part of the history and, we believe, much more of the future.

Applied anthropology in the Israeli academe is no longer a "foreigner" or a distant relative in the family of anthropology. We are getting closer to the place we deserve in the heart of our discipline. We believe that this is happening due to the interest and enthusiasm of the students, who feel the need and desire to make a real contribution to this troubling and complex world. An equally important factor is the support of a few members of the older generation (who remember their own contribution in the early stages of anthropology in Israel). It is up to us, the present active and committed applied anthropologists, to complete the job of establishing applied anthropology in the center of the anthropology identity and endeavor in the Israeli academy and Israeli society.

NOTES

1. Applied anthropology has been defined in a spectrum of meanings. There is a narrow meaning: work supported by and reported to a community organization, government agency, et cetera, or any work done for an organization that needs/wants cultural research to function better, evaluate their programs, or advocate for their members. There is also a broader meaning to applied anthropology: work done with more than theoretical notions in mind or work done to assist people in their lives in some direct and meaningful way. There is applied work in Israel across this spectrum.

2. Much work of applied anthropology in Israel (as elsewhere) exists in the form of reports and projects. Material, if at all available, is written in Hebrew. Most of the material cited here appears in English-language books and journals. The choice was often one of availability for the English reader and not necessarily the best example of an individual's work. If any of our colleagues feels slighted, we ask their forgiveness.

REFERENCES

Abramovitch, H.
   1986   There Are No Words: Two Greek-Jewish Survivors of Auschwitz. Psychoanalytic Psychology 3(3): 201–216.
Abu-Rabia, A.
   1993   Educational Anthropology in Bedouin Society. Practicing Anthropology 15(2):21–23.
   1994   Negev Bedouin and Livestock Rearing: Social, Economic and Political Aspects. Oxford: Berge.
   1999   Refuah Bedouit Marsortit (Traditional Bedouin Medicine). Tel-Aviv: Department of Defense.
Amnesty International
   2000a   AI in Action: Refugees. In Amnesty International Report 2000. Pp. 281–282.
   2000b   AI in Action: Human Rights Education. In Amnesty International Report 2000. P. 281.
Ashkenazi, M.
   1985   Studying the Students: Information Exchange, Ethiopian Immigrants, Social Workers, and Visitors. Israel Social Science Research 3(1–2):85–96.
Ashkenazi, M., and A. Weingrod
   1985   Introduction: From Falasha to Ethiopian Jews. Israel Social Science Research 3(1–2):3–8.
Cohen, E.
   1968   Social Images in an Israeli Development Town. Human Organization 21:163–176.
   1970   Development Towns—the Social Dynamics of "Planted" Communities in Israel. In Integration and Development in Israel. S. N. Eisenstadt, R. Bar-Yoseph, and C. Adler, eds. Pp. 587–617. Jerusalem: Israel Universities Press.
   1972   The Black Panthers and Israeli Society. Jewish Journal of Sociology 14(1): 93–109.
Cohen, E., L. Shemgar, and Y. Levy
   1962   Absorption of Immigrants in Development Towns. Jerusalem: Hebrew University—Department of Sociology (in Hebrew).
Deshen, S. A.
   1966   Conflict and Social Change: The Case of an Israeli Village. Sociologia Ruralis 6:31–51.
   1970   Immigrant Voters in Israel: Parties and Congregations in a Local Election Campaign. Manchester: Manchester University Press.

Durst, R., S. Minuchin-Itzigsohn, and K. Jabotinsky-Rubin

1993   Brain Fag Syndrome: Manifestation of Transculturation in an Ethiopian Jewish Immigrant in Israel. Journal of Psychiatry 30(4):223–233.

Elam, Y.

1972   The Social and Sexual Roles of the Hima Women. Manchester: Manchester University Press.

1978   Use of Force among Moroccan and Georgian Immigrants to Israel. Societies 9(4):35–54.

1980   Georgian Immigrants in Israel: Anthropological Observations. Jerusalem: Hebrew University—Kaplan School of Economics and Social Sciences (in Hebrew/English summary).

Gluckman, M.

1961   Anthropological Problems Arising from the African Industrial Revolution. In Social Change in Modern Africa. A. Southall, ed. Pp. 67–81. London: Oxford University Press.

Goldberg, H. E.

1972   Cave Dwellers and Citrus Growers: A Jewish Community in Libya and Israel. Cambridge: Cambridge University Press.

1984a Disadvantaged Youngsters and Disparate Definitions of Youth in a Development Town. Youth and Society 16(2):237–256.

1984b Greentown's Youth: Disadvantaged Youth in a Development Town in Israel. Assen: Van Gorcum.

Halper, J.

1985   The Absorption of Ethiopian Immigrants: A Return to the Fifties. Israel Social Science Research 3(1–2):112–139.

1993   Between Practicing and Engaged Anthropology in Israel. Practicing Anthropology 15(2):27–30.

2003   Planning as a Tool of Political Control. Planners Network. Internet Journal, Winter Edition. Electronic document, http://www.plannersnetwork.org/htm/pub/archives/155/halper.htm.

Halper, J., and A. Nudelman

1993   Applied, Practicing and Engaged Anthropology in Israel. Practicing Anthropology 15(2):3–4.

Handelman, D.

1975   Bureaucratic Transitions: Development of Official-Client Relationships in Israel. In Transaction and Meaning. B. Kapferer, ed. Pp. 223–274. Philadelphia: ISHI.

1977   Work and Play among the Aged: Interaction, Replication and Emergence in a Jerusalem Setting. Assen: Van Gorcum.

Handelman, D., E. Basker, and D. Sprinzak

1981   The "Miftan" as a Rehabilitative and Educational Institution. Hebrew University NCJW Research Institute for Innovation in Education (mimeo).

Handelman, D., and E. Leyton

1978   Bureaucracy and Worldview: Studies in the Logic of Official Interpretation. St. John's, Newfoundland: Memorial University of Newfoundland Institute of Social and Educational Research.

Kalifon, S. Z.

1997   Applied Anthropology in Israel: Doing Applied Work Without Really Trying. In The Global Practice of Anthropology. M. L. Baba and C. E. Hill, eds. Pp. 179–197. Studies in Third World Societies, Publication No. 58. Williamsburg, VA: College of William and Mary Press.

Kalka, I.

1993   The Anthropologist as AIDS Activist. Practicing Anthropology 15(2):24–26.

Kressel, G.

1977   Bride-Price Reconsidered. Current Anthropology 18:441–458.

Levy, A., S. Cooper, and A. Elizur

1986   Degradation and Rites of Degradations in a Closed Psychiatric Ward. Israel Journal of Psychiatry and Related Sciences 33(4):275–285.

Marx, E.

1967   Bedouin of the Negev. Manchester: Manchester University Press.

1988   Rehabilitation of Refugees in the Gaza Strip. Tel-Aviv: Tel-Aviv University Dayan Center (in Hebrew/ English summary).

Minkovitz, M.

1967   Old Conflicts in a New Environment: A Study of a Moroccan Atlas Mountains Community Transplanted to Israel. Jewish Journal of Sociology 9(2):191–208.

Minuchin-Itzigsohn, S., R. Ben-Shaul, A. Weingrod, and D. Krasilovsky

1984   The Effect of Cultural Conceptions on Therapy. A Comparative Study of Patients in Israeli Psychiatric Clinics. Culture, Medicine and Psychiatry 8:229–254.

Nader, L.

1974   Up the Anthropologist—Perspectives Gained from Studying Up. In Reinventing Anthropology. D. Hymes, ed. Pp. 284–311. New York: Vintage Books.

1980   The Vertical Slice: Hierarchies and Children. In Hierarchy and Society. G. M. Brittan and R. Cohen, eds. Pp. 31–43. Philadelphia: ISHI.

Nevo, N.

1986   Unpaid Work in the Rural Family in Cooperative Farming. Israel Social Science Research 4(1):112–139.

1993   The Anthropologist in a Rural Bureaucracy: Chances for Survival. Practicing Anthropology 15(2):44–56.

Nudelman, A.

1993   Understanding Immigrant Adolescents. Practicing Anthropology 15(2):13–15.

1994   Health Services to Immigrant and Refugee Population: Patient and Provider Cross-Cultural Perspective. Collegium Anthropicum 18(2):189–194.

2000   From Research to Intervention: The Input of Anthropology in a Sexual Health Education and Aids Prevention Program for Ethiopian Immigrant Adolescents in Israel. In The Anthropology of Africa: Challenges for the 21st Century. P. Nchoji Nkwi, ed. Proceedings of the 9th Annual Conference of the Pan African Anthropological Association, ICASSRT Monograph 2:33–36.

2002   Sexual Health Education in Residential Schools in Israel: An Interactive Approach. In Education for Health Topics, Values and Praxis, FICE Romania and IRECA-FICE Israel. I. Neacsu, E. Grupper, and T. Mares, eds. Pp. 113–121. Bucharest: Semne Press.

Palgi, P.

1963   Immigrants, Psychiatrist and Culture. The Israel Annals of Psychiatry and Related Disciplines 1(1):43–58.

1975   The Traditional Role and Symbolism of Hashish among Moroccan Jews in Israel and the Effects of Acculturation. In Cannabis and Culture. V. Rubin, ed. Pp. 207–216. The Hague: Mouton.

1993   How It All Began . . . A Personal Saga. Practicing Anthropology 15(2):5–8.

Palgi, P., M. Goldwasser, and H. Goldman

1955   Typical Personality Disturbances of Iraqi Women in Light of their Cultural Background. Megamot 1(3):236–242 (in Hebrew).

Patai, R.

1953   Israel between East and West. Philadelphia: Jewish Publication Society.

Peres, H.

1998   Return to Womanhood: Construction of a Redefined Feminine Identity in the Hebrew Israelite Community. In The Hebrew Israelite Community, Prophetic Change for a New Reality. P. Hare, ed. Pp. 65–80. Lanham, MD: University Press of America.

Rosen, C.

1985   Core Symbols of Ethiopian Identity and Their Role in Understanding the Beta Israel Today. Israel Social Science Research 3(1–2):55–62.

Rosenfeld, H.

1958   Processes of Structural Change within the Arab Village Extended Family. American Anthropologist 60(6):1127–1139.

1970   On Determinants of the Status of Arab Village Women. In Integration and Development in Israel. S. N. Eisenstadt, R. Bar Yoseph, and C. Adler, eds. Pp. 429–440. Jerusalem: Israel Universities Press.

Scheper-Hughes, N.

2003   Human Kidneys: The New Cash Crop. New Internationalist, March 2003 (e-journal).

Shabtay, M.

1993   Absorption of Ethiopians through the Israeli Defense Forces. Practicing Anthropology 15(2):16–17.

2000   Identity Reformulation among Ethiopian Immigrant Soldiers in Israel: The Case of Ethiopian-Israeli Soldiers. *In* Language, Identity and Immigration. E. Olshtain and G. Horenczyk, eds. Pp. 141–154. Jerusalem: Magness Press, the Hebrew University.

2003a   "ReGap": Music and Identity among Young Ethiopians in Israel. Criticalarts 17(1/2).

2003b   From Jerusalem to Ethiopia and Back: From Identity Confusion to Committed Identity. Adult Education in Israel 7:141–167.

Shokeid, M.

1968   Immigration and Factionalism: An Analysis of Factions in Rural Israeli Communities of Immigrants. British Journal of Sociology 19:385–406.

1971   The Dual Heritage. Manchester: Manchester University Press.

2002   An Israeli's Voyage: Tel-Aviv-New York and Between. Tel-Aviv: Yediot Books.

Snyder, C. R., P. Palgi, et al.

1982   Alcoholism among the Jews of Israel. Journal of Studies on Alcoholism 43(7):623–654.

Tal, L.

1993   An Anthropologist on a Community Rehabilitation Project. Practicing Anthropology 15(2):18–20.

Weil, S.

1995   It Is Futile to Trust in Man: Methodological Difficulties in Studying Non-Mainstream Populations with Reference to Ethiopian Jews in Israel. Human Organization 54(1):1–9.

Weingrod, A.

1962a   Administered Communities: Some Characteristics of New Immigrant Villages in Israel. Economic Development and Cultural Change 11:69–84.

1962b   Reciprocal Change: A Case Study of a Moroccan Immigrant Village in Israel. American Anthropologist 64(1):115–131.

1966   Reluctant Pioneers: Village Development in Israel. Ithaca, NY: Cornell University Press.

Willner, D.

1965   Politics and Change in Israel Administered Communities: The Case of Land Settlement. Human Organization 24(1):65–72.

1969   Nation-Building and Community in Israel. Princeton, NJ: Princeton University Press.

THE PRACTICE OF ANTHROPOLOGY IN GREAT BRITAIN

SARAH PINK
Loughborough University

British applied anthropology has emerged from the difficult relationship with academic anthropology that characterized its trajectory during the last century. It is flourishing in the 21st century supported by the leading anthropological associations of the UK along with new practicing organizations. This chapter examines how applied anthropology in Great Britain has both developed as a response to and is being used to intervene in an increasingly globalised world. It will also discuss several examples of current anthropological work in public and private sectors as a response to global changes taking place in the country. Key Words: Great Britain, industry, policy, government, applied anthropology

The history of applied anthropology in Britain is inextricable from the political, economic, and institutional contexts in which social anthropology has developed as an academic discipline. Shore and Wright (1997)[1] identify the origins of British applied anthropology as part of the "Colonial Gaze." As they note, Evans-Pritchard's (1951) and Firth's (1981) writings tended to define applied anthropology "in the rather narrow terms of its value for government" (1997:141). Indeed, although anthropologists had opportunities to engage in applied work in industry during the middle 20th century, they did not take these up. Anthropology's colonial legacy is fundamental to understanding the historical context of both academic and applied anthropology in Britain.

In the existing literature there is some variety in how the development of applied colonial anthropology is characterized. Kuper (1996) suggests that anthropologists were reluctant to do applied work during the colonial period and those that attempted applied work performed very poorly. There was, he claims, "never much of a demand for applied anthropology from Whitehall or from the colonial government" (1996:110). However, Mills' (2002) detailed analysis of the relationship between applied and "pure" anthropology in the era of the Colonial Social Science Research Council (CSSRC) (1944–62) suggests rather more activity in applied anthropology, played out within the context of competition and debate between personalities and departments in British anthropology.

NAPA Bulletin 25, pp. 123–133, ISBN 1-931303-28-2. © 2006 by the American Anthropological Association. All rights reserved. Permissions to photocopy or reproduce article content via www.ucpress.edu/journals/rights.htm.

The split between the "pure" and applied that prevails in British anthropology today (discussed below) was to some degree established in this earlier context through the agenda of the CSSRC. Mills (2002) describes how during these years there were clear tensions between the practical anthropology advocated by Malinowski and the scientific academic anthropology of Radcliffe-Brown and his followers. This emerged as a "contest between what we now call 'pure' and 'applied' versions of anthropology" played out between personalities and departments. Max Gluckman at that time at Oxford supported a more theoretical anthropology while Raymond Firth and Audrey Richards at the London School of Economics supported the practice of anthropology in a more public arena. The CSSRC's initial emphasis was on the practical application of anthropology to a research agenda in the colonies. The sort of applied work carried out initially consisted of a series of commissioned surveys and ethnographies. By the 1950s, the political context in the colonies had begun to change, with their independence becoming increasingly on the agenda. The interests of the CSSRC had shifted to, for example, initiating studies of comparative election procedures. Fueled by concern that the Government should not be seen to fund research in and thus interfere with its now ex-colonies, the CSSRC was wound up in 1961. At this time (as has recurred throughout history) assumptions about the gendered nature of anthropological endeavor were also at play. Kuper notes how some regarded applied anthropology "as less intellectually demanding, and therefore as best suited to women" or the inexperienced anthropologist (1996:104–105). This did not always mean, however, that women played a subordinate role. Applied anthropology in the colonies was certainly influenced by Audrey Richards from her position on the CSSRC and as director of the CSSRC-funded Makere Institute in Uganda (Mills 2002).

The historical relationship between British anthropology and colonialism is well-known; however, Mills has also documented a lesser-known series of encounters between anthropologists and industrialists, led by Israel Sieff, a cofounder of Marks and Spencers (the department store chain) in Britain. The case illustrates well how the relationship between the "pure" and the applied developed after the era of applied colonial anthropology. Mills (2005) describes how "Sieff spent a great deal of time during the early 1950s wooing both academics and his business colleagues with his vision of anthropology's potential contributions to industrial welfare and personnel 'problems.' " However, during the 1950s British anthropology gained funding from the Carnegie and Rockefeller institutes as well as having its history of CSSRC sponsorship. Moreover, with the establishment of the Association of Social Anthropologists of Britain and the Commonwealth (ASA) in 1946, the discipline had defined itself as a scholarly profession, to the exclusion of the wider range of interested parties who made up the membership of the Royal Anthropological Institute (RAI).

The leading anthropologists at this time were, under these circumstances, in a position to decline to shape their research agendas to meet the needs of industry. Here again the contest between pure and applied anthropology was played out, and the former gained a distinct advantage. Despite some anthropologists' enthusiasm that they could provide industrialists with practical advice about staff relationships and productivity, the overall message to industry was that anthropologists' work was more exploratory; it would produce problems and question but would not necessarily offer the sets of solutions they required. The interest in this work subsequently declined and in time anthropology and industry went separate ways (Mills 2005).[2] This reflected what Shore and Wright described as "British anthropology's tendency to cloak itself in lofty detachment and scientific objectivity, and to shun the idea of active involvement" (1997:141), which persisted into the late 20th century. However this 1950s encounter provides an interesting historical contrast to the burgeoning relationship between anthropology and industry that is developing in the rather different political and economic context in which anthropology exists in Britain today.

It was not until the late 1970s that applied anthropology began to regain momentum. Shore and Wright discuss the setting up of a series of small voluntary organizations that addressed the role of anthropology in various fields such as medical anthropology, social and community work, and nursing. The Group for Anthropology in Policy and Practice (GAPP) was established to support applied interests and provided both training courses and networking for anthropologists working in the same fields. In 1988 a combination of these groups, supported by the Wenner Gren Foundation, formed the British Association for Social Anthropology in Policy and Practice (BASAPP), which changed its name to "Anthropology in Action" in 1993. BASAPP had its own journal (*Anthropology in Action*), provided a forum and series of events for applied anthropologists, and had a membership working in diverse areas of applied anthropology. Nevertheless, Shore and Wright characterized its work as "fragmentary, uncoordinated and reactive, lacking a 'defined corpus of theory' and an 'organised body of knowledge' " (1997:140). Indeed it was not to survive, as " 'Anthropology in Action' ceased to be a membership organization with a program of activities in May 2000, although its journal of that name" continues (Wright 2005). Notwithstanding this, since the turn of the century there is in fact increasing divergence and demand for applied anthropology in Britain.

The increase demand for anthropological work created a need to document its growing uses in the country. In 2001 I was invited to join the ASA Committee as Networking Officer. Part of my brief time in this role was to initiate closer links with anthropologists working outside the academy. In order to systematic document the diversity, depth, and breadth of applied anthropology in the country, I organized the Applications of Anthropology Seminar Series.[3] It was funded by the current embodiment of what was the CSSRC, the Economic and Social Research Council (ESRC), and the ASA and C-SAP (the Centre for Teaching and Learning in Sociology, Anthropology and Politics) with the following aims: (1) to examine existing debates about the role of applied anthropology, (2) to review the professional nonacademic areas and activities anthropologists are engaged in, (3) to explore collaborations between anthropologists working in and outside academic departments, (4) to examine the needs of current users of anthropology, (5) to report on the implications of this for training in anthropology, and (6) to promote awareness about anthropological methods. Some outcomes of this project are discussed in the following sections.

In 2003 Paul Sillitoe called for anthropology to "promote its professional identity beyond the academy" in what he sees as obvious areas for practice "such as development, forensic science, the media, the 'culture' industry, heritage work, museums and galleries, teaching, intercultural relations, refugee work and the travel industry." In addition he listed less obvious potential areas "such as law, banking, social work, human resources, retailing, management and the armed forces" (2003:2). Lamenting anthropology's current lack of a professional profile, he hoped that going public would increase student numbers and prevent nonanthropologists posing as members of our profession. Sillitoe's complaint was not totally ungrounded: The public profile of social anthropology as a "useful" discipline certainly needs further development. However, one of the lessons learned from the Applications of Anthropology Seminar Series is that by 2003 anthropologists had begun to make inroads into both the professions that Sillitoe considered "obvious" and the professions that he considered "less obvious." We found a healthy presence in public and private sectors. Moreover, many of these practicing anthropologists are clearly located in a global context shaped by, among other things, new communications technologies, war and the threat of terrorism, tourism, migration, refugees and asylum seekers, and a search for global products and markets.

Although there is no complete register of applied anthropologists in Great Britain, the Applications of Anthropology Seminar Series and the results of a questionnaire it developed have provided a substantial overview of the range of private and public sector organizations in which applied anthropologists work. Applied anthropologists have found growing niches in areas such as civil service, the public and welfare sector, research, design and development in business, the media industries, and legal cases.

In British government departments there is an increasing interest in anthropology, and the number of anthropologists engaged in roles that inform government policy is increasing. For example, anthropologists are employed as civil servants by the Ministry of Defence (MOD), where they provide a range of research services to the government working in interdisciplinary groups (see Hills 2005). Another anthropologist is employed as a senior research officer in the Higher Education Division of the Department for Education and Skills.[4] Such roles involve providing research that can inform the decision making of powerful policy makers in government. However, the work of anthropologists in the British civil service also involves much more than carrying out anthropological research; they need to be able to interpret statistical data and use a range of quantitative and qualitative methods. Their work is unlikely to involve actually doing fieldwork; instead they produce work that is anthropologically informed. In addition to these salaried roles in government departments, anthropologists also undertake work for the British public sector from their bases in academic institutions. For example, Hart (2005) describes her experiences of doing research commissioned by the National Health Service focusing on a series of issues related to organizational change and staffing issues within the organization. While these government uses of applied anthropology seem to be increasing, the importance of anthropology in what has perhaps been its more established niche—overseas development—is shifting if not decreasing. As Green (2005) outlines, her work for DFID in social development requires not her anthropological skills as a fieldworker with in-depth contextual knowledge but rather her ability to make anthropologically informed assessments according to policy requirements. Nevertheless the role of anthropologists in development is a critical force, focusing particularly on issues of indigenous knowledge (Sillitoe et al. 2002).

In the private sector a similar employment structure exists. Anthropologists might be employed by a company, commissioned to undertake a project for a company through their university, work as freelance consultant, or be employed by a research agency. Anthropologists employed in industry appear to have more opportunities to do fieldwork themselves; however, much of their work is in interdisciplinary teams and many of their tasks might involve management and other roles that would be informed by anthropology rather than being anthropological in themselves. Companies such as Kodak and Unilever employ anthropologists or commission studies undertaken by academic anthropologists or research consultants that employ Ph.D. anthropologists. London-based agencies such as Sapient, Happy Dog, and Ideas Bazaar also work with anthropologists to develop anthropologically informed ethnographic research projects for public sector and business clients (Roberts 2005).

Another example of current possibilities for anthropologists is the British legal system—a niche where anthropologists are required to work in a quite different way from the above. Here anthropologists are required to work as independent sources because of their in-depth knowledge or expertise about one particular culture or subculture and its historical and contemporary beliefs and practices. An example that is necessarily unique to British anthropology is the case of foxhunting. In 1999 Marvin, who had already developed academic anthropological research in this area, was asked to produce a "neutral" paper for a committee set up by the home secretary to undertake a major inquiry into foxhunting in the context of contemporary debates about whether hunting with dogs should be banned. Following this in 2002, when foxhunting was banned in Scotland, Marvin was asked to write a report on the social and cultural impact of this ban, to be used in the legal case for an appeal against the ban (Marvin 2005). A second example that is not unique to British culture and politics but part of a broader global issue is the role played by anthropologists as expert witnesses in legal cases in British courts (see Good 2003)—for example, in cases where immigrants to Britain use their home "cultural traditions" to justify homicide or when asylum seekers who are in fear of victimization in their home country make an appeal (Schwander-Sievers 2005).

Finally, an emergent niche not yet fully developed is the potential for the application of anthropology in the public media domain. There is a history of postgraduates in visual anthropology finding work in media production and anthropologists have (notably in the 1970s and 1980s) been consultants to documentary film projects (see Henley 2005). British anthropologists have yet to take on the role of media personalities and public commentators, as they have for example in Norway (Eriksen 2003). There have been some moves in this area: Some anthropologists report having been approached by both current affairs programs and popular television shows. However, anthropologists are yet to make a full impact on the British media sphere. The increasing use of visual and new media technologies and methodologies in the research and representation practices is a significant area for applied anthropological work. Ethnographic research often involves using video or photography, intranet, and multimedia representation of visual research to support the dissemination of research products within organizations. The skills and training of visual anthropologists in this niche is becoming identified as the emergent field of applied "visual anthropology" (Pink 2004).

A long-established focus on applied anthropology in Britain has been an anthropology in and of organizations. This has recently been surveyed by Gellner and Hirsch (2001) in their edited volume that covers a range of organizational contexts, including management in industry and the public sector (Chapman 2001; Ouroussoff 2001); ethnography in science laboratories (Hine 2001) and museums (MacDonald 2001); and welfare, policy, and local authority contexts including divorce procedures (Simpson 2001), a children's therapeutic unit (Pulman-Jones 2001), a computer access project (Mascarenhas-Keyes 2001), rural development work (Mosse 2001), and local authority and policy (Abram 2001). Gellner and Hirsch discuss the roles anthropologists who study policy and powerful public and private organizations have in making explicit how polices and power structures might impact on other people's realities in contexts of inequalities based on gender, ethnicity, and other identity factors. They suggest that the distinctions between the projects of doing anthropology for and in/of organizations are not necessarily clear-cut. Anthropologists who have not been contracted to analyze the organization itself nevertheless tend to end up doing an informal and most probably never disseminated "anthropology of" the organization they work for/in, as well as carrying out the projects they are commissioned or employed to do. Such understandings inform the way we present our results to and generally communicate in any given organizational context. In some cases they may be essential for the research to be able to work effectively (see Mascarenhas-Keyes 2001). Much of this contemporary applied work in/for organizations falls within the substantive foci of applied anthropology in Britain discussed by Shore and Wright (1997), who highlighted the relationship between applied anthropology and policy. They noted that, in the early 1990s, public sector and policy-oriented applied anthropology focused on "working on management and organizational change in the government, non-government and private sectors" (1997:140). While this critical anthropology of policy clearly still exists in Britain, it is now coupled with the emphasis on using anthropological methodologies to produce research results (the "product" that clients need) that forms the basis of the studies discussed in the first part of this section.

THE RELATIONSHIP BETWEEN APPLIED AND ACADEMIC ANTHROPOLOGY

As I noted above, the relationship between applied and academic anthropology in Britain has been troubled from the outset, manifesting itself in the contesting discourses between applied and "pure" anthropologists. This has meant that there have been few opportunities for useful exchanges between applied and academic anthropology in the past. However, in the 21st century support for applied anthropology in Great Britain by the key institutions, the RAI and ASA, has increased. The ASA actively supports training and networking in applied anthropology. The GAPP courses continue under the direction of the ASA and are funded by the ESRC, the Applications of Anthropology Seminar Series was an ASA initiative, and "Apply," the ASA applied anthropology network (established in 2003), is active in the organization of events and the development of on-line resources. Also in 2003, the Berghahn Books series "Studies in Applied Anthropology" was set up specifically to publish volumes that bridge the gap between applied and academic anthropology.

Many other connections between applied and academic anthropology are undocumented and represented by personal and professional relationships and networks that link academic anthropologists with nonacademic user organizations. These contacts sometimes result in consulting, co-supervising of research students, and other collaborative ventures; for instance, the ESRC and MOD have a joint research studentship and funding source for applied work, and a few private and public sector organizations offer student placements and internships. Some British universities also provide anthropological consultant services. For example, the Edinburgh Resource Centre at the University of Edinburgh employs anthropologists who supply consults to the Social Development. The Centre is involved in initiatives with organizations such as the Department for International Development (DFID). In addition, in the commercial sector, anthropologists are beginning to create their own research agencies and consultant units working with business and public sector clients to provide anthropologically informed research.

KEY ISSUES IN APPLIED ANTHROPOLOGY

Many issues faced by British applied anthropologists are general to applied anthropologists in other contexts—covering ethics, ownership of research materials, and often feelings of being excluded from the academy. Other issues specific to applied anthropologists involve their relationship to the discipline as a whole and the availability of applied training in Britain.

British social anthropology has always been defined largely by its fieldwork method—long-term ethnographic fieldwork—derived from the tradition established by Malinowski and his students. Many British anthropologists have taken on board the need for new approaches that are appropriate to the new global and local contexts in which we live—such as multisited ethnography (Marcus 1995) and a new type of fieldwork that involves researching people's lives in their homes (Miller 2001). However, the short-term nature of much applied anthropology fieldwork has led to the question of whether this is "real" ethnography or anthropology. Participants in the Applications of Anthropology Seminar Series argued that such short-term projects are often based on longer-term experience in the field they are working in or that, because their work is informed by anthropological principles and questions, it is undoubtedly anthropological. This is true even though they may be engaged in anthropologically informed research or decision making at management and policy-making levels. Such work is anthropological and suggests that defining anthropology by its method might no longer be suitable in the contemporary global context (for either academic or applied anthropology). However, since much applied anthropology work is not published in academic journals or books, its practitioners do not often participate in anthropological debates. The result is that such research tends to be excluded from the existing anthropological literature, and thus it does not achieve a profile in this academic sphere. Therefore, under circumstances where data might be jointly owned or confidential and where time constraints do not allow for the production of an academic monograph or shorter work, applied anthropology projects frequently remain disseminated only to those who commissioned them.

In Britain, little postgraduate training in applied anthropology is available. Applied methods are very infrequently taught at the postgraduate level in British universities, and many Ph.D.-level anthropologists therefore lack the skills they need to be able to engage successfully with organizations and their research needs. Such training has been managed by GAPP for the last ten or more years (funded by the ESRC), and academic departments have not engaged with its provision. Future training possibilities, however, might bridge this gap for both applied and academic anthropologists.

CONCLUSION: APPLIED ANTHROPOLOGY AND GLOBAL DEVELOPMENTS

Global developments over the past decade are inevitably interwoven with the growth and development of British anthropology. For example, in government the recruitment of anthropologists is directly linked to the changing context in global security. Collinson (2003) suggests that during the 1990s a combination of factors—such as the end of the Cold War, the rise in importance of asymmetric warfare, and an increasing emphasis on peacekeeping and humanitarian operations—led to an emphasis on the importance of examining the social, historical, and psychological context of conflict and of the often unique insights that social scientists are able to provide in this respect. A number of themes, such as the increasing trend toward multisited research in a context of disrupted human lives caused by transnational migration and movement of migrant workers, refugees, and asylum seekers, have affected developments in both academic and applied anthropology. These global situations provide a context for applied anthropologists in Britain to develop projects that focus on ethnic minority and cultural issues within Britain. Most of the work in these situations was discussed earlier in this chapter, such as working as an expert witness in the legal system or providing understandings of ethnic minority experiences and issues in education or health.

Other demographic changes in Britain—for example, changing gender roles, the growing aging population, and the increase in people living alone—mean that there are new sets of consumers for industry to learn about, again an area where anthropologists can provide in-depth contextual studies. Applied anthropology, to some degree, is being used in Britain to direct public and business policy in the face of a changing culture and society in Britain. Indeed, it appears to be in these contexts that the value of anthropologists as analysts of the detail of changing societies and new markets as well as the dynamics of the workplace within the organization has been realized.

In Britain our everyday lives might involve purchasing a new cleaning product or computer, reading in the paper about changes in education policy, efforts to retain nursing staff in NHS hospitals, or the conviction of an asylum seeker accused of rape or murder, or watching the TV news about a fuel strike and seeing an advert for a bank. Unlikely as it might seem, in the processes by which these diverse objects and representations, or the policies that they are based on, have been produced, an applied anthropologist could well have been at work. Where we are less likely to find British anthropologists is in the seat of public commentator on radio, on television, or in the newspapers, although this may be set to change in the near future. Nevertheless, there is still work to be done. British applied anthropology is gaining a stronger and more influential profile as it finds its place both inside and outside the academy. However, to realize its full potential, more networking, training, and promotion are needed within both academic and public contexts.

NOTES

Acknowledgments. It would have been impossible for me to write this chapter without the support of a number of individuals and organizations. Much of the knowledge presented here originates from the Applications of Anthropology Seminar Series that I convened in 2003. I have acknowledged individual contributions in the text; other contributions must be credited to the discussions developed with the seminar participants. The seminar series was funded by the ESRC and co-funded by the ASA and C-SAP and supported by Loughborough University. I would like to particularly thank Sue Wright for recommending me for the task of writing this chapter and David Mills (C-SAP), Richard Fardon (Chair of the ASA), and Hilary Callan (Director of the RAI) for their comments on an earlier draft of this chapter.

1. This chapter builds on Shore and Wright's chapter in the first global anthropology text by Baba and Hill (1997). I would like to thank Sue Wright for recommending me for this task. This chapter differs from Shore and Wright's original work in that it has been developed with reference to new literature on the historical and contemporary context of British applied anthropology and, ten years on, describes a new field of opportunities for applied anthropologists in Britain. See Shore and Wright 1997 for a more detailed examination of the colonial legacy of British anthropology.

2. My brief summaries here are based on David Mills' excellent and detailed analyses of the history of British social anthropology. Mills' work is recommended for any follow-up reading on British applied anthropology during this period.

3. Many of the ideas and comments made in this chapter are based on the discoveries and discussions from the Applications of Anthropology Seminar Series. While the opinions expressed in this chapter are my own, I would like to acknowledge that the input of the speakers and participants in the three seminars held between March and September 2003 has been crucial to the formation of my thinking on this. Wherever possible I have endeavored to cite individuals; much of what I have to say here, however, is attributable to these seminar discussions rather than to myself or any other individual. I hope not to have misrepresented anyone or neglected to give credit where due.

4. Stella Mascarenhas-Keyes, a social anthropologist (DFES), was a speaker at the second Applications of Anthropology Seminar Series (June 2003).

REFERENCES

Abram, S.

    2001 Amongst Professionals: Working with Pressure Groups and Local Authorities. *In* Inside Organisations: Anthropologists at Work. D. Gellner and E. Hirsch, eds. Pp 183–204. Oxford: Berg.

Baba, Marietta L., and Carole E. Hill, eds.

    1997 The Global Practice of Anthropology. Studies in Third World Societies, No. 58. Williamsburg, VA: College of William and Mary Press.

Collinson, P.

    2004 Anthropology in the Ministry of Defence. *Anthropology in Action, Vol 10*, (1).

Chapman, M.

    2001 Social Anthropology and Business Studies: Some Considerations of Method. *In* Inside Organisations: Anthropologists at Work. D. Gellner and E. Hirsch, eds. Pp. 19–34. Oxford: Berg.

Eriksen, T. H.

    2003 The Young Rebel and the Dusty Professor: A Tale of Anthropologists and the Media in Norway. Anthropology Today 19(1):3–5.

Evans-Pritchard, E.

    1951 Social Anthropology. London: Routledge and Kegan Paul.

Firth, R.

    1981 Engagement and Detachment: Reflections on Applying Social Anthropology to Social Affairs. Human Organisation 40:193–201.

Gellner, D., and E. Hirsch, eds.

    2001 Inside Organisations: Anthropologists at Work. Oxford: Berg.

Good, T.

    2003 Anthropologists as Expert Witnesses: Political Asylum Cases Involving Sri Lankan Tamils. *In* Human Rights in Global Perspective: Anthropological Studies of Rights, Claims and Entitlements. Richard Wilson and Jonathan Mitchell, eds. Pp. 93–117. London: Routledge.

Green, M.

    2005 Social Development, Institutional Analysis and Anthropology? *In* Applications of Anthropology. S. Pink, ed. Oxford: Berghahn: 110–129

Grillo, R.

    1994 The Application of Anthropology in Britain, 1983–1993. *In* When History Accelerates: Essays on Rapid Social Change: Complexity and Creativity. C. Hann, ed. London: Athlone Press. 300–316

Hart, E.

    2005 Applications of Anthropology in the National Health Service. *In* Applications of Anthropology. S. Pink, ed. Oxford: Berghahn. 145–168

Henley, P.

    2005 Anthropologists in Television: A Disappearing World? *In* Applications of Anthropology. S. Pink, ed. Oxford: Berghahn. 170–190

Hills, M.

    2005 Anthropology at the Centre: Reflections on Research, Policy Guidance and Decision Support. *In* Applications of Anthropology. S. Pink, ed. Oxford: Berghahn. 130–144

Hine, C.

    2001 Ethnography in the Laboratory. *In* Inside Organisations: Anthropologists at Work. D. Gellner and E. Hirsch, eds. Pp. 61–76. Oxford: Berg.

Kuper, A.

    1996 Anthropology and Anthropologists. London: Routledge.

MacDonald, S.

    2001 Ethnography in the Science Museum, London. *In* Inside Organisations: Anthropologists at Work. D. Gellner and E. Hirsch, eds. Pp. 77–96. Oxford: Berg.

Marcus, G.

    1995 The Modernist Sensibility in Recent Ethnographic Writing and the Cinematic Metaphor of Montage. *In* Fields of Vision. L. Devereaux and R. Hillman, eds. Berkeley: University of California Press. 35–55

Marvin, G.

    2005 Research, Representations and Responsibilities: An Anthropologist in the Contested World of Foxhunting. *In* Applications of Anthropology. S. Pink, ed. Oxford: Breghahn. 191–208

Mascarenhas-Keyes, S.

    2000 Understanding the Working Environment: Notes toward a Rapid Organisational Analysis. *In* Inside Organisations: Anthropologist at Work. D. Gellner and E. Hirsch, eds. Pp. 205–220. Oxford: Berg.

Mills, D.

    2001 Behind Closed Doors. *In* Home Possessions. D. Mills, ed. Oxford: Berg. pp. 1–19

    2002 British Anthropology at the End of the Empire: The Rise and Fall of the Colonial Social Science Research Council 1944–1962. Revue d'Historie es Sciences Humaines 6:161–188.

    2005 Dinner at Claridges? Anthropology and the Captains of Industry 1947–1955. *In* Applications of Anthropology. S. Pink, ed. Oxford: Berghahn.

Mosse, D.

    2001 Social Research in Rural Development Projects. *In* Inside Organisations: Anthropologists at Work. D. Gellner and E. Hirsch, eds. Pp. 157–182. Oxford: Berg. 55–70

Ouroussoff, A.

    2001 What Is an Ethnographic Study? *In* Inside Organisations: Anthropologists at Work. D. Gellner and E. Hirsch, eds. Pp. 35–58. Oxford: Berg.

Pink, S., ed.

    2004 Applied Visual Anthropology. Special Issue of Visual Anthropology Review 20(1).

Pulman-Jones, S.

    2001 Observing Other Observers: Anthropological Fieldwork in a Unit for Children with Chronic Emotional and Behavioural Problems. *In* Inside Organisations: Anthropologists at Work. D. Gellner and E. Hirsch, eds. Pp. 117–136. Oxford: Berg.

Roberts, S.

    2005 The Pure and the Impure? Reflections on Applying Anthropology and Doing Ethnography. *In* Applications of Anthropology. S. Pink, ed. Oxford: Berghahn. 72–89

Schwander-Sievers, S.

    2005 Making a Difference?: The Anthropologist as "Cultural Expert" in Legal Cases. *In* Applications of Anthropology. S. Pink, ed. Oxford: Berghahn. 209–228

Shore, C., and S. Wright

    1997 Colonial Gaze to Critique of Policy: British Social Anthropology in Policy and Practice. *In* The Global Practice of Anthropology, Studies in Third World Societies, No. 58. M. L. Baba and C. E. Hill, eds. Pp. 139–154. Williamsburg, VA: College of William and Mary Press.

Sillitoe, P.

    2003 Time to Be Professional? Guest Editorial in Anthropology Today 19:1.

Sillitoe, P., A. Bicker, and J. Pottier

    2002 Participating in Development. London: Routledge.

Simpson, B.

    2001 Swords into Ploughshares: Manipulating Metaphor in the Divorce Process. *In* Inside Organisations: Anthropologists at Work. D. Gellner and E. Hirsch, eds. Pp. 97–116. Oxford: Berg.

Stadhams, D.

    2004 Look to Learn: A Role for Visual Ethnography in the Elimination of Poverty. Applied Visual Anthropology (S. Pink, ed.), a Guest-Edited Issue of Visual Anthropology Review 20(1):45–58.

Wright, S.

    2005 Machetes into a Jungle? A History of Anthropology in Policy and Practice 1981–1996. *In* Applications of Anthropology. S. Pink, ed. Oxford: Berghahn. 27–54

APPLIED ANTHROPOLOGY IN CANADA: HISTORICAL FOUNDATIONS, CONTEMPORARY PRACTICE, AND POLICY POTENTIALS

ALEXANDER M. ERVIN AND LORNE HOLYOAK
University of Saskatchewan

Canadian domestic or on-shore applied anthropology is examined beginning with historical background from the Nineteenth through to the mid-Twentieth Century. It is only through the exponential growth of Canadian anthropology in the 1960s that its applied branches find their niches. Applied anthropology diversifies first into primary emphases on policy critiques, development, and northern and Aboriginal issues and then secondarily to resource industries, multiculturalism, immigration, health, and advocacy. Key Words: Canada, development, multiculturalism, advocacy, policy

Disclaimers are necessary before we review the highlights of Canadian applied anthropology. We cannot access the entire literature since much of applied research remains unpublished and largely "fugitive." University-based applied anthropology is likely over-represented here in contrast to what might be discovered as the strengths of nontraditional, full-time practice.

We cannot substantially deal with development work being done offshore. This is practiced at a level commensurate with most developed countries and through agencies such as the Canadian International Development Agency (CIDA) and the International Development Research Centre (IDRC), both federally funded. It also involves various NGOs and universities with their counterparts in a wide range of countries and the hiring of individual Canadian anthropologists in developing countries.

It is most likely that Canadian anthropology's involvement in international development could warrant a substantial chapter in itself; however, the rest of the present chapter is directed to anthropological practice within Canadian borders.

CANADIAN APPLIED ANTHROPOLOGY BEFORE THE 1970S

For a long time Canadian anthropology was underdeveloped and academic in the form of salvage ethnology related to Native peoples. As a historic footnote, some minimal applied activities can be seen through the work of 19th-century natural historian/

NAPA Bulletin 25, pp. 134–155, ISBN 1-931303-28-2. © 2006 by the American Anthropological Association. All rights reserved. Permissions to photocopy or reproduce article content via www.ucpress.edu/journals/rights.htm.

geologist George Mercer Dawson of the Geological Survey of Canada. Beginning in 1875, he surveyed the West Coast and ethnographically described the Haida, Shuswap, and Kwakiutl while making recommendations to the government for their humane treatment and inclusion in commercial fisheries. Dawson lobbied for the establishment of the Anthropological Survey of Canada at the National Museum of Man in Ottawa. He intended it to provide background information for enlightened administration of Canadian Native peoples (van West 1976), yet the subsequent history of the institution tended to reveal more antiquarian interests. As early-20th-century footnotes, National Museum anthropologists Edward Sapir and Diamond Jenness appealed for the preservation of cultural traditions such as the potlatch and the sun dance that were under threat of being made illegal, but their support was not successful.

Much later, Jenness engaged in some policy analysis with his multivolume comparison of Eskimo Administration in Canada (1964), Labrador (1965), Alaska (1962), and Greenland (1967). This work is monumental, but some of his policy recommendations vis-à-vis Canadian Inuit (or Eskimo) are controversial. In his final synthesis he advocated large-scale relocations of Inuit to southern Canadian cities where they would undergo assimilation and absorption into an industrial economy. Most of the remaining Inuit were to be placed in larger settlements to provide them with effective services. These recommendations were meant to overcome the dilemmas of a collapsed fur trade, extreme poverty and poor health, presumed lack of other sources of income, and a dramatic population explosion beyond the capability of local resources (Jenness 1968:62–63). However, the suggestions would have almost guaranteed the loss of their culture. Fortunately the recommendations for southern relocation were not heeded, and these flaws in policy analysis should not diminish Jenness's enormous contributions to Canadian anthropology. Yet, for newer generations of Canadian applied anthropologists, they should serve as historical lessons of what to avoid.

Applied anthropology finally gains its foothold in Canada with the work of Harry Hawthorn of the University of British Columbia (BC). With Native participation his first activity in 1948 was to organize a conference on the topic of Indian welfare. That same year, he supervised a project for the federal government investigating the proposed extension of Old Age Pensions to Indians. Shortly after this, he conducted a multidisciplinary background study for the BC government, examining the tensions between the Doukabhour religious sect and the general population. Then, he did another investigation for the federal government, focused on the conditions of BC Indians (Hawthorn 1955; Hawthorn et al. 1958).

Contemporaneously, at the other end of the country in the early 1950s, the establishment of the Stirling County Study by Alexander Leighton (1959) in southern Nova Scotia has been internationally significant in the development of transcultural psychiatry and cross-cultural psychiatric epidemiology. Although initially directed out of Cornell University, it has been an exemplar of collaboration with Canadian scholars, most notably Marc-Adélard Tremblay of Laval University.

The next significant marker is the Hawthorn-Tremblay report; *A Survey of the Contemporary Indians of Canada* was a two-volume comprehensive investigation of topics like education, economic development, health, and band administration. Intended as a major policy review for the Department of Indian Affairs, it was compiled by a team of approximately fifty researchers, the majority of whom were anthropologists. It contained 151 recommendations and called for a special status of "citizenship plus" for Aboriginal people (Hawthorn et al. 1967). But, with the coming to power of Pierre Trudeau's administration, which favored assimilatory policies, the recommendations were not acted upon. However, some Native leaders and federal bureaucrats have looked upon the report favorably and, after over 30 years, it still has its influence on a slowly emerging set of policies directed toward self-determination (Weaver 1993).

In the 1960s there was growing attention to development in Canada's Northwest and Yukon Territories, strategic areas with regard to minerals, oil and gas, national sovereignty, and defense. Infrastructures like those in southern Canada were being consolidated through what could be considered as "neocolonial" approaches. Policies and services (such as health, education, and economic development) were being consolidated for both Indians and Inuit primarily through the establishment of larger settlements. Accordingly, the federal Northern Coordination and Research Centre employed numerous anthropologists to conduct community studies as policy backgrounders and to monitor impacts of community changes.

Then, because of increased urbanization, prosperity, and the postwar baby boom, Canadian universities expanded their campuses and admissions, and many new universities were formed. Where there had been one autonomous anthropology department (Toronto) there were 21 by the end of the decade, as well as 14 expanded and combined departments of sociology and anthropology. Yet even today, numbers are still relatively small, with only about 400 university-based social anthropologists in the country. Over half of the newly stocked anthropology departments typically consisted of immigrant anthropologists from the United States, Britain, and Commonwealth countries. Canadian anthropology, then, could be characterized as being cosmopolitan in its perspectives, rather than being distinctively national. However, a more genuine Canadian anthropology is emerging as the immigrant anthropologists have crystallized their new Canadian identities, attended to Canadian research topics, and, more importantly, trained a new generation of Canadian anthropologists.

APPLIED ANTHROPOLOGY IN CANADA, 1970–2004

Although sparsely populated by other national standards (31,000,000 people living primarily in a narrow 200-mile band north of the American border) and beyond that still having a vast, almost frontier-like territory, the country is quite complex and pluralistic. It is intensively industrialized and a major exporter of industrial, agricultural, mineral, fisheries, and forestry products. Politically a minor international player, economically Canada is a member of the G-8 and frequently (for better or worse) a major supporter of "free trade" policies. It is highly urbanized and characterized by considerable ethnic pluralism. The country has attracted large-scale immigration, most recently from non-European developing countries. Social indicators and living standards, on the aggregate, would suggest a highly favored nation. But, the country also contains extremes of regional disparities, lingering vestiges of internal colonialism, and significant pockets of poverty and poor health, especially regarding its Aboriginal people, that resemble conditions in underdeveloped countries. There have been many unresolved issues regarding the political structure of the society. Although generally a stable country, there has been sporadic unrest with potentials for social violence and endemic racism especially in the context of the misunderstandings and mistreatments of Aboriginal or First Nations peoples. Such contexts provide the rationale for an applied anthropology to address a multitude of issues.

ABORIGINAL SELF-GOVERNMENT AND NORTHERN DEVELOPMENT

Research in both northern development and Aboriginal self-determination continues to predominate and probably represents almost 75 percent of onshore activity. The work of the late Richard Salisbury (1986; Salisbury et al. 1972) and his colleagues at McGill and McMaster Universities, including Harvey Feit (1985; Feit and Beaulieu 2001) and Colin Scott (Scott and Webber 2001), relates to both the themes of northern development and Aboriginal self-government. It includes social impact studies and program evaluations in the planning and outcomes of the James Bay Hydroelectric Project begun in the early 1970s. That mega-project involved major floodings and diversions of waters and led to equally massive changes in indigenous Cree society, some of which can be viewed as quite detrimental. Nonetheless, there has developed a significant regionalization of Native society and government, which was previously absent, and a sophisticated political competence that has enhanced self-determination. Furthermore as part of the agreement, a guaranteed annual income program was established. Unexpectedly, that has actually increased the participation of Cree trapping in their domestic economies. There have been other benefits through the development of an infrastructure that supports further development—much of which is directed by a new leadership within the 7,000 Cree. While downplaying their own contributions, Salisbury and his colleagues probably played significant roles in the development of the more positive dimensions of the programs resulting from the agreement.

Other studies by Canadian anthropologists have been major contributions in the more generic field of social impact assessment. One centers on the Mackenzie Valley pipeline hearings that, in the 1970s, indefinitely postponed the building of a pipeline from rich Arctic sources of oil and gas to southern Canada. The work of Michael Asch (1982) and other anthropologists, as well as the significant testimonies of the peoples themselves, confirmed the serious potential disruptions of the local Dene peoples. A political agreement was reached, whereby oil and gas development cannot proceed until outstanding issues of land claims and treaty infringements have been resolved.

The other highly significant project is the Inuit Land Use and Occupancy Study, which was directed by Milton Freeman in the early to mid-1970s. It was jointly conceived by Inuit Tapisarat (an Inuit political advocacy group) and the Department of

Indian Affairs and Northern Development. About twenty social (primarily anthropologists) and environmental scientists, along with several scores of Inuit partners, reconstructed detailed regional patterns of land and resource use and occupancy. The three-volume report (Freeman 1976) provided information about the distribution of fish and game as well as their habits, movements, and concentrations. It made remarkable use of Inuit ecological knowledge in compatibility with social and environmental science. This baseline study provided much of the justification for the development of a new Inuit territory, called Nunavut (The People's Land), separated from the former Euro-Canadian- and Dene-dominated Northwest Territories. Its creation in 1999 enabled Inuit self-government and control over their destiny and local resources.

Another significant development has been the highly sophisticated policy analysis regarding Aboriginal peoples by scholars such as Noel Dyck (1985), and in collaboration with James Waldram (Dyck and Waldram 1993). Michael Asch (1984, 1997) has presented a number of works related to Native rights and public policy, as has Sally Weaver, whose *Making Canadian Indian Policy: The Hidden Agenda* (1981) set a high standard for the frequently neglected desirability for anthropologists to "study up" in order to effectively understand policy making as a process. This study examined how, during the 1960s, high-level federal bureaucrats and politicians developed a policy that was essentially assimilatory but was intended to provide "just" solutions for Canada's Native peoples. Their product, an (unintentionally) ironically and aptly named "White Paper," was based on the cultural assumptions of well-educated, but naive, bureaucrats. That assimilatory approach was resisted by emerging Native organizations that united to meet this threat of termination of treaty obligations.

Overall, probably at least several hundred anthropologists are engaged in applied studies involving Canadian Native people. Other notable research could include Hedican's (1986, 1995), Tanner's (2000, 1979), and Waldram's (1985, 1988, 1993) work on socioeconomic development in the subarctic regions of northern Canada, Slobodin's (1966) work on Métis identity, Paine's (1971, 1977) studies on interethnic relations in the North, Dyck's (1997) research on education, and many others.

HEALTH

There is an extensive medical anthropology in Canada, most of it directly related to policy and practice. This includes the work of Joseph Kaufert and William Kooladge in the Department of Community Medicine at the University of Manitoba. In a pioneering collaboration they have worked with health workers in training programs to establish Natives as health workers, interpreters, and advocates for Winnipeg hospitals. Also at Manitoba, John O'Neil and Patricia Kaufert have been engaged since the mid-1980s in a long-term, participatory project in the Eastern Canadian Arctic engaging with issues surrounding obstetric care and Aboriginal control of health delivery (O'Neil et al. 1993).

Regarding Aboriginal people and medical anthropology, O'Neil's (1986a) analysis of adolescent suicide and his (1986b) and Speck's (1987) critiques of medical services are noteworthy. Waldram (1990) has done pioneering work on Native health utilization patterns and needs in cities, and Warry (1992), besides making interesting theoretical observations, describes innovations in collaborative research undertaken in studies relevant to the transfer of health services to Aboriginal control.

Lock and Wakewich-Dunk's (1990) study of chronic responses to stress among Greek immigrant women in Canada and Lock and Bibeau's (1993) reflections on the practice of medical anthropology in Canada are also worthy of attention. A number of chapters in a work by Waldram et al. (1995) dealing with contemporary Aboriginal health issues in the context of the provision of services, the role of Aboriginal medicine, self-determination, and policy directions have a particularly applied aspect.

A notable practicing medical anthropologist is Frank Wagner, who has worked at the Ontario Ministry of Health and the Ministry of Community and Social Services, addressing key policy issues as part of the development of health care legislation and policy, programs, and services for persons with disabilities. He is currently the cochair of the Hospice Palliative Care Network, a joint initiative with Mt. Sinai Hospital in Toronto. In this capacity he has helped to develop and deliver an interdisciplinary model of home palliative care.

Usher Fleising at the University of Calgary has been involved in a number of projects involving health and health science policy in Canada. A prominent example is a multi-authored study (Caulfield et al. 2001) that addresses the policy implications of genetic testing technologies for Canada's public health care system.

Multiculturalism, Ethnicity, and Immigrant Resettlement

Canada annually admits about 250,000 immigrants. About three-quarters now come from nontraditional sources—Asia, Latin America, the Caribbean, and Africa. But the country was already significantly multicultural before these recent shifts in immigration. About 40 percent of the population representing non-British, non-French, and non-Aboriginal populations could be classified as multicultural, and about 10 percent of the overall population can be considered as constituting "visible minority" categories. It is interesting to note that approximately every three years, Canada takes in about the equivalent of its total Aboriginal population through such immigration.

In spite of that, little anthropological attention has been devoted to these phenomena. This is surprising, since anthropologists are exceptionally well-equipped to provide policy analysis and practical advice on these topics. But multiculturalism and immigration are not completely neglected, and the existing policy analysis and research on ethnicity and ethnic groups, ethnic relations, racial discrimination, and immigration and refugee resettlement all show potential for anthropological growth.

In the broad field of ethnicity, the work of Norman Buchignani is significant for his (1982) theoretical overview and for his work with South Asian–Canadians as a whole (Buchignani et al. 1985) and Indo-Fijians in particular (1983). Doreen Indra, along with her colleagues Louis-Jacques Dorais and Kwok B. Chan (Chan and Indra 1987; Dorais et al. 1988), has provided syntheses of the Southeast Asian experiences in Canada.

Research on racism and race relations is becoming more urgent for understanding tendencies that seem to be escalating during the current periods of high immigration and drastic, unsettling economic restructuring. Racism provides significant obstacles to some aspects of successful immigrant and ethnic group integration. So far, much of this research is centered in southern Ontario and much of it comes out of York University (Henry 1978; Kallen 1982). Stanley Barrett, of Guelph University, has examined, in his provocatively titled book *Is God a Racist?* (1987), the underlying assumptions of right-wing racist groups in southern Ontario. His most chilling observation is how ordinary and respectable members actually are in the other aspects of their lives.

Another subdomain for anthropological analysis and practice is that of immigrant resettlement, especially as related to government-sponsored immigrants or refugees. An overview has been provided by Merry Wood (1988), a researcher on the Task Force on Mental Issues Affecting Immigrants and Refugees. Some anthropologists have examined the processes in local context. Lisa Gilad (1990) studied the resettlement experience, with regard to Eastern Europeans, Southeast Asians, and Latin Americans, in St. John's, Newfoundland, which has been a major stopping point for refugee claimants because of the proximity of Gander Airport, a strategic refueling point for international flights. Linda Havers (1993) tackled the sensitive topic of Vietnamese street gangs in Calgary, and Linda Fuchs (1991) analyzed support needs and systems among Southeast Asian women in Saskatoon. Another example is Hess and Smith's (1984) research on the predicaments of Salvadorian, Guatemalan, and Haitian refugees in Montreal.

Since the early 1980s, approximately 200 community-based immigrant resettlement organizations have sprung up across the country to assist in the resettlement of hundreds of thousands of refugees from about forty ethnicities and nationalities. A few anthropologists, such as David Bai (1992) in Edmonton, have worked with agencies in helping to design and evaluate programs. One of us (Ervin) completed a needs assessment for a resettlement agency in Saskatoon. It involved service providers and immigrants from 35 countries. It revealed a much greater need for programming and services related to immigrant health and family counseling. Suggestions of the needs for augmented and flexible, competency-based, second-language training, plus greatly expanded employment readiness training, were also reinforced, as was the need for expanded, integrated, and relatively intensified adult education. In this case, this research was combined with a modest practitioner-training program, and some of its graduates went on to work with immigrant settlement agencies.

Anthropology of Resource-Based Industries

A small group of anthropologists in Atlantic Canada have been involved in fisheries research in an interdisciplinary and international context. Some of that work lays out the major parameters and policy dimensions of the various fishing industries and ethnographically describes fishermen and their communities. Variables and dimensions have included social structure of work and communities, modes of production (e.g., family fishing to industrialization), communication, competition, labor–management relations, adaptations of fishermen, impacts of technology, modernization and government regulations, resource management, and current crises surrounding depletion of stocks, occupational safety, job satisfaction, and so forth (Anderson and Wadel 1972).

In the late 1970s, just after Canada had declared jurisdiction over a 200-mile offshore territorial limit, Raoul Anderson (1978) of Memorial University advocated a major review of fisheries from a human science perspective, rather than simply from technological, commercial, or biological perspectives. Such a review at that opportune time could have led to a major restructuring of decision making among fishermen, their kin and communities, bureaucrats, unions, commercial interests, and other important stakeholders. Unfortunately, according to Davis (1991:89), these exceptionally perceptive and anthropologically based policy suggestions went largely unheeded.

Canada's Atlantic fisheries face an unprecedented crisis, with a complete moratorium on northern cod fisheries and greatly restricted quotas regarding most of its other fish stocks. This has created considerable grief, hardship, and uncertainty among fisherman, their families, and their communities. Ironically, Anderson (1988) was commissioned in the late 1980s by the Newfoundland Department of Fisheries to assess the social and cultural impact of reduced access to cod fishing.

Using the Digby Neck region of Nova Scotia, Davis (1991) demonstrates that there was a post–World War II drive to expand and industrialize the industry to provide fish processors and consumers with more catch. This was done by providing subsidies to those buying larger boats and increasing their capital investment and through various programs to foster the consolidation of packing and processing industries. But then, because of some earlier stock reductions in the 1970s, resource management policies tried to reduce the number of fishermen who were chasing too few fish. This was done through creating expensive licensing for limited entry into specific fisheries (e.g., lobster, scallops) and maintaining excessive bureaucratic regulations and inspections. These reduced the flexibility required by captains in shaping their adaptations and instead encouraged overspecialization, vertical integration, and the industrialization of the industry. In these regards, the work of Marion Binkley (1990) documents declines in occupational safety and job satisfaction.

Agriculture, especially in Western Canada, is undergoing a crisis similar to that of the East Coast fisheries. Caught between a trade subsidies war involving the United States and the EU, Western Canadian farmers have been struggling and disappearing, along with their communities, at alarming rates due to low returns and high costs of production that have favored agribusiness and the consumer. Rural sociology and agricultural economics have largely lost their earlier holistic- and political economic-styled perspectives on agriculture and farming communities. A few (Ervin 1985; Hedley 1979) have attempted to portray this domain in multidimensional, holistic, ecological, and political economic perspectives in Saskatchewan and Alberta. Of note is the recent assistance that an American anthropologist, Kendall Thu, has been giving Canadian hogwatch organizations in their resistance to the proliferation of intensive livestock operations in the production of pork.

Canada is one of the world's largest producers in both mining and forestry, but not much anthropological research has been done in these domains. The ample anthropological potential for contributions to social forestry can be seen in Julian Wake's (1990) review and through the example of consulting work done by practicing anthropologist William Horswill, who has worked with tribal governments in British Columbia helping to establish harvesting contracts, map traditional land use, and negotiate through forest use conflicts with non-Natives. Similarly, Leyton's (1975) work with Newfoundland miners and Williamson's (1974) book describing the changes experienced by Inuit relocated for underground work in nickel mining, Rouse's (1993) study of miners' attempts to control the quality of their work situation, and Rouse and Fleising's (1995) contrasting of workers' and management's organizational cultures at a coal mine show the value of anthropological approaches in the study of this often stressful occupation.

ADVOCACY AND PARTICIPATORY ACTION RESEARCH

Although not unique to Canada, Canadian anthropologists are making noticeable contributions to the anthropology of advocacy and participatory or action-styled research. One "whistle-blowing" exercise, which attracted a lot of media attention, is Elliot Leyton's (1975) *Dying Hard*, where he documents the suffering, social consequences, and inadequate compensations for Newfoundland fluorspar miners who were dying from the consequences of silicosis, lung cancer, and mining accidents. He followed up on this research through the media, by lobbying government, and through the preparation of a special report on workers' compensation.

Another example is Dara Speck's (1987) exposure of inadequate health services for Native peoples. In this passionate ethnography, she expands on the tragic and unnecessary death of a young Kwakiutl girl to appendicitis and medical malpractice. She shows how this incident is not isolated but related to local Indian–white relations, impediments to self-determination, and inadequate health services. In *As Long as the Rivers Run*, James Waldram (1988) demonstrates parallels between the ways that the federal government made treaties with Native peoples in the last century and the ways current provincial governments have negotiated hydroelectric mega-projects in the North. In both cases, the processes were rushed, compensations were inadequate, promises were broken, and political expediency was paramount for catering to the presumed energy needs of Euro-Canadians. Relocated communities are subjected to loss of economic self-sufficiency, ecological disruption, dietary delocalization, inadequate compensations, and social unrest.

Beyond such case studies, there is a significant theoretical literature that conceptualizes the practice of advocacy, both relating and contrasting it to normal social science. The most notable of these is Robert Paine's (1985) collection, where he examines the pitfalls of advocacy, explores the nature of advocational "truths," and shows how advocacy needs to be introduced early into anthropological curricula and professional training. He suggests that the profession should more positively rethink its acceptance of advocates and advocacy. In *Beyond the Breast-Bottle Controversy*, Penny Van Esterik (1989) effectively classifies types of anthropological advocacy. She also demonstrates the value of unraveling the assumptions behind various advocacy positions. Even when they are allied, as with feminist and traditional Laleche-styled advocacies in the case of the bottle-versus-breast-feeding controversy, there can be profound and unexamined differences of assumption and strategy.

The work of Michael Ames, curator of the Museum of Anthropology at the University of British Columbia, could be considered under the rubric of advocacy anthropology. Ames (1986) has been advocating the democratization or "deschooling" of museums, by making collections and curators more available to the general public and allowing museums to assist the public to become more involved in the promotion and regeneration of its various traditions. Beyond this, articles by Asch (2001), Ervin (1990), Hedican (1995), Ryan (1985), Waldram (1993), and Williamson (1999) also contribute to the growing conceptualization of advocacy, as well as providing case examples and calls for action.

Regarding advocacy, in 1994 a national campaign of lobbying was conducted through the auspices of the Society of Applied Anthropology in Canada (SAAC) and through its journal *Proactive*. That journal carried an article by Norwegian anthropologist Georg Henriksen (1994) that outlined the predicament and circumstances of the Mushuau Innu of Davis Inlet, Labrador. These included the lack of sanitation and clean water, high rates of infectious illness, suicide, alcoholism and solvent abuse, extreme poverty, welfare dependencies, and isolation from traditional subsistence opportunities. These people had been relocated, for administrative convenience, to an island not readily accessible to their traditional caribou hunting grounds. The Innu were petitioning to have their community relocated to a place of their own choosing, within their sacred territories, and with opportunities to more fully return to caribou hunting. More importantly, they felt that this would be the ideal location to begin their healing, especially as it pertained to children and youth, who were the principal victims of the stresses. Public attention, through radio, television, and newspapers, had been drawn to this very isolated community, when there had been a very serious outbreak of suicide and substance abuse (gasoline and glue-sniffing) among children and youth.

In 1994 SAAC's members and some colleagues in the international anthropological community responded to a campaign of support, through letters and petitions, directed to the prime minister, the Minister of Indian Affairs, and the Newfoundland Government. Eventually, the federal government agreed to the Innu appeal and in 2003 they were relocated to a new community at their chosen location on the mainland. The anthropological advocacy may have had some significance but has to be viewed as of an auxiliary nature, secondary to the growing political competence of the Innu themselves.

Relevant to Newfoundland and Labrador is that anthropologists there (primarily situated in St. John's and associated with Memorial University) have provided remarkable leadership in the realm of anthropological advocacy. Besides the work of Elliot Leyton, Robert Paine, and the Davis Inlet campaign mentioned above, Neis (1992) writes of the early-1960s influence of anthropologists and sociologists on an emerging opposition to a rather authoritarian provincial government: Included was their research relevant to fisheries and resettlement policies that had been oppressive to outport fishermen and their families. Gordon Inglis worked closely in research and advocacy roles with

Newfoundland unions and revealed and supported needs for more humane service delivery in isolated communities. Adrian Tanner was a major catalyst for the establishment of the Indian and Inuit Support Group, whose members engaged in public education and public criticism of government policy as related to Aboriginal issues in the 1970s and 1980s and continued through with support for the Innu (Tanner et al. 1995). Following that was the full-time policy and advocacy work done by Peter Armitage, a practitioner graduate of the Memorial program working on land claims, social justice issues, and self-determination, for the Naskapi-Montagnais Innu Association in Labrador, actively using acquired media skills and technical ones associated with impact assessment.

Related to advocacy is participatory action research where those most affected design, conduct, and analyze their own research and then act upon the findings. They usually have the supplemental guidance of trained social science researchers, who place themselves in equal or even subordinate positions. That is also well-represented in Canada and has been led by the efforts of Joan Ryan and her colleague Michael Robinson (Ryan and Robinson 1996) through the Arctic Institute of North America. This work related to efforts of various Dene communities in the Mackenzie district of Canada's northern territories and included both economic and cultural preservation initiatives. The most well-known is Ryan's (Ryan and Robinson 1990) work with the Ft. McPherson Gwich'in collecting linguistic, oral historical, and traditional ecological knowledge, for the purposes, among other things, of enhancing the local school curriculum. Wayne Warry's (1992) work with First Nations people in southern Ontario and John O'Neil's (O'Neil et al. 1993) liaisons with Inuit both attest to the value of these styles of collaboration in the health field.

APPLIED ANTHROPOLOGY IN FRANCOPHONE CANADA

Literature regarding applied anthropology in Québec is referred to throughout this review. As with many other facets of Canadian society, applied anthropology in this country must confront what has in the past been referred to as the two solitudes of English and French Canada. However, this stereotype, while accurate to a degree, does not reflect the complexity of the nation or the discipline. In fact, many francophone anthropologists in Canada work and publish in English, and some vice versa. Not surprisingly, there is a great deal of collaboration between colleagues that crosses linguistic boundaries. Yet it is necessary to recognize that this collaboration takes place mostly in Quebec, with its French-speaking majority and large English-speaking minority. Thus, while not a separate tradition, applied anthropology in Quebec, in both French and English, is (dare we say it?) distinct. This distinctiveness is most evident in French-language journals produced in Canada.

Pilon-Le (1984), while consistent with the trend toward rural studies in Quebec, has focused on the impact of agricultural policies on farm inheritance and consequently upon production. In a similar vein, the work of Bariteau (1977) on the structural impediments to the fishing industry in the Magdelan Islands is relevant to questions of regional development.

There are three nodes of applied anthropology in the province of Québec. At Laval University since 1972, there has been a continuing effort to conduct formal research on Native studies that would be deliberately and consistently participatory in nature. The fruits of these efforts are described in some detail in an article by Tremblay (1988:9). At McGill University in Montreal a tradition of applied anthropology has evolved around development studies. The early history of this focus involved research with the James Bay Cree (Chance 1968; Salisbury 1986). Salisbury has also provided overviews of applied anthropology in anglophone Québec (1977). The development stream at McGill continues today with both domestic and international foci. Université de Montréal is noted for its work in international development and also for its domestic work in medical anthropology (Corin et al. 1990).

For more details on Québecois anthropology, see Bariteau and Genest (1987), Gold and Tremblay (1982), and Tremblay (1990).

THE INSTITUTIONALIZATION OF APPLIED ANTHROPOLOGY IN CANADA

Since the 1970s, an infrastructure has emerged that attempts to support a more consistent and professional application of anthropology in Canada. In 1973 the Canadian Anthropology Society, Société canadienne d'anthropologie (CASCA), separated from an organization dominated by sociologists. Although still primarily academic in orientation, CASCA has explored issues of public policy, the state of the art of application, and the possible certification of practicing anthropologists. More germane, for a while, was the Society of Applied Anthropology in Canada (SAAC) founded in 1981. During its short history, it achieved several accomplishments: the establishment of a set of ethical guidelines; a prize (the Weaver-Tremblay Award) for accomplished practice; the cosponsorship of the Canadian Applied Anthropology Project (a documentation of "fugitive" reports being accumulated by Wayne Warry at McMaster University); and a newsletter that morphed into a journal—*Proactive*. This journal promoted practicing nonacademic anthropology, as well as policy analysis, and provided examples and information for the sake of students aspiring to nonacademic careers. Unfortunately, because of small numbers, widely distributed across a very large country, and a failure to gain a succession in leadership, SAAC and *Proactive* folded in 1995. CASCA has filled the gap somewhat, now offering the Weaver-Tremblay Award and having a number of applied sessions every year at its annual congresses. A recent positive development has been the revival of a dormant local practitioner organization—the Society for Applied Anthropology in Manitoba (SAAM)—with 30 members meeting monthly in Winnipeg (see www.saaminc.org). SAAM publishes a newsletter, *Anthropology in Practice*, and has published two books from its proceedings: One (Chodkiewicz and Brown 1999) is on the impacts of hydroelectric development in northern Manitoba, and the other (Chodkiewicz and Wiest 2004) will be on globalization and communities.

SAAC's paid membership used to range from about 80 to 160, and 99 members completed detailed information about themselves for a directory. The proportion that they represented of the total number of practicing anthropologists who retained an anthropological identity is hard to extrapolate. A guess is that they might constitute about one-quarter to one-third of that constituency. Among the 99, 51 were academically affiliated, primarily as tenured faculty, 7 were students or status undetermined, and 41 were practicing, nonacademic anthropologists. Of that group, 11 were associated with federal or provincial agencies, and another 11 were associated with nongovernmental organizations, such as Aboriginal lobby groups, addiction research foundations, and so forth. Nineteen were in some sort of private practice associated with consulting, in areas like social impact assessment, education, social forestry, and others.

It can be estimated that several thousand people received master's or doctoral degrees from Canadian anthropology departments from the early 1970s until now. The number receiving baccalaureates in anthropology probably reached 15 to 20 thousand during the same period, along with many others since. To what extent do they practice anthropology, or have these people just been liberally educated and gone on to other nonanthropological endeavors?

From an awareness of a few graduates of our own program at the University of Saskatchewan, we know that a portion is using some anthropological skills, although significantly modified by on-the-job experiences and realities. One graduate has been an executive director of an immigrant settlement agency, another has been an executive director of an ex-convict assistance agency, others work for United Way, another is a policy adviser for a First Nations government, while others are social workers and counselors with multicultural clients, policy researchers, and so forth. Such lists presumably could be compounded many times across the country.

In spite of such penetrations of anthropologically trained people in nontraditional sectors, there remains a challenge to crystallize and focus capacities to more directly train our students for practice. This requires continuous linkages with nonacademic anthropologists to better understand how to prepare more competently beyond academic cloning, our students for the job market.

While surveying Canadian anthropology programs, we found some applied directions of note. McGill University, while not offering a specific program in applied anthropology, does have numerous faculty specializing in either medical systems or development. McGill also has the Centre for Society, Technology and Development (STANDD), a research center dominated by anthropologists that provides a training ground and research opportunities for graduate students in development anthropology. Carleton University also offers a number of courses in development and applied anthropology. Of significance is the undergraduate degree with concentration in power and everyday life, which offers students the opportunity to focus on power relations, development, and globalization. York University offers three undergraduate course streams that may be broadly construed as applied, including colonialism, development, and globalization; medical anthropology and science studies; and social justice and human rights. At the graduate level, emphases include advocacy and social justice; environment and development; and medical anthropology—all topics that can be parlayed into applied expertise. Simon Fraser offers an undergraduate applied social research stream. This specialization does not appear to extend necessarily to the graduate level. Numerous Canadian universities offer courses related to development, applied anthropology, or medical anthropology, but without offering specific undergraduate course streams. However, McMaster University now offers graduate programs (master's and doctoral) in the anthropology of health, which are stepping-stones to applied careers.

Yet, as they have anecdotally reported, many Canadian practicing anthropologists have emerged from on-the-job training rather than through more direct skill transmission from their university education. Canadian applied and practicing anthropologists have been primarily trained from within generic academic programs, where one or two courses, if that, might be devoted to application or policy. For many university departments, the overwhelming emphasis is on theory and ethnographic content, more subject to trends dominating academic anthropology than to anticipating the needs for policy analysis and application.

Many who teach in Canadian anthropology departments feel that applied anthropologists best emerge out of a general academic and liberal education, where they learn the foundations of a sound academic anthropology that is later transferred to practice. Given the generally high quality of work cited in this article, there is sometimes merit to this idea. Yet it should be noted that the vast majority of this work has been produced by people at the Ph.D. level who have been safely positioned as tenured and only act part-time as applied anthropologists out of their academic departments. They control the curriculum as well. The issue to be resolved is how to make the best use of training opportunities at the undergraduate and master's levels so that many more of our graduates can contribute their anthropological insight to society on a much more sustained level. A minority would say that we explicitly need to foster a practitioner corps.

The overwhelming majority of teachers of anthropology have been trained with such a strong academic orientation that they are rarely aware of the pressures of full-time practice or the realities of how to communicate policy analysis and recommendation. Some seem to feel that they are somehow engaged in worthy advocacy or application when they have described or decried a situation in some learned journal, book, or conference presentation. While laudable, these efforts are mostly of little to no influence, because they have not been communicated to policy makers, media, nongovernmental organizations, advocates, and the public.

Few Canadians choose, as have many Americans, to perceive applied sociocultural anthropology as the fifth subdiscipline. When that happens, training programs tend to go much beyond traditional academic approaches, where practitioner education (usually at the master's level) emphasizes public policy analysis, intensive exposure to qualitative and quantitative methodology, program planning, internships, and multidisciplinary exposures to domains, such as urbanization, health care delivery, and so forth.

We piloted such a program at Saskatchewan but it could not be sustained because our resources were downsized drastically during the budget crises of the 1990s, although we still try to maintain its thrust as much as possible at the undergraduate level.

CONCLUSIONS

The editors of this volume have asked us to address a few questions, for which, alas, we may only be able to provide cursory responses. Impacts of globalization—certainly Canadian communities and peoples are no less subject to globalization than are communities and peoples in any other part of the world. In fact, since Canada is a member of the G-8 and an early participant in attempts at global economic integration, especially through NAFTA, it has much experience in this domain. However, the issues do not yet seem to have a marked impact on anthropological policy discourses in Canada. Certainly most Canadian anthropologists are very much plugged into global networks of collaboration through publication, research, Internet connection, and conference attendance. For instance, indigenous issues and the ethnopolitics of identity are shared among Canadian, Australian, New Zealand, and American anthropologists. Much more potential remains—one example, the impact and global connections of the spectacular expansion of diamond mining in Canada's Northwest Territories engaging Dene communities in its investment, extraction, and marketing. Another example is the impact of globalized corporate food production through vertically integrated intensive livestock operations and meatpacking plants. Already mega-factory farms on the Canadian prairies are producing for the massive Asian market and increasingly employing Mexican migratory labor in both factory farms and meatpacking plants with major changes in the political economy and community structures of the Canadian West taking shape. Globalization also results in the extensive movement of populations, which manifests itself in diaspora communities and refugees. In turn, the question of how these communities are to be integrated into Canadian society, and how they can be provided with appropriate social services, is one that is beginning to draw the attention of anthropologists. Not to be ignored is the effect of global population movements on the Canadian-born community and attitudes toward the influx of new Canadians. A further elaboration of this is found in the phenomenon of international travel as a vector for the transmission of infectious disease agents, with attendant implications for medical anthropology. These remain just a few examples.

Contributions to theory, method, and substantive advances in knowledge—the majority of Canadian applied and policy analyses over the last three decades have been focused on issues of First Nations/Aboriginal rights and self-determination and have been informed by a broad political economy relevant to the conflicts of the nation-state and its relations to minority nations within its boundaries. The substance of the most noticeable contributions of Canadian anthropology is contained within that framework. During this period, some significant advances for Aboriginal peoples have occurred—treaties, partial recognitions of nationhood, expansions of land bases and jurisdictions, and other measures of self-determination. These can be seen through the James Bay Agreement, Nunavut, and many other individual treaties. Anthropological policy discourses, framed by the broad theories of political economy, may have played auxiliary yet minor roles in their accomplishment. Still there is considerable work to be done at all levels to create more meaningful impacts on the lives of most First Nations people. Beyond political economy, Canadian anthropologists in their relatively small numbers (compared to the U.S., Britain, and Mexico, for example) are contributing commensurately to contemporary method and theory in many domains of practice.

Beyond these questions, what are the accomplishments of a practice- and policy-oriented anthropology in Canada? A professional and institutional beachhead has been established. Organizations have been formed, classes taught, and practitioners produced through generic anthropological training. Several textbooks have been published (Hedican 1995; Ervin 2005). Some areas, such as Native self-determination and socioeconomic development, have been fairly well-developed, and medical anthropology has rapidly grown as a sustainable domain.

Social impact assessment has been well established in the country, a by-product of a need to monitor proposals and consequences for mega-projects in our Northern hinterlands. Advocacy is a major dimension of Canadian practice, and theoretical inquiry about its place in anthropology has been a significant contribution to global anthropology. A number of Canadian anthropologists are starting to make major advances in the processes of collaborative and participatory research styles, and such approaches represent a wave necessary for future sharing of knowledge with the public.

Still, there are a number of things that need to be resolved—training for one. Those of us involved in practice need to communicate more effectively. Reports are often written in the style of academic theses or scholarly books and do not make use of executive summaries and other effective ways of framing useful knowledge and policy suggestions. The problem of retrieving the fugitive knowledge of application needs to be dealt with.

Even though Canadian anthropology has significantly devoted itself to Aboriginal issues, its impact is less than could be expected. Aboriginal people themselves have sometimes indicated their often very critical perspectives about our shortcomings, and, to many, we are frequently perceived as unwelcome or ambivalent participants.

Anthropologists, while respecting and attempting to resolve their historical relationships to Aboriginal peoples, should consider expanding practice to other mainstream policy domains. This chapter has pointed out the practical importance of the studies of immigration, multiculturalism, and resource-based industries that could be amplified. More attention to anthropologically underdeveloped urban issues would effectively enlarge anthropological spheres of practical concern in Canada. Among those expanding the scope of applied social research beyond Aboriginal societies is Pamela Down at the University of Saskatchewan. Her research on various aspects of the sex trades and the exploitation of and violence against women in various social groups has resulted in a number of reports and submissions to NGOs and the legislative and judicial branches of government. These scattered examples show the potential for mainstreaming anthropological expertise.

Such topics need not be considered the exclusive domain of sociologists. Much is needed that is empirical, community-based, and participatory or collaborative in style. Practicing anthropologists have much to offer the network of urban social planning councils, policy think tanks, as well as thousands of government and community-based, nongovernment service agencies and organizations. Anthropologists have tended to avoid these settings for more exotic fields. By doing so, they also tend to reinforce the weak public image of anthropology as an arcane and frequently irrelevant subject, as well as limiting the job potentials of their students.

But, to conclude, in spite of such challenges, considering applied anthropology's brief existence and small numbers in Canada, it has undergone very rapid growth, and it contains much potential and already a surprising amount of relevant content, contribution, and maturity.

NOTES

This chapter is an updated version of an article written by A. M. Ervin, entitled "Anthropological Practice in Anglophone Canada: Multiculturalism, Indigenous Rights and Mainstream Policy Potential," published in the *Global Practice of Anthropology* (1997) and edited by Marietta Baba and Carole Hill. Information for this update was gathered through a literature search and survey of relevant websites. In some cases faculty at Canadian universities were interviewed about local programs and activities. A solicitation for information (in English and French) about applied anthropology in Canada was sent out through the Canadian Anthropology Society (CASCA) Listserv to all of its members. This met with some success, but although this revised version of the original does contain an expanded examination of anthropological practice in francophone Canada, it is not as extensive in that regard as we had hoped.

REFERENCES

Ames, M.
    1986   Museums, the Public and Anthropology. Vancouver: University of British Columbia Press.
Anderson, R.
    1978   The Need for Human Sciences Research in Atlantic Coast Fisheries. Journal of Fisheries Research Board of Canada 35:1031–1049.
    1988   Cod Stock Allocation and the Inshore/Nearshore Fishing Sector: The Social and Cultural Implications of Reduced Access. St. John's: Department of Fisheries Government of Newfoundland and Labrador.
Anderson, R., and C. Wadel, eds.
    1972   North Atlantic Fishermen: Anthropological Essays on Modern Fishing. St. John's: Institute of Social and Economic Research, Memorial University of Newfoundland.
Asch, M.
    1982   Capital and Economic Development: A Critical Appraisal of the Recommendations of the Mackenzie Valley Pipeline Commission. Culture 2(1):29–41.
    1984   Home and Native Land: Aboriginal Rights and the Canadian Constitution. Toronto: Metheun.
    2001   Indigenous Self-Determination and Applied Anthropology in Canada: Finding a Place to Stand. Anthropologica 43(2):201–209.
Asch, M., ed.
    1997   Aboriginal and Treaty Rights in Canada: Essays on Law, Equality and Respect for Difference. Vancouver: University of British Columbia Press.
Bai, D.
    1992   Canadian Immigration Policy and the Voluntary Sector: The Case of the Edmonton Immigrant Services Association. Human Organization 51(1):23–35.

Bariteau, C.

　1977　Les Limites du rôle des Coopératives dans le développement d'une région Capitaliste: l'Exemple Madelinot. Revue de l'Université de Moncton 10(1):27–39.

Bariteau, C., and S. Genest

　1987　Axes majeurs et developpements recent de 1'anthropologie au Quebec. Anthropologie et Societes 11:117–143.

Barrett, S. R.

　1987　Is God a Racist?: The Right Wing in Canada. Toronto: University of Toronto Press.

Binkley, M.

　1990　Work Organization among Nova Scotian Offshore Fishermen. Human Organization 49(4): 395–406.

Buchignani, N.

　1982　Anthropological Approaches to the Study of Ethnicity. Toronto: The Multicultural Historical Society of Ontario.

　1983　Determinants of Fijian-Indian Social Organisation in Canada. In Overseas Indians—A Study in Adaptation. G. Kurian and R. Srivastava, eds. New Delhii: Vikas Publishing.

Buchignani, N., D. Indra, and R. Srivastava

　1985　Continuous Journey: A Social History of South Asians in Canada. Toronto: McClelland and Stewart Ltd.

Caulfield, Timothy A., Michael M. Burgess, Bryn Williams-Jones, Mary-Ann Baily, Ruth Chadwick, Mildred Cho, Raisa Deber, Usher Fleising, Colleen Flood, Jan Friedman, Rhoda Lank, Terrance Owen, and John Sproul

　2001　Providing Genetic Testing Through the Private Sector—A View from Canada. Isuma—Canadian Journal of Policy Research 2(3):72–81.

Chan, K., and D. Indra, eds.

　1987　Uprooting, Loss and Adaptation: The Resettlement Process of Indochinese Refugees in Canada. Ottawa: The Canadian Public Health Association.

Chance, Norman A., ed.

　1968　Conflict in Culture: Problems of Developmental Change among the Cree. Ottawa: St. Paul University.

Chodkiewicz, Jean-Luc, and Jennifer Brown, eds.

　1999　First Nations and Hydro-Electric Development in Northern Manitoba. Winnipeg, Manitoba: The Centre for Rupert's Land Studies at the University of Winnipeg.

Chodkiewicz, Jean-Luc, and R. E. Wiest, eds.

　2004　Globalization and Community: A Canadian Perspective. Winnipeg, Manitoba: Department of Anthropology, University of Manitoba Anthropology Papers No. 34.

Corin, E., G. Bibeau, J. Martin, and R. Laplante

　1990　Comprendre pour soigner autrement: Pour régionaliser les services de santé mentale. Montréal: Les presses de l'Université de Montréal.

Davis, A.

　1991　Dire Straits: The Dilemmas of Fisher, the Case of Digby Neck and the Islands. St. John's: Institute of Social and Economic Research, Memorial University of Newfoundland.

Dorais, L.-J., K. Chan, and D. Indra, eds.

　1988　Ten Years Later: Indochinese Communities in Canada. Montreal: Canadian Asian Studies Association.

Dyck, N.

　1997　Differing Visions: Administering Residential Schooling in Prince Albert 1876–1995. Halifax: Fernwood Publishing.

Dyck, N., ed.

　1985　Indigenous Peoples and the Nation State. Institute of Social and Economic Research. St. John's: Memorial University of Newfoundland.

Dyck, N., and J. Waldram

　1993a　Anthropology, Public Policy and Native Peoples in Canada: An Introduction to the Issues. In Anthropology, Public Policy and Native Peoples in Canada. N. Dyck and J. Waldram, eds. Montreal: McGill-Queens.

Dyck, N., and J. Waldram, eds.

1993   Anthropology, Public Policy and Native Peoples in Canada. Montreal: McGill-Queens Press.

Ervin, A. M.

1985   Culture and Agriculture in the North American Context. Culture 5(2):35–51.

1990   Some Reflections on Anthropological Advocacy. Proactive 9(2):24–28.

1997   Trying the Impossible: Relatively Rapid Methods in a City-wide Needs Assessment. Human Organization 56:324–334.

2005   Applied Anthropology: Tools and Perspectives for Contemporary Practice. 2nd edition. Boston: Allyn and Bacon.

Feit, H.

1985   Legitimation and Autonomy in James Bay Cree Responses to Hydroelectric Development. *In* Indigenous Peoples and the Nation State. N. Dyck, ed. St. John's: Institute of Social and Economic Research, Memorial University of Newfoundland.

Feit, H., and R. Beaulieu

2001   Voices from a Disappearing Forest: Government, Corporate, and Cree Participatory Management Practices. *In* Aboriginal Autonomy and Development in Northern Quebec and Labrador. C. Scott, ed. Pp. 119–149. Vancouver: University of British Columbia Press.

Freeman, M., ed.

1976   Inuit Land Use and Occupancy Project: A Report. 3 vols. Ottawa: Department of Supply and Services.

Fuchs, L.

1991   Factors Affecting Levels of Happiness among Southeast Asian women in Saskatoon. *In* Immigrants and Refugees in Canada. S. P. Sharma, A. M. Ervin, and D. Mintel, eds. Saskatoon: University of Saskatchewan.

Gilad, L.

1990   The Northern Route: An Ethnography of Refugee Experiences. Institute of Social and Economic Research, Social and Economic Studies No. 39. St. John's: Memorial University of Newfoundland.

Gold, G., and M.-A. Tremblay

1982   After the Quiet Revolution: Quebec Anthropology and the Study of Quebec. Ethnos 47:103–133.

Havers, L.

1993   Vietnamese Street Gangs: Foreign Import or Domestic Product. Proactive 12(2):35–46.

Hawthorn, H., ed.

1955   The Doukabhours of British Columbia. Vancouver: University of British Columbia and J. M. Dent and Sons.

Hawthorn, H., C. S. Belshaw, and S. M. Jamieson

1958   The Indians of British Columbia. Toronto and Vancouver: University of British Columbia and University of Toronto Press.

Hawthorn, H., M.-A. Tremblay, A. C. Cairns, F. G. Vallee, S. M. Jamieson, J. Ryan, and K. Lysyk

1967   A Survey of the Contemporary Indians of Canada: Economic, Political, and Educational Needs and Policies, Parts I and II. Ottawa: Indian Affairs Branch.

Hedican, E.

1986   The Ogoki Guides: Emergent Leadership among the Northern Ojibwa. Waterloo: Wilfred Laurier University Press.

1995   Applied Anthropology in Canada: Understanding Aboriginal Issues. Toronto: University of Toronto Press.

Hedley, M.

1979   Domestic Commodity Production. *In* Challenging Anthropology. D. Turner and G. Smith, eds. Toronto: McGraw Hill, Ryerson.

Henriksen, G.

1994   The Mushuau Innu of Davis Inlet: Self Government, Innovation and Socio-Cultural Continuity. Proactive 13(1):2–23.

Henry, F.

1978   The Dynamics of Racism in Toronto. Ottawa: Secretary of State.

Hess, S., and C. Smith
   1984   Repression and Exile: A Study of Salvadorian, Guatemalan, and Haitian Refugees in Montreal. Montreal: McGill University Program for the Anthropology of Development.
Jenness, D.
   1962   Eskimo Administration: I. Alaska. Montreal: Arctic Institute of North America.
   1964   Eskimo Administration: II. Canada. Montreal: Arctic Institute of North America.
   1965   Eskimo Administration: III. Labrador. Montreal: Arctic Institute of North America.
   1967   Eskimo Administration: IV. Greenland. Montreal: Arctic Institute of North America.
   1968   Eskimo Administration: V. Analysis and Reflections. Montreal: Arctic Institute of North America.
Kallen, E.
   1982   Ethnicity and Human Rights in Canada. Toronto: Gage.
Leighton, A.
   1959   My Name Is Legion: Foundations for a Theory of Man in Relation to Culture. New York: Basic Books.
Leyton, E.
   1975   Dying Hard: The Ravages of Industrial Carnage. Toronto: McClelland and Stewart.
Lock, M., and G. Bibeau
   1993   Healthy Disputes: Some Reflections on the Practice of Medical Anthropology in Canada. Health and Canadian Society 1(1):147–177.
Lock, M., and P. Wakewich-Dunk
   1990   Nerves and Nostalgia: Expression of Loss among Greek Immigrants in Montreal. Canadian Family Physician 36:253–258.
Neis, B.
   1992   The Uneasy Marriage of Academic and Policy Work: Reflections on the Newfoundland and Labrador Experience. In Fragile Truths: Twenty-Five Years of Sociology and Anthropology in Canada. W. K. Carroll, L. Christiansen, R. Currie, and D. Harrison, eds. Pp. 334–349. Ottawa: Carleton University Press.
O'Neil, J.
   1986a   Colonial Stress in the Canadian Arctic: An Ethnography of Young Adults Changing. In Anthropology and Epidemiology. C. R. Janes, R. Stall, and S. M. Gifford, eds. Dordrecht: Reidel.
   1986b   The Politics of Health in the Fourth World: A Northern Canadian Example. Human Organization 45(2):119–128.
O'Neil, J., J. Kaufert, P. Kaufert, and W. Koolage
   1993   Political Considerations in Health Related Participatory Research in Northern Canada. In Anthropology, Public Policy and Native Peoples in Canada. N. Dyck and J. Waldram, eds. Montreal: McGill-Queens Press.
Paine, R., ed.
   1971   Patrons and Brokers in the East Arctic. St John's: Institute of Social and Economic Research, Memorial University of Newfoundland.
   1977   The White Arctic: Anthropological Essays on Tutelage and Ethnicity. St John's: Institute of Social and Economic Research.
   1985   Anthropology and Advocacy. St. John's: Institute of Social and Economic Research, Memorial University of Newfoundland.
Pilon-Le, Lise
   1984   La Relève Agricole au Québec: Problèmes Juridiques et Économiques du Transfert de la Ferme Spécialisée. In Les Politiques Agro-alimentaires et leurs Conséquences sur le Milieu Rural. Pp. 250–280. Actes du Colloque France-Québec de 1983: CNRS-INRA-FNSP.
Rouse, M. J.
   1993   Folk Technology in a High Tech Industry: Cultural Objects in a British Columbia Coal Mine. Proactive 12(2):46–58.
Rouse, M. J., and U. Fleising
   1995   Miners and Managers: Workplace Cultures in a British Columbia Coal Mine. Human Organization 54:238–249.

Ryan, J.

1985   Decolonising Anthropology. *In* Anthropology and Advocacy. Robert Paine, ed. Pp. 208–215. St. John's: Institute of Social and Economic Research, Memorial University of Newfoundland.

Ryan, J., and M. P. Robinson

1990   Implementing Participatory Action Research in the Canadian North: A Case Study of the Gwich'in Language and Cultural Project. Culture 10(2):57–73.

1996   Community Participatory Research: Two Views from Arctic Institute Practitioners. Practicing Anthropology 18(4):7–12.

Salisbury, R.

1977   Anthropology in Anglophone Quebec. *In* Applied Anthropology in Canada. J. Freedman, ed. Pp. 136–147. Ottawa: Canadian Ethnology Society.

1983 L'anthropologie appliqué au Canada: Problèmes et horizons. *In* Conscience et Enquête. M.-A. Tremblay, ed. Pp. 208–218. Ottawa: National Museum of Canada.

1986   A Homeland for the Cree: Regional Development in James Bay, 1971–1981. Kingston and Montreal: McGill-Queens Press.

Salisbury, R. et al.

1972   Development and James Bay: Socio-economic Implications of the Hydro-electric Project. Montreal: McGill University Press.

Scott, C., and J. Webber

2001   Conflict between Cree Hunting and Sport Hunting: Co-Management Decision Making at James Bay. *In* Aboriginal Autonomy and Development in Northern Quebec and Labrador. C. Scott, ed. Pp. 149–175. Vancouver: University of British Columbia Press.

Slobodin, R.

1966   Metis of the Mackenzie District. Ottawa: Canadian Research Centre for Anthropology.

Speck, D.

1987   An Error in Judgment: The Politics of Care in an Indian-White Community. Vancouver: Talon Books.

Tanner, A.

1979   Bringing Home Animals: Religious Ideology and Mode of Production of the Misstassini Cree Hunters. St. John's: Institute of Social and Economic Research, Memorial University of Newfoundland.

2000   The Innu of Labrador. *In* Endangered Peoples of the Arctic, Struggles to Survive and Thrive. Milton Freeman, ed. Pp. 75–92. Westport, CT: Greenwood.

Tanner, A., P. Trimper, Mary Mackey, and Mark Shrimpton

1995   Utshimassits Relocation, Initial Environmental Evaluation. Jacques Whitford Environment, St. John's for Mushuau Innu Renewal Committee and Mushuau Band Council. Task Force on Mental Health Issue Affecting Immigrants and Refugees.

Tremblay, M.-A.

1977   L'anthropologie appliquée a 1'Université Laval 1956–1966: Les stratégies et les processus de 1'mtervention. *In* Applied Anthropology in Canada. J. Freedman, ed. Hamilton: Canadian Ethnology Proceedings No. 4.

1988   Anthropological Research and Intervention at Laval University since the Sixties. The Western Canadian Anthropologist 5(Dec.):3–28.

1990   Les Fondements historiques et theoriques de la pratique professionnelle en anthropologie. Quebec City: Laval Universite, Laboratoire d'anthropologie.

Van Esterik, P.

1989   Beyond the Breast-Bottle Controversy. New Brunswick, NJ: Rutgers University Press.

van West, J.

1976   George Mercer Dawson: An Early Canadian Anthropologist. Anthropological Journal of Canada 14:8–13.

Wake, J.

1990   Social Forestry in British Columbia. Proactive 9(2):3–14.

Waldram, J.

1985   Hydroelectric Development and Dietary Delocalization in Northern Manitoba, Canada. Human Organization 44(1):41–50.

1988   As Long as the Rivers Run: Hydroelectric Development and Native Communities in Western Canada. Winnipeg: University of Manitoba Press.

1990   Physician Utilization and Urban Native People in Saskatoon, Canada. Social Science and Medicine 30:579–589.

1993   Some Limits to Advocacy Anthropology in the Native Canadian Context. In Anthropology, Public Policy and Native Peoples in Canada. N. Dyck and J. Waldram, eds. Kingston and Montreal: McGill-Queens Press.

1997   The Way of the Pipe: Aboriginal Spirituality and Symbolic Healing in Canadian Prisons. Peterborough, ON: Broadview Press.

Waldram, J., A. Herring, and T. K. Young

1995   Aboriginal Health in Canada: Historical, Cultural and Epidemiological Perspectives. Toronto: University of Toronto Press.

Warry, W.

1992   The Eleventh Thesis: Applied Anthropology as Praxis. Human Organization 51(2):155–164.

Weaver, S.

1981   Making Canadian Indian Policy: The Hidden Agenda. Toronto: University of Toronto Press.

1993   The Hawthorn Report: Its Use in the Making of Canadian Policy. In Anthropology, Public Policy and Native Peoples in Canada. N. Dyck and J. B. Waldram, eds. Kingston and Montreal: McGill-Queens Press.

Williamson, R. G.

1974   Eskimo Underground. Uppsala, Sweden: Uppsala University.

1999   The International Fur Ban and Public Policy Advocacy: The Significance of Inuit Cultural Persistence. Practicing Anthropology 21(1):2–9.

Wood, M.

1988   Review of the Literature on Migrant Mental Health. Santé/Culture/Health 5:1–93.

PRACTICING ANTHROPOLOGY IN PORTUGAL

ANA ISABEL AFONSO

FCSH—Universidade Nova de Lisboa

The rise of anthropology in Portugal is examined within the framework of several cycles of development. The chapter discusses how the consolidation of anthropology at university level was the main focus until the 90's. Applied anthropology, as distinctive from academic anthropology received very little attention. Consequently, there was an absence of an institutionalization of applied anthropology in the country. Nowadays, however, two main trends converge that supports the growth of applied anthropology and is providing work for anthropologists outside academia. First, anthropology departments in Portugal have stabilized their staff quotas resulting in very few positions open for anthropologists at the university level. Second, global changes are impacting the social framework of the country and, consequently, opening up new horizons of research and practice for social scientists. Several examples of these opportunities are discussed which is creating an optimism about the various niches for new and relevant anthropological practices. Key Words: Portugal, colonialism, community, applied/ practice, research

From a simplified and panoramic viewpoint, the history of the construction and consolidation of anthropological discourse in Portugal can be traced through three main cycles of development, each of them directly or indirectly associated to practical concerns. I agree with van Willigen when he states, "Awareness of history does much to reduce the antipathy that exists between theoretical and applied anthropologists. Historical awareness teaches a number of important points, perhaps most important among them, that the theoretical realm is historically based on application" (1993:17).

THE RISE OF ANTHROPOLOGY IN PORTUGAL

The Proto-Anthropology Stage

The first stage runs from mid–19th century to the Second World War, and was dominated by the emergence of a proto-anthropology and influenced by Romantic currents of that time (Branco 1986; Leal 1998). During this period, thematic interests led by eminent

NAPA Bulletin 25, pp. 156–175, ISBN 1-931303-28-2. © 2006 by the American Anthropological Association. All rights reserved. Permissions to photocopy or reproduce article content via www.ucpress.edu/journals/rights.htm.

scholars centered on collecting inventories of oral traditions (Coelho 1985), material culture (Rocha Peixoto 1990[1]), and local or regional customs (Vasconcelos 1933), mostly collected in rural settings. At the same time, anthropologists also worked in overseas colonies whose studies were promoted by the dictatorial regime since the 1930s. The scientific aim of this research was to produce ethnological maps for the political objective of ensuring the control over local groups. Several expeditions to overseas territories were organized, giving priority to the collection of anthropometric data, whose immediate utility was used for better management of indigenous forced labor. The research expeditions that took place overseas, beyond their scientific interest, were promoted and sponsored by governmental institutions interested in the knowledge produced in order to design policies that would ensure the preservation of the colonies.

Transcripts of reports from that time (Moutinho 1982) seem grotesque to us nowadays, and, as has been mentioned, this kind of anthropology represented the most conservative tendencies of regime colonial ideologies (Cabral 1991:31).

Interest in studies of indigenous populations of the colonies emerged by the end of the 19th century when the international political situation (especially following the Conference of Berlin and the British Ultimatum of 1891) shook the basis of the Portuguese Empire. The maintenance of the colonies (either in political or economic terms) deserved great investment that constituted a heavy responsibility for the government and for the Portuguese people in general. Portugal entered an era of a profound socioeconomic crisis that left the country in a difficult situation and motivated a search for a national identity. This search involved national perception of the Portuguese colonies, whose existence was perceived to be threatened. Intellectual elites, disappointed with Portuguese imperial destiny, turned to history and popular culture in order to find the lost national splendor. This led to profuse ideological production around national identity—a search for the roots, conditions, and circumstances of existence of the Portuguese nation (Pereira 1998:v, my translation).

This "lost national splendour" was associated with rural life and popular culture. Overseas it was associated with a sort of civilization mission that contributed to generate a hegemonic relationship between colonizers and autochthonous groups. These policies were supported by "scientific" data from physical anthropology, the main thrust of the first colonial anthropology. Actually, since the end of the 19th century, anthropology was considered the "total science of Man," whose physical features were seen like important issues that would clarify human nature. The studies of skulls assumed that craniological characteristics were correlated with psychological capabilities. As a consequence, these types of studies were given priority and support from the government. Portuguese colonial regime took advantage of the anthropological interest in physiological features. Anthropobiological studies led to evaluation of the capabilities and skills of indigenous populations (Schouten 2001:164). Mendes Correia (1934) coordinated some initial expeditions to African colonies and East-Timor. The materials collected during fieldwork (especially within African groups) led to publications about controversial issues such as working skills, educability, impulsivity, and global intelligence.

Apart from these research projects, throughout this cycle very few anthropological courses were organized at university level, and the first ones that appeared (Anthropology,

Human Paleontology, and Archaeology; and Anthropometry) were clearly situated in the domain of physical anthropology, as part of undergraduate degree programs in biology or medicine. Beyond these subsidiary courses delivered at main Portuguese universities, in 1906, the Escola Superior Colonial (Higher Colonial School), in association with the Sociedade de Geografia de Lisboa (The Lisbon Geographical Society), developed diplomas in anthropology that integrated subjects like Colonial Ethnology and Indigenous Policy in the curriculum.

Thus, on the one hand, the development of folk-ethnological studies in the Iberian geographical context, during the 20th century, focused on recreating "traditional" or "popular" ways of life within the domestic scenario (Gómez 1997:303, my translation), while, on the other hand, emphasis was placed, especially since the 1930s, on studies produced as a consequence of scientific missions undertaken in the overseas territories. These two convergent orientations have contributed very incisively to the development of anthropological studies in Portugal.

Establishment of Cultural and Community Studies

By the end of the 1940s, with the pioneering studies of Jorge Dias (1907–73), Portugal entered a new stage in the history of the discipline (Dias 1948a, 1948b) that extended until the revolution in 1974. A brief summary of his career illustrates the influence he has had in the modernization of anthropology in Portugal.

Jorge Dias obtained his undergraduate degree at the University of Oporto, where he studied German philology. His interest in archaeology and ethnography led him to pursue a graduate program in Volkskunde in Germany, where he defended a PhD thesis about a Portuguese village named Vilarinho da Furna (northwest Portugal). Returning to Portugal at the end of the 1940s, he began working at the Centro de Estudos de Etnologia Peninsular in Oporto, where he was responsible for the ethnographic studies section. With a small working team (which included, besides his wife, Margot Dias, Ernesto Veiga de Oliveira, Fernando Galhano, and Benjamim Pereira), several research projects were developed, sponsored by Instituto de Alta Cultura (Estate Culture Foundation).

As other authors have pointed out (Branco 1986; Cabral 1991; Pereira 1998), Jorge Dias' first anthropological works denote the influence of the German ethnologist Richard Thurnwald (1869–1954) and are especially concerned with wide-ranging surveys and aim at mapping different features of material cultural of the peasant world. The study "Os Arados Portugueses e as suas prováveis origens" (Portuguese Ploughs and Their Possible Origins), published in 1948, illustrates his approach to community studies. Afterwards, similar studies were conducted that focused on other domains of material culture (such as popular architecture, traditional technologies, and music instruments).

The topics approached by this small group clearly began to separate the domain of anthropobiology (which had dominated the activities of anthropologists) from this emergent new field of anthropology, which was basically "cultural." However, the process took time and the truth is that the first projects carried out continued to be dominated by the older methods and presentation of anthropology used in the country. In fact, the techniques and style of the publications with a cultural perspective were quite similar to the contents of the works of the anthropobiologists (with all his measurements, typologies, and morphological systemizations) and these first cultural anthropology collections. For example, the graphic style of the artist Fernando Galhano, who collaborated with Jorge Dias' group, was very similar to illustrations in the Biological Manuels. His ethnographic drawings of the "objects of culture" exhibited, in fact, the same detail that his contemporaries dedicated to the graphic description of plants and animals (see Museu de Etnologia 1985). As a consequence, most of the work of his pioneering teams became visible in a particular place—the museum—where the collected ethnographic materials were archived, catalogued, and described in a similar manner to the specimens collected for natural history museums.[2,3]

Jorge Dias' first visit to the United States, in the 1950s, when he fell under the influence of North American culturalism through the disciples of Franz Boas, marks a turning point in his career. This influence would be seen in his monograph Rio de Onor—uma comunidade agro-pastoril (Rio de Onor—an agro-pastoralist community) (Dias 1953). While the emphasis given to material cultural and traditional technologies related with agricultural activities is still evident, this publication inaugurates community studies in Portugal based on intensive fieldwork and participant observation.

Jorge Dias' career as an anthropologist balanced research at CEEP[4] with teaching. He delivered courses on Ethnology at Coimbra and Lisbon Universities and collaborated with the Instituto Superior de Ciências Sociais e Política Ultramarina[5] (Higher Institute of Social Sciences and Overseas Policy), where he was responsible for the teaching of subjects such as Cultural Anthropology, Regional Ethnology, and Indigenous Institutions. At that time, it was in this school that the colonial officers received a complementary formation, which aimed to introduce them to different dimensions of overseas territories and indigenous populations.

Afterwards, Jorge Dias was invited by the Portuguese Overseas Ministry to participate in the scientific campaigns that were being carried out at the African colonies, and from 1957 to 1961 he was charged to be the coordinator of the Missões de Estudo das Minorias Étnicas do Ultramar Português (Expeditions for the Study of Ethnic Minorities from Portuguese Overseas). The main objective of these expeditions, promoted and sponsored by the colonial government, was the study of the cultural and social dimensions of the dominated groups for the purpose of ensuring control of eventual rebellion nucleus or movements of independency. A generalized sense of discomfort and tension characterized the relationship between colonial administrators and some autochthonous groups. The work of Jorge Dias represented the political recognition of the importance of the cultural and social dimensions of the discipline, which signaled a break from the domain of anthropobiology. "Sociocultural" studies were emancipated from physical anthropology, which as previously discussed, dominated colonial studies. His reports to the colonial board, particularly carried out in Mozambique, illustrated the discriminatory attitudes of intolerable racism in the colonies. They called for a better understanding of colonized peoples and addressed the scientific importance of the collection of ethno-graphic materials. Besides the reports produced for the government, which are the object of an interesting analysis by Rui Pereira (1998:V-LII), the four volumes on the Macondes from Moçambique, first published between 1964 and 1970, constitute the most representative of all ethnographic monographs produced by the Portuguese school (Pereira 1998:V). Addressing the reports produced by Jorge Dias during such expeditions, Rui Pereira underlines precisely this dimension:

> The reading and analysis of the 'Reports' would demonstrate that the scientist never omitted political considerations, being critical as regards colonial administration, sometimes gently, other times incisively, but also believing in the political mission and role of Portuguese participation in colonial Africa [...], never avoiding the clarification, however, that 'the most important report will be the monographic study of the Macondes.' [Pereira 1998:XXXIII]

In reality, the observation of situations related to the exploitation of the colonial labor force led Jorge Dias to address explicit criticism regarding the controversial relationships between colonial officers and indigenous populations. By assuming a role that nowadays we would consider as an advocacy-anthropology strategy, the criticism of this pioneer social anthropologist was sometimes reinforced by particular proposals of concrete measures aiming to ameliorate the social and economic conditions of the people under study. Citations of his reports are illustrative of his approach:

> I have visited entire villages in Macomia region where it was hard to find people. Upon my arrival I would only meet blind or defective persons, because the others had run away when they knew a white man was coming. They are terrified by the procedures of colonial officers when they invade their villages to recruit labor, acting through ignorance or cruelty. I have collected several data about these problems. [Dias 1957, cited in Pereira 1998:XLV]

While promising, this line of anthropological practice would have little continuity in the years that followed in Portugal. With the colonial war, which continued throughout the 1960s, anthropological work would be temporarily abandoned, considering the risks inherent to conducting research under the circumstances of armed conflict.

The Institutionalization of Academic Anthropology

The revolution of 1974 (and the decolonization process that took place) gave rise to the third stage of anthropological development in Portugal (see Areia 1986). The transition from the authoritarian regime to democracy in the country brought about important social, political, economic, and cultural changes in universities and scientific research. Universities underwent strong restructuring, either with respect to the staff or in terms of the contents of courses. After decades of contention in several scientific domains, the years following the revolution were a period of academic expansion, particularly in the social sciences, which previously had little representation at higher education levels under dictatorial regime. New democratic regimes brought about an overall restructuring of the university. The structures that supported colonial administration quickly became obsolete. The staff of these institutions was integrated into the new university departments.

Throughout this stage the first undergraduate degree courses were established (all in Lisbon), new university departments were founded, and a professional association of anthropologists was established—the APA (Associação Portuguesa de Antropologia)—directed successively by a series of academics. A great part of the synergies of this stage focused on creating the basic conditions in order to ensure the institutionalized reproduction of anthropological knowledge. This involved the formation of human resources, the necessity to provide libraries with accessible references, and the cataloguing of materials accumulated in the main anthropological museums, as well as the conduct of fieldwork research according to modern standards. All these efforts took time to accomplish, finally reaching levels of success in the last decade.

As stated above, if we exclude physical anthropology, anthropology teaching was rather inexpressive during the period preceding the revolution in 1974. Previously, academic teaching of anthropological subjects was isolated and sporadic, and the discipline became autonomous within universities after the revolution. Branco (1986:94) underlines this trend: "A support structure was created that would consolidate and produce autonomy in a scientific domain—specialized university teaching."

The next section will discuss, in some detail, the establishment of applied anthropology in Portugal.

The Establishment of Academic and Applied Anthropology[6]

The brief history of the discipline, culminating in the consolidation of anthropology at university level (Cordeiro and Afonso 2003), explains the state of infancy that characterizes the institutionalization of applied anthropology in Portugal. This does not mean, however, that no applied studies have been pursued. Indeed, throughout the 20th century, and more recently, applied studies have been present, most of which were conducted by academics. While, in the past, these kinds of studies were mostly directly commissioned by governmental institutions to researchers, nowadays they are developed through agreements established between university departments (or research centers) and external public and private institutions.

Between the end of the 1970s and the beginning of the 1980s, three new undergraduate degree courses appeared in Lisbon: the first at Universidade Nova (1978), the second at the Instituto Superior de Ciências Sociais e Políticas, previously ISCSPU, and the third at ISCTE (Instituto Superior the Ciências do Trabalho e da Empresa) (1982). The staff of these recently founded departments derived from the reorganization of tiny dispersed groups more or less involved in the teaching of subjects related with anthropology[7] and also from the incorporation of young graduates that had returned to Portugal after having pursued their studies abroad.[8] Later, this initial staff would be joined by young undergraduates who finished their first degrees in the new departments.

In this particular context of turbulence and overall restructuring within the universities, it is difficult to separate academic and applied anthropology. The starting point of this period of institutionalization lies, precisely, in their convergence. Actually, research projects carried out by young anthropologists were associated with their academic career, and the main purpose of anthropological work was to ensure the reproduction of specialized anthropological knowledge in a scenario of great competition between different branches of the social sciences. The structure of the first undergraduate degree programs reflects this central concern, and the shape of the courses, apart from slight differences between institutions, was centered on anthropological theory and ethnographic reading, aiming to provide a solid grounding in the discipline.

But as anthropology departments have stabilized their staff quotas, the profile of the courses has been questioned and re-evaluated. This has resulted in the inclusion of new subjects and syllabus updating, which aims to reduce the hiatus between anthropological theory and its practice. Thus, disciplines on methods and techniques are being reinforced[9] where students are encouraged to think critically about the application of ethnographic concepts and methods to a particular applied research context, which usually implies long-term fieldwork.

Another example is found in efforts to integrate interdisciplinary subjects[10] in order to give the student a certain familiarity with other disciplinary perspectives, which eventually could facilitate entry into the labor market by opening access to jobs not exclusively in the domain of anthropology. Generally speaking, however, the profile of main course programs has remained predominantly associated with theoretical anthropology and the number of graduates is increasing exponentially.

By 1990, the inception of anthropology as an autonomous discipline ceased to constitute a problem, with three programs functioning full-time in three universities in the capital city of Lisbon. Anthropological disciplines have also been integrated as compulsory or optional courses in undergraduate degree programs in other domains of the social sciences (e.g., sociology, communication studies, psychology, law, and international studies). This expansionist trend was maintained over the last decade, when two other undergraduate degree programs opened in public universities situated in cities in other parts of the country—at the Universidade de Coimbra (1992) and recently in Miranda do Douro, in an extended branch of the Universidade de Trás-os-Montes e Alto Douro (1998).[11]

We find in these new curricula the same concern with classic anthropological subjects but also strategies that make them different from earlier courses in other university departments. For example, the undergraduate course at Coimbra University, framed within a longer tradition of biological anthropology practiced at the Museu e Laboratório Antropológico (see Areia 1986), provides a hybrid structure, associating the sociocultural dimension to biological anthropology and enabling the student to organize and select her/his own curriculum and orientation. In the case of the most recent undergraduate degree program opened at the UTAD (which serves especially the northern hinterland), the title of the degree (Antropologia Aplicada ao Desenvolvimento) clearly shows its emphasis and orientation to applied anthropology. As the document presenting the course states,

Students enrolled in 'Applied Anthropology' will be familiarized with anthropological methods and techniques of research, and trained to use them in the design, elaboration and evaluation of concrete projects, either related with development anthropology or with other domains of application. [UTAD 2003:3]

The proliferation of courses in higher education is accompanied by the inception of research centers at the universities and by the diffusion of knowledge through scientific circuits, which arose through the publication of new anthropological journals.[12]

This could be regarded as reflecting a positive step towards the consolidation of a disciplinary domain. However, we find that in the 21st century, the public image of the anthropologist remains rather encapsulated within the university space. Yet these niches where anthropology teaching is reproduced and anthropological research carried out are limited and incapable of absorbing the growing number of graduates that year after year finish their studies. Thus, having solved the problem of institutionalization, we now face the challenges of establishing careers in applied anthropology.

In fact, since positions within university departments and museums are now few and far between, and the teaching of anthropology at secondary school (as an optional subject) has been cancelled, there are not many opportunities for young graduates to enter the job market. Indeed, anthropology competes rather at a disadvantage with other social sciences, inasmuch as it still lacks a strong professional profile and continues to be linked, in the public mind, with a certain exotic dilettantism as well as with the practices derived from anthropometric research of the first generation of anthropologists. The present situation of a hostile job market faced by successive cohorts of undergraduates suggests, then, that some caution is necessary in celebrating the expansionist process. As has happened in other national contexts, the debate around anthropological practice has begun to enter scientific agendas and questions the uses of anthropological knowledge.

The need to restructure academic curricula as well as to open new horizons for research and the application of anthropological knowledge in the contemporary world stand out, in my mind, as the main challenge faced by university departments today. Furthermore, questioning of the current teaching model is felt to be urgently needed as attempts are made to match anthropology teaching to the possible roles young graduates could fulfill in society at large. An example of this commitment is drawn from recent experiments carried out in two representative departments—at ISCTE and UNL.

The Department of Anthropology at ISCTE launched, in 1998, an in-service vocational training, which involved the establishment of agreements between the institute and different types of external institutions (museums, NGOs, private companies, municipal councils), where graduates, sponsored by PRODEP,[13] could be engaged, during one year, in specific projects. For the majority of students who decided to undertake such training, this constituted a first contact with the labor market that was supervised under the joint coordination of the institutions in question and teachers of the department.[14]

Inspired by this pioneer experiment, the latest restructuring that occurred in the department of anthropology at UNL[15] has also introduced a similar opportunity of in-service vocational training, but as an optional semester integrated into the undergraduate degree program. This optional semester (which is carried out in an external institution under the joint supervision of a member of that institution and a teacher from the university), constitutes an alternative to a minor in a different disciplinary area or to an ethnographic research project and essay based on individual fieldwork. The possibility of completing the necessary credits to obtain a degree in anthropology in a particular work setting is concerned with increasing the employability of future graduates by attempting to bridge the gap between the university and the outside world of potential applied work.

Previously, students had to carry out and write up a compulsory final research project to get their degree in anthropology (as fundamental research was the condition sine qua non for the degree). The introduction of this 'Applied Anthropology' optional area in the curriculum in the UNL course renders undergraduate formation much more flexible. It opens up new horizons of applicability of anthropological knowledge not strictly linked to university teaching or to basic research.

The ISCTE experiment of in-service vocational training, albeit recent, is regarded in a very positive manner by students and teachers in Portugal. In addition to making the testing of new methodologies possible for research and intervention in the field of anthropology, vocational training provides greater involvement between teachers and students as well as between the educational institution and civil society (Cordeiro and Afonso 2003:178). Beyond this, the particular success of some of the students that have pursued vocational training is contributing to the construction of a public image of the anthropologist by making more visible his specialized knowledge and the advantages of ethnographic method in the approach of sociocultural issues of the contemporary world.

While the present situation can lead to the conclusion that conditions for the institutionalization of applied anthropology in Portugal have not so far been created, there are signs that things are moving in that direction. In particular, there have been recent attempts (timid and not always consensual) within different anthropology departments to revise the curricula of undergraduate degree programs, aiming to promote a more adequate articulation between anthropology teaching and its potential social uses.

EMERGING AREAS OF ANTHROPOLOGICAL PRACTICE

Although we cannot speak of applied anthropology in Portugal as an autonomous disciplinary sub-domain with its own organizational structure separate from fundamental anthropology, a confluence of interests between basic research and anthropological practice, clearly motivated by practical problems of overall society, has been evident since the pre-disciplinary stage of anthropology. As stated above, this orientation was particularly remarkable within colonial contexts, with the carrying out of expeditions commissioned by institutions related with colonial government.

But apart from a few exceptions,[16] it is also clear that the interest for applied anthropology, which timidly emerged within the colonial context, found little echo amongst future anthropologists. We can see in this abandonment the effects of political turbulence that accompanied the decolonization process, turning the former colonies into hostile and even dangerous anthropological terrains. But it can also be regarded as a general post-revolution intellectual tendency, which, in several scientific domains, involved the uncritical rejection of old paradigms.

In a certain way, we may say that "the baby was thrown out with the bath water." Applied anthropology came to be associated with its worst connotations, reflecting connivance with the procolonial dictatorial political regime, as synonymous with indirect rule, or second line anthropology—non-scientific and purely ideological.

The negative image associated with the concept of *applied anthropology* would take time to dissolve, and it is only recently that the debate around anthropological practice was relaunched in the national scientific arena. This situation is not alien to the progress of the institutionalization of the discipline by itself but it also reflects the strong appeal made to the social sciences to test their potential applicability (or social utility) in a context of political, economical, social, and cultural transformations.

Since the revolution of the 1970s and the entrance of Portugal in the European Community (in 1986), important changes have occurred in the country that affect several domains of society (education, legislation, health care, family relations, environment, demographic patterns, public works, motorization of society). Before the revolution, Portugal was a poor and peripheral country, with deficient communications, that lacked basic infrastructures in several places from north to south hinterland, and had high levels of illiteracy and restricted access to university, an increasing number of emigrants (both for political and economic reasons), and notorious social and economic differences.

Nowadays, the majority of these figures have changed, and the resulting modernization of the country generated social problems that deserve the special concern of the social scientists. Their particular way of observing and analyzing these problems are being recognized as important in contributing to attempts of solving the problems brought about by recent global changes. As a consequence, anthropologists, along with other social scientists, are being commissioned by non-academic public or private enterprises to participate in applied projects. Unfortunately, the outcomes of these kinds of studies are generally materialized through massive reports, access to which is not always possible. Due to this circumstance and in the absence of a complete characterization of the current state of practicing anthropology in Portugal, my contribution offers only a partial view and risks leaving in the shadow important works.

The brief review that follows is intentionally restricted to applied projects, recently developed, that have been the object of publication in scientific journals. The projects mentioned cover a diverse range of substantive foci of applied work, such as anthropology of work, environment, social impact analysis, and migration. A synopsis of four projects illustrates the focal problems privileged and also the institutional frames within which they were carried out. To a certain extent, these examples can be seen as illustrative of potential niches of applied work that are emerging in Portugal due, to some extent, to changes caused by development and globalization processes.

Anthropology of Work

Based on long-term research carried out in a refining plant, Paulo Granjo produced a pioneering study in the domain of practicing anthropology, particularly in the area of work relations and danger. The project was funded by JNICT (Junta Nacional de Investigação Científica e Tecnológica)[17] and was conducted from 1994 to 1997. The author addresses the question of risk, arguing that the dominant ideology of management, the concern in maximizing the production, and the processes of hierarchy and dependence work together, maximizing the dangers already existing in industrial settings (Granjo 1998:89). By discussing the relationship between theoretical and applied research, the results of this innovative ethnographic study underline the importance of human relations factors in the work place, the understanding of which could contribute to minimize danger, namely through informal learning and reproduction of professional skills and knowledge. The author also stresses the relevance of interdisciplinary team-work to carry out this kind of research, within which knowledge exchange could contribute to objectively dealing with organizational problems that arise in such settings.

Environmental Studies

The project "Social Management of the Natural Resources in South-eastern Algarve" took place in a "natural park" in the coastal area of Algarve (the southernmost region of Portugal). It was a result of an official agreement between the Instituto de Conservação da Natureza (Institute for Nature Protection) and a research center (CEAS—Social Anthropology Research Center, which is linked to ISCTE). The park's board commissioned anthropological research among fishing communities in order to collect and to systematize data about the "maritime" and "coastal" human settlements inside the park's territory. This territory covers over 18.400 hectares, corresponding to 60 kilometers of Algarve's eastern coast, and includes the surrounding marshes and dune areas of three important cities (Faro, Olhão, and Tavira). The rapid urbanization of the region and the chaotic development of mass tourist industry inside and around the park led to inflammable situations of conflict that were fueled by lobbies that operated at national, regional, and local levels (Ramos et al. 2003:158).

In order to do anthropology in this controversial context, a small research team, consisting of four anthropologists, began working in the area in March 1999 and conducted a two-year project in anthropological research within the park's limits. The initial draft proposal presented to the park aimed to address the following topics: (1) social and economic profile of the fishing and shellfish-gathering settlements; (2) study of the traditional techniques for fishing and shellfish production and gathering; (3) description of the means and equipment used in the pursuit of these activities; (4) inquiry into indigenous knowledge of the sea and the lagoon; and (5) study of local oral traditions.

The final text introduced some changes. As the research was carried out, it became obvious that park administration should be considered one of the groups under study through deconstructing how they perceived anthropologists' research goals. This new orientation conveyed a different meaning from the agenda initially suggested and had a strong impact on the diffusion (or lack of diffusion) of the research outcomes. But in the opinion of the anthropologists, this was the price to pay for what they considered to be a scientific anthropological approach.

Social Impact Analysis

The construction of the mega-dam Alqueva, in river Guadiana—which would originate an enormous reservoir in the driest zone of the country (south hinterland)—had great impact in the region at environmental, economic, political, and social levels. The construction work, started in the early 1990s, was financed with European funds for its implementation. The submersion of the village of Luz—situated in one of the zones of the reservoir, with an urban area of circa 16 hectares—and the inevitable move of its 363 inhabitants (in 2001) represented a serious social problem that deserved urgent intervention.

Framed by Plano de Minimização de Impactes do Alqueva (Program for Minimizing Impacts from Alqueva), which was coordinated by EDIA,[18] different interdisciplinary work teams were constituted to carry out a series of studies funded by the enterprise. They focused on the planning of the new village, including the houses, public services and equipment, and space for monuments, with a special concern for the process of reinstallation, which would take place in 2002.

A small group of anthropologists (including a visual anthropologist) participated in different stages of the project, namely during the move to the New Luz village. They carried out cultural research for the purpose of easing the resettlement of the villagers. The most delicate phase took place when the graves were transferred to the new cemetery. The anthropologists stated that "Within a community whose inhabitants were already seriously affected by the submersion of their village, the transference of the cemetery represented a violent invasion of privacy and touched the sacred relation of the people with Death, which was felt as totally disrupting social and familial harmony" (Saraiva 2003:110, my translation). An interesting dimension of the project was related to the conception of a local museum (see Saraiva et al. 2003) situated in the monumental area of the new village, which was dedicated to the memory of the submerged village. The museum was conceived as a radical testimony to the village submerged by the waters from Alqueva reservoir.

In this respect, the Sala da Memória (Memory Room) constitutes a privileged and innovative space in the construction of a memorial archive and is supported by audio-visual records collected throughout the project and complemented with materials offered by the village inhabitants themselves. This archive is more than a collective and cumulative family album. Rather, "it is a dynamic space of interaction and reinvention, participating and influencing present and future reality" (Mourão and Costa 2003:103, my translation).

Migration

The final example of applied anthropological research involves a research project entitled "Presentes e Desconhecidos: uma análise antropológica sobre mobilidade e mediação com populações migrantes no Concelho de Loures"[19] (Baptista and Cordeiro 2002). Its purpose was to analyze immigrant settings in a municipality situated on the periphery of Lisbon—where the immigrant population had remarkably increased in the previous decade—and propose to identify type-situations associated with migratory and installation processes.

The study was commissioned in 2000 by the Department of Social Affairs of the Loures Municipality, who sponsored it, making an official agreement with CEAS[20] (a research center at ISCTE). The two-year research project was carried out by a small work team of sociologists and anthropologists and, in methodological terms, was based on the intertwining of two main sources: daily press and ethnographic fieldwork. The researchers state that their purpose was to attempt to illustrate how immigration is frequently associated with diversified forms of obscurity and marginality of migrants. Aided by an array of media materials, they describe the dynamics that are involved with immigrants' settlement in a particular territory (Baptista and Cordeiro 2002:40, my translation). In order to carry out their mandate, they organized the project around four main lines of inquiry linked to key issues in the approach of the problem: (1) territory and mobility (where are the immigrants?); (2) immigrant and foreigner (how do immigrants identify themselves?); (3) citizen and undocumented non-citizen (is there an immigrant social condition?); and (4) institutional and informal (how are immigrants assisted?).

Although the authors considered the research as an exploratory study (where the period of one year dedicated to fieldwork was felt to be rather short), the outcomes of the research gave a voice to the immigrants' experience. The results of this project consist mainly in the production of knowledge supported by ethnographic method, particularly in ascertaining the migrants' perspective. This knowledge can be used (in a greater or lesser way) in designing particular policies that aim to find proper solutions to migrant problems—anthropologists rarely are involved in designing such policies—or in direct action. Again, in Portugal, anthropologists have little power in bringing about changes via policy formulation. The role of anthropologists that participated in the applied projects outlined above was essentially one of consultant or, in some cases, that of specialized analyst. In the final analysis, it is not the anthropologist but the entity that funds such projects that has been responsible for the conception of the policy programs and for the concrete actions that will be implemented.

Although, as I have suggested, applied anthropology in Portugal is still in its infancy, it is important to mention that a progressive openness toward a diversified range of topics, clearly motivated by practical problems of contemporary societies and often brought about by development and globalization, is emerging among academic anthropologists. These problems are often still framed in theoretical terms, which indicates a transitional phase toward the acceptance of expanding the work of anthropologists toward integrating theoretical and applied anthropology. Indeed, paradigmatic examples of this kind of approach address several content areas with great potential in terms of anthropological practice, such as Education Anthropology (Iturra 1990, 1994), Medical Anthropology (C. Bastos 1999), Ethnic Minorities (Bastos and Bastos 1999), Work and Unemployment (Casal 2000), Post-Colonial Identities and History in Africa (Dias 2002), Social

Movements (Godinho 2001), Urban Anthropology (Cordeiro et al. 2003), Car Culture (Ramos et al. 2003), and Anthropology of Tourism (Silva 2004).

PRACTICING ANTHROPOLOGY IN A MULTIETHNIC NEIGHBORHOOD: A CASE STUDY

My recent participation in a project in the area of local development is the starting point for a brief retrospective concerning some key issues that arose during this research. The project, "Antropologia e Desenvolvimento local: um estudo piloto no bairro da Bela Vista" (Anthropology and Local Development: A Pilot Study in Bela Vista), took place in the satellite-city of Setúbal (50 km from Lisbon), for one year (which included six months of initial fieldwork), starting in November 1999. As occurs with similar applied anthropology projects, an official agreement was established between the municipality and CEEP[21]—a research center at UNL. The project was part of a larger program of urban rehabilitation of the city of Setúbal—ORUS[22]—whose objectives consisted in its physical and environmental valorization, as well as in the improvement of socioeconomic conditions of the inhabitants that lived within the intervention area.

The Bela Vista estate neighborhood located in the proposed area of intervention was considered a problematic social setting. It was characterized by conflicts and aggressive behavior between intra- and interdomestic groups, fragile economic conditions, dependency, racism, and the absence of social amenities, which had contributed to the proliferation of a very negative image. The majority of the buildings were constructed in the early 1970s and the decades that followed, totaling about 1,200 apartments.

At the very beginning, the Bela Vista estate neighborhood was planned to host internal migrants that were coming to the city to work in local industries, but following the 1974 revolution and industrial crisis in the region, the newcomers would come mostly from the former Portuguese colonies as refugees from the political and military violence that followed decolonization, especially in Angola and Mozambique.

The aim of the study (as initially stated) was to promote case studies in the area that contributed to a better understanding of the inhabitants' ways of living and expectations in order to be able to design specific policies that might contribute to fulfilling the population's needs. Thus, an anthropological approach was particularly appropriate and allowed close interaction with the inhabitants, which would facilitate entry into the neighborhood and the identification of the most pressing problems of its inhabitants. The first step was then to organize a small work team, constituted by four anthropologists and coordinated by myself and Adolfo Casal (both academics in the anthropology department of UNL).

The development of the project included three main stages, whose results would be written up in progress reports:

1. Data gathering (6 months): detailed social map of the neighborhood and surveying of its main problems; analysis of the use and appropriation of space

(to include gender, age, and ethnic differences); processes of change within the neighborhood (based on different histories of installation).

2. Intervention proposals (3 months): surveying of inhabitants' potential and expectations as regards sustained development in different domains of everyday life; needs assessment and identification of concrete measures that would match population goals.

3. Discussion of the proposals (3 months): analysis and discussion of action measures with local agents, considering their priority, adequacy and eventual implementation.

To the preliminary draft proposal of the project, Setúbal Municipality added a fourth stage that previewed the foundation of a local observatory that would be responsible for the evaluation of the intervention measures. The observatory would be constituted by a mixed team, integrating scientific consultants and local agents.

The particular circumstance surrounding this project—namely, the perspective of being engaged in applied anthropology, producing anthropological knowledge that could contribute to ameliorate the lives of our research subjects—was felt, without doubt, to be a stimulating challenge that we were proud to accept. However, as research evolved, we began to requestion methods and strategies that we have tried to consolidate, by attempts and failures, throughout the project. One of the most problematic issues addressed the old question, Who is the research for?

The design phase of the project focused on the inhabitants of Bela Vista neighborhood as the main object of research. As we entered the field and became familiar with the area's main problems, however, we felt that it was fundamental to redirect our attention to include the relationships established among the inhabitants of the neighborhoods and the different institutions, governmental or non-governmental, that had a strong presence in the barrio. The inclusion of these dimensions, albeit important, would bring, we felt, ethical dilemmas. It became difficult to maintain a neutral position as regards the role of the institutions within the neighborhood and especially the questionable role of the municipality, which delegates to the NGOs (and on other formal organizations) the role of managing the social problems of Bela Vista. Within this controversial scenario, how should we manage the information? What would be published and not published in the reports? To whom should our research be addressed? To the inhabitants? To the institutions (NGOs and other)? To the municipality? None of these questions was entirely answered during the project and we decided to produce an ethnographic description of Bela Vista, as dense as possible, approaching different groups and their relations (which included not only the inhabitants but the institutions with whom they interact as well).

The reports contained citations transcribed from the interviews that addressed several dimensions of social life in the barrio including frequently used critical statements about the failure of the municipality to fulfill the inhabitants' expectations. Several topics approached important issues that could indeed have led to interesting lines of reflection in order to implement specific policy programs. However, it became clear in the course of this applied project that our client (the municipality?) was more interested in the possession of the information than in its discussion and analysis vis a vis solving social problems in the area. The project ended with the writing of the reports, and the phase of the project concerned with intervention measures was not carried out.

This leads to another key issue. The working team role, having been excluded from eventual participation in direct action, as was stated in the objectives of the project, was restricted to that of "information producer." This information, which was supposed to contribute to identifying specific measures for improving the social and economic conditions of the Bela Vista inhabitants, ended up as the exclusive property of our main client (the Setúbal Municipality, who funded the study). The only echo we have had from the research, despite all our commitment and expectancies, has appeared from time to time in the media, following turbulent events at Bela Vista. Transcripts of our reports have been arbitrarily cited by Setúbal Municipality in order to justify government disregard of social problems occurring in Bela Vista estate neighborhood.

The ending point of this project is therefore rather paradoxical. Launched with the aim and impetus of doing applied anthropology, the main outcomes of this experiment will be reflected in the domain of fundamental research. As was concluded by Jorge Dias about his fieldwork among the Maconde from Mozambique (see above), in our opinion, the results of this research were mainly the ethnography that was written. Indeed, beyond the production of an ethnography of an urban multiethnic neighborhood, the project opened new horizons of future theoretical research. At this moment, some members of the work team are engaged in projects that address studies of gypsy groups, a topic motivated by the expressive numbers of gypsy families amongst Bela Vista inhabitants.

CONCLUSION

In this chapter, I have suggested that throughout the sequential cycles that characterize the history of anthropology in Portugal, the applied domain was given little attention in national scientific agendas. Recently, however, an increasing involvement in applied anthropology has flourished. This recent trend is reflected in a national concern about the purpose of higher education degree programs and the increasing governmental support of collaborative research projects. Both these developments are fueled by the need for social scientists to solve practical social problems in the nation. Thus, recent trends in anthropology in Portugal are framed by continuous movement between academia and society at large. This is particularly the case where accelerated changes, influenced by globalization processes, linked to the growing mobility of populations and goods in a worldwide system.

At the national level, both internal and external factors catalyzed these overall changes. During the 1970s the fall of the dictatorial political regime and the decolonization process that followed constituted influential endogenous factors. In the 1980s Portuguese integration in the European Union also introduced profound changes in the country, either in terms of legislation or with regard to the implementation of modernization policies in several areas of society (environment, health care, housing, and public works). During the last decade, the effects of these changes were clearly visible in the social composition of the country. Portugal, in common with other south European nations, quickly attracted the influx and establishment of large numbers of immigrants, which has had important social, cultural, political, and economic repercussions for the nation. These global changes are opening up new horizons of research for social scientists, which leads them to project new focal issues, addressing problems of the contemporary world, and to strengthen interdisciplinary dialogue.

NOTES

Acknowledgments. I would like to acknowledge Graça Cordeiro and Manuel João Ramos for the comments on my first draft, as well as Jill Dias and Carole Hill for the English revision of the manuscript.

1. Ethnographic essays written by Rocha Peixoto (1866–1909), posthumously collected in a single volume.

2. Several museums (local and regional) that were created during the expansionist period will be, side by side with the universities, the most important job market niches for the future generation of anthropologists.

3. In 1962 Jorge Dias was charged Director of the Museu de Etnologia in Lisbon—a museum that derives from an old educational museum at Instituto Superior de Estudos Ultramarinos (Overseas Studies Institute). There he would have had to organize all the materials that were collected especially during overseas expeditions.

4. Centro de Estudos de Etnologia Peninsular (Peninsular Ethnology Research Center).

5. ISCSPU was responsible for the formation of colonial administrative officers and from 1969 onwards, organized a two-year degree course entitled Curso Complementar de Ciências Antropológicas e Etnológicas (Complementary Degree Course of Anthropological and Ethnological Sciences).

6. The term *anthropological practice* is used in the text synonymously with *applied anthropology*, according to the definition proposed by J. van Willigen: "applied anthropology is a complex of related, research-based, instrumental methods that produce change or stability in specific cultural systems through provision of data, initiation of direct action, and/or the formation of policy. This process can take many forms, varying in terms of problem, role of the anthropologist, motivating values, and extent of action involvement" (van Willigen 1993:8).

7. At Universidade Nova, for example, were integrated academics coming from the old ISCSPU (Social and Political Sciences Overseas Institute) and also some geographers coming from Faculdade de Letras de Lisboa (Faculty of Arts).

8. The department of anthropology, at ISCTE, could be seen as the most expressive in this kind of recruitment.

9. In the undergraduate degree program at UNL, a research seminar was introduced in which the students have to carry out a final research project based on fieldwork experience (called monografia—monograph).

10. E.g., ISCSP, where first semesters include a range of subjects introducing several domains of the social sciences (such as Law, Economics, Demography, Sociology, Social and Economic History).

11. In the 1990s, there appeared also a new undergraduate degree program in the private university Fernando Pessoa, in Oporto (1990), but at this moment the course has just closed.

12. Three examples illustrate this trend: *Ethnologia* (edited by Departamento de Antropologia da UNL); *Etnográfica* (edited by CEAS—Centro de Estudos de Antropologia Social at ISCTE); and *Arquivos da Memória* (edited by CEEP—Centro de Estudos de Etnologia Portuguesa at Universidade Nova de Lisboa).

13. Programa de Desenvolvimento Educativo para Portugal (Program for the Development of Education in Portugal)—European Union funds.

14. As regards some of the external institutions (namely, Museu Nacional de Etnologia, which has privileged contacts with the national network of museums), this first experience could lead either to future contracts—commissioned from any museum from the network and mediated by the National Museum—or motivate the graduates to pursue their studies by enrolling in a masters/PhD program.

15. This recent restructuring took place in the 2003–2004 academic year, following the overall restructuring of the social sciences faculty at UNL, which has adapted the curricula of the degree courses to a student-oriented model, influenced by Anglo-Saxon major/minor structure.

16. The PhD research carried out by Adolfo Casal on social change and development, based on fieldwork conducted in postcolonial Mozambique from 1977 to 1983, constitutes an exception within this hiatus of applied studies. The author's analysis focuses on rural development strategies led by political authorities, which were implemented through concentration of the scattered population into local centers and the setting up of cooperatives (Casal 1996).

17. Nowadays named FCT—Fundação para a Ciência e a Tecnologia (Nacional Foundation for Science and Technology)—which is the main national scientific foundation.

18. Empresa de Desenvolvimento e Infra-estruturas do Alqueva (Enterprise for the Development and Alqueva Infra-structures).

19. Present and unknown: an anthropological analysis about mobility and mediation with migrant populations in Loures municipality.

20. Centro de Estudos de Antropologia Social (Social Anthropology Studies Center).

21. Centro de Estudos de Antropologia Portuguesa (Research Center of Portuguese Anthropology), with which I collaborated while the project was carried out.

22. ORUS—Operação de Reabilitação Urbana de Setúbal (Program for the Urban Rehabilitation of Setúbal).

REFERENCES

Areia, Manuel
    1986   A investigação e o ensino da Antropologia em Portugal após o 25 de Abril. Revista Crítica de Ciências Sociais 18:138–152.

Areia, Manuel, and M. Rocha
    1985   O ensino da antropologia—Cem anos de Antropologia em Coimbra. Pp. 13–60. Coimbra: Instituto de Antropologia, Universidade de Coimbra.

Baptista, Luís, and Graça Cordeiro
    2002   Presentes e Desconhecidos. Reflexões antropológicas acerca do fluxo imigratório no concelho de Loures. Sociologia, Problemas e Práticas 40:23–43.

Bastos, Cristiana
    1999   Global Responses to AIDS: Science in Emergency. Bloomington: Indiana University Press.

Bastos, J. Gabriel, and Susana Bastos
    1999   Portugal Multicultural. Situação e estratégias identitárias das minorias étnicas. Lisboa: Fim-de-Século.

Branco, Jorge
    1986   Cultura como Ciência? Da Consolidação do Discurso Antropológico à Institucionalização da Disciplina. Ler História 8:75–102.

Branco, Jorge, and M. João Ramos, org.
    2003   Estrada Viva? Aspectos da Motorização na Sociedade Portuguesa. Lisboa: Assírio e Alvim.

Cabral, João
    1991   Os Contextos da Antropologia. Lisboa: Difel.

Casal, Adolfo
    1996   Antropologia e Desenvolvimento. As Aldeias Comunais de Moçambique. Lisboa: IICT.
    2000   A civilização do Trabalho, a cultura do desemprego e o risco de exclusão social. Etnología 9–11:191–210.

Coelho, Francisco
    1985   [1879] Contos Populares Portugueses. Lisboa: D. Quixote.

Cordeiro, Graça, and Ana Isabel Afonso
    2003   Cultural and Social Anthropology in the Portuguese University: Dilemmas of Teaching and Practice. In Learning Fields: Educational Histories of European Social Anthropology. Vol. 1. D. Dracklé, I. Edgar, and T. Schippers, eds. New York, London: Berghahn Books.

Cordeiro, Graça, Luís Baptista, and António Costa, eds.
    2003   Etnografias Urbanas. Oeiras: Celta.

Dias, António

1948a   Os Arados Portugueses e as suas prováveis origens. Coimbra: IAC.

1948b   Vilarinho da Furna, uma aldeia comunitária. Porto: Afrontamento.

1953   Rio de Onor, comunitarismo agro-pastoril. Porto: IAC.

Dias, António, and Margot Dias

1964   Os Macondes de Moçambique. Lisboa: JIU.

Dias, Jill

2002   Novas identidades africanas em Angola no contexto do comércio atlântico. In Trânsitos coloniais: Diálogo críticos luso-brasileiros. Cristiana Bastos, Miguel Vale de Almeida, and Bela Feldman-Branco, coords. Lisboa: ICS.

Godinho, Paula

2001   Memória da Resistência Rural no Sul—Couço (1958–1962). Oeiras: Celta.

Gómez, Luís

1997   Cien Años de Antropologías en España y Portugal (1870–1970). Etnográfica 1(2):297–317.

Granjo, Paulo

1998   A Antropologia e a Abordagem da Indústria e do Risco: Legitimidade e Experiência de Terreno. Etnográfica 2(1):73–89.

Iturra, Raul

1990   Fugirás à Escola para Trabalhar a Terra. Lisboa: Escher.

1994   O Processo Educativo: Ensino ou Aprendizagem? Porto: Afrontamento.

Leal, João

1998   Tylorean Professors and Japanese Corporals: Anthropological Theory and National Identity in Portuguese Ethnography. Aix-en-Provence: Actes du Colloque Anthropologie et la Mediterranée.

Mendes Correia, António

1934   Valor psico-social comparado das raças coloniais. In Trabalhos do primeiro Congresso Nacional de Antropologia Colonial. Pp. 385–393. Porto: Editora 1ªExposição Colonial Portuguesa.

Mourão, Catarina, and Catarina Costa

2003   Imagens e sons para o Museu da Aldeia da Luz. In 2003 Museu da Luz. C. Saraiva, B. Pereira, and M. George, coord. Pp. 99–104. Aldeia da Luz: Catálogo da Exposição.

Moutinho, Mário

1982   A etnologia colonial portuguesa e o Estado Novo. In O Fascismo em Portugal (Actas do Colóquio, Faculdade de Letras, Março, 1980). Lisboa: Regra do Jogo.

Museu de Etnologia

1985   Desenho Etnográfico de Fernando Galhano (Exhibition Catalog). Lisbon: I.I.C.T./Museu de Etnologia (vol. I Portugal; vol. II Africa).

Pereira, Benjamim

2003   O Museu da Luz. Etnográfica 7(1):209–212.

Pereira, Rui

1986   Antropologia Aplicada na política colonial do Estado Novo. Revista Internacional de Estudos Africanos 4–5:191–235.

1998   Introdução à reedição de 1998. In Os Macondes de Moçambique. Vol. 1. J. Dias, ed. Lisboa: CNCDP/IICT.

Ramos, M. João et al.

2003   Managing Natural Resources in Eastern Algarve, Portugal: An Assessment of the Policy Uses of Local Knowledge(s). In J. Pottier, A. Bicker, and P. Sillitoe, eds. Pp. 155–170. London: Pluto Press.

Rocha Peixoto, António

1990   Etnografia Portuguesa: Obra etnográfica completa. Lisboa: D. Quixote.

Saraiva, Clara

2003   Aldeia da Luz: Entre Dois Solstícios, A Etnografia Das Continuidades e Mudanças. Etnográfica 7(1):105–130.

Saraiva, Clara, Benjamim Pereira, and M. João George, coord.

2003   Museu da Luz. Aldeia da Luz: Catálogo da Exposição.

Schouten, Maria Johanna

2001   Antropologia e Colonialismo em Timor português. Lusotopie:157–171.

Silva, Maria, coord.

2004   Outros Trópicos. Novos Desafios Turísticos. Novos Terrenos Portugueses. Lisboa: Horizonte.

UTAD

2003   Proposta de Reestruturação da Licenciatura em Antropologia Aplicada ao Desenvolvimento, Miranda do Douro. Working document.

van Willigen, John

1993   Applied Anthropology: An Introduction (revised). London: Bergin & Garvey.

Vasconcelos, José Leite

1933   Etnografia Portuguesa. Tentame de sistematização. Vol. I. Lisboa: Imprensa Nacional.

WHAT'S IN THE NAME 'APPLIED ANTHROPOLOGY'?
AN ENCOUNTER WITH GLOBAL PRACTICE

Marietta L. Baba
Michigan State University

Carole E. Hill
University of North Carolina–Asheville

This chapter is a reflective essay that explores the contextual influences upon the naming and non-naming of applied anthropology in different nations and regions of the world. Using a historical and comparative method, the chapter is deliberately designed to present a perspective that does not originate from or end up in the United States. By comparing diverse contexts chronologically, the chapter suggests alternative ways of understanding the reasons why applied and practicing anthropology have evolved so distinctively in different places. The chapter suggests that applied and practicing anthropology, indeed all of anthropology, is inextricably bound to its historical and cultural contexts, meaning that there are important differences in the way the discipline is understood and practiced across different nations and regions. Moreover, historical shifts in context have resulted in important changes in the way the discipline is practiced over time. The chapter also argues that if processes of globalization are indeed transforming the nature of connectedness and boundaries across nations, then there are consequences for the distinctive forms of applied and practicing anthropology observed across nations, with an emphasis on those in the United States. The authors postulate that some of the differences observed between applied and practicing anthropology in the United States and elsewhere are beginning to blur, and that the unique model of applied anthropology that developed in the United States during the last quarter of the 20th century is destined to be transformed into one that is more integrated into the mainstream of the discipline and, indeed, into all of global anthropology.
Key Words: global anthropology, practicing anthropology, United States, globalization, historical and cultural context

> We need to anthropologize the West: show how exotic its constitution of reality has been; emphasize those domains most taken for granted as universal (this includes epistemology . . .); make them seem historically peculiar as possible; show how their claims to truth are linked to social practices and have hence become effective forces in the social world. [Rabinow 1986:241]

Historical accounts of applied anthropology's development are represented well in the disciplinary literature from both European and North American sources (see Foster 1969;

NAPA Bulletin 25, pp. 176–207, ISBN 1-931303-28-2. © 2006 by the American Anthropological Association. All rights reserved. Permissions to photocopy or reproduce article content via www.ucpress.edu/journals/rights.htm.

Bastide 1973; Partridge and Eddy 1978; Gardner and Lewis 1996; Bennett 1996; and van Willigen 2002). These reviews sometimes begin with an exposition of the colonial roots of applied anthropology and often end up describing its florescence in America during the final quarter of the 20th century.[1] North American histories suggest that developments in the United States reflect a mature and ideal form of applied anthropology. Apparently, only in the U.S. exist (1) formal academic training programs for distinctively identified applied anthropologists, (2) national and local professional organizations devoted to the application and practice of anthropology, *and* (3) full-time professional anthropologists working in various roles across occupational fields outside the academy. No other nation has developed such an established institutional infrastructure for applied and practicing anthropology. Reasons for this are not immediately clear.

The elaborate infrastructure in the U.S. does not preclude that anthropologists in other nations do not apply or practice anthropology. As this volume and the previous work (Baba and Hill 1997) demonstrate, anthropologists in many countries may predominantly practice or may practice in addition to other occupational roles. Nevertheless, they have not developed special institutional mechanisms that parallel those found in the U.S. and generally have not named their application or practice as such. It is simply called anthropology, not applied anthropology or practicing anthropology.[2] Our claim is that naming is an integral component of the constitution of reality (and, in this case, the "anthropologizing" of that reality), as a name may reflect a distinctive and separate cognitive construct with unique cultural meaning (Strauss and Quinn 1997). By focusing on the domain of applied anthropology, often taken for granted in the United States, we may contribute to making it "seem as historically peculiar as possible" (Rabinow 1986:241) and reveal the institutional structures and practices conducive to its flourishing in the U.S. As Chambers noted, the histories of applied anthropology have been written without much more than a "nod" to the social and political contexts, "a significant weakness in a field which is clearly molded to such contexts" (Chambers 1987:310). In addition, an effort to "anthropologize" this domain may enable us to detect factors impeding the naming of applied and practicing anthropology in other nations and regions.

In this reflective essay, we explore the contextual influences upon the naming and non-naming of applied anthropology. Our method is historical and comparative and is designed to gain access to perspectives that originate and develop in areas outside the U.S. We, as the authors, draw upon our American experiences and literature; however, an important body of evidence is supplied by various and, generally, non-American authors in this and the previous collection (Baba and Hill 1997). Because of this expansion in perspective, some conclusions reached are different from those traditionally received. We view these two collections on the global practice of anthropology as cultural assemblages that allow us to explore the contexts of knowledge and practice in anthropology situated across the First, (formerly) Second, and Third Worlds.[3] By comparing these diverse contexts chronologically, we hope to gain a better understanding of why applied and practicing anthropology evolved distinctively in different places.

Our exploration shows that all of anthropology, and not only applied and practicing anthropology, is inextricably bound to its historical and cultural contexts, meaning that there are important differences in the way the discipline is understood and practiced. Moreover, historical shifts in context have perpetuated important changes in the discipline's practice over time (and we mean practice within the entire anthropological community, not only in the work of applied anthropologists[4]). The implications of contextual relevance are significant and salient for all anthropologists. Unless American anthropologists wish to suggest that we possess the 'one true way' to practice anthropology, we need to give serious consideration to alternative ways of knowing and practicing, some of which are already being adopted by our counterparts elsewhere in the world.

We also argue that if globalization is transforming the nature of connectedness and boundaries across nations, then there are likely consequences for the distinctive forms of applied and practicing anthropology discovered in this volume, as well as our known forms in the U.S. Our investigation leads us to postulate that some differences we have observed between applied and practicing anthropology in the United States and elsewhere are beginning to blur and that the unique regime of applied and practicing anthropology developed in the U.S. over the last quarter of the 20th century is destined to be transformed and more integrated into the mainstream of the discipline and, indeed, into all of global anthropology.

A RE-FORMED VIEW OF APPLIED AND PRACTICING ANTHROPOLOGY

The Naming of Applied Anthropology in Its Colonial Context: 1880–1945

The initial naming of applied anthropology may be traced to the colonial regime of Great Britain, where anthropologists first sought to convince administrators to fund their fieldwork in the absence of other means of support.[5] According to Adam Kuper:

> From its very early days, British anthropology liked to present itself as a science which could be useful in colonial administration. The reasons are obvious. The colonial governments and interests were the best prospects of financial support, particularly in the decades before the discipline was granted recognition by the universities. [1983:100]

Before World War II, the British colonial government provided virtually no funding for social science research in Africa, the main theater of anthropological operations (Mills 2002). There was funding for training colonial administrators in anthropological and ethnographic skills, thereby founding, at Oxford, the first anthropology department (van Willigen 2002). Subsequently, some colonial governments created positions for a government anthropologist (e.g., southern Nigeria) and even sponsored applied studies that anthropologists could perform. Otherwise, anthropologists had to be creative in their search for funds. According to Kuper (1983), leading anthropologists such as Malinowski and Radcliffe-Brown became known in the 1920s and 1930s for touting the practical virtues of anthropology and ethnography as a means to address colonial problems, but this was primarily a sales pitch for securing ad hoc research funding. Kuper (1983) argues that, once the money was in hand, anthropologists were likely to do what amounted to a bait and switch, conducting a basic research investigation, while assuming that the colonial sponsor could extract the necessary information from it without the anthropologists' help. Kuper (1983) asserts that many British anthropologists at the time were functionalists or liberals and, therefore, were theoretically or ideologically disinclined to aid and abet the administrators' interests in understanding social change (which many anthropologists viewed as dangerous; i.e., change could be damaging to the people anthropologists studied, and to anthropology itself, as it might wipe out the discipline's subject matter). Needless to say, these proclivities did not endear the anthropologist to the administrator (the latter often stereotyping the former as a "romantic reactionary," Kuper 1983:114). Another anthropological practice of the time was to assign one's protégé or a junior scholar to do an applied study, as such work was thought to be better suited to less well prepared individuals. Kuper states that:

> When, more or less reluctantly, the anthropologist 'did some applied work,' he tended to pick one of a limited range of topics. (I say he, but applied work was often regarded by the more mandarin as less demanding intellectually and, therefore, as best suited to women. Malinowski's first student to be dispatched to do a study of 'culture change' in Africa was chosen because it was thought she was still too new to anthropology to do a conventional tribal study) . . . (anthropologists participated) only grudgingly (as a rule) in the little studies dreamt up by the administrators, and accept(ed) the view that they should not speak out on matters of policy, not being 'practical men.' [1983:110–112]

Kuper goes on to argue that "the reality is that British anthropologists were little used by the colonial authorities, and despite their rhetoric when in pursuit of funds, they were not particularly eager to be used" (1983:116). Other scholars have noted, however, that there was complicity and symbiosis between anthropologists and colonial administrators during the era of British empire, as the anthropologists used the *promise of applied solutions* to extract funds for research, and this is how the initial theoretical foundation of social anthropology was formulated (Mills 2002; see also chapter on Great Britain in this volume).

Our interpretation of the foregoing is that early colonial practices generated the structures for what became a two-tier model of knowledge production in anthropology and that this model provided the grounds upon which theory and practice were later separated. The first tier was reserved for freewheeling 'pure' theory, with the 'other' or second tier intended for more short-term, derivative 'applied' studies. In accordance with the paternalistic tendencies of colonialism, the theorists were given 'right of first refusal' to the second tier. However, it was generally considered peripheral work. By implication, those who were assigned to work on the second tier could not choose to work on the first tier. Initially, this incipient two-tier structure was not quite so cut-and-dried, because there were few academic positions available and anthropologists had to be flexible regarding postings.

The context shifted in the 1930s and 1940s with significant changes in British colonial policy and the beginning of World War II. As a response to critics who charged that the colonies were isolated and not 'developing' economically, the British decided to engage in more affirmative administrative planning that could provide a stimulus to the economic growth of the colonies (Mills 2002). Funding began to flow toward social science research in Africa during the 1930s through a number of mechanisms, including grants from the Carnegie Corporation and Rockefeller Foundation. Some of these funds allowed anthropologists to free themselves from a triangular relationship involving colonial patrons and subjects and move toward a dyadic relationship with subjects that represented the academic model (Pels and Salemink 1999). In the 1940s the British enacted the Colonial Development and Welfare Act (CDWA), a legislative reform agenda for the colonies that finally provided substantial government funding for social science research in the colonies, including funds for anthropology. The principal contextual shift prompting this official change in policy was the start of World War II in 1939 and Britain's need to respond to those who criticized its empire (especially the Americans).

Mills (2002) provides a detailed account of the Colonial Social Science Research Council (CSSRC), which was established to set and implement policy for the allocation of research funds that would fulfill the CDWA mandate. Initially, it was anthropologists at the London School of Economics (LSE) who became most closely affiliated with the CSSRC (Raymond Firth and Audrey Richards). Both were protégés of Malinowski, one of applied anthropology's great early advocates. They embraced the reformist goals of the CDWA integrating scientific and pragmatic research objectives. Mills (2002:171) notes:

> There is a little doubt that the members of the CSSRC saw themselves as intellectual pioneers, leading the way both in mapping out uncharted territories of African social research problems, and in trail-blazing the new possibilities for a problem-oriented multidisciplinary social science.

The CSSRC recognized the importance of advancing the knowledge base and viewed both fundamental and pragmatic research as pursuant to this goal since little was known about human society in Africa. While colonial social problems provided a context within which research was framed, anthropology was able to transform such research into a satisfying theoretical product. This enabled the discipline to gain legitimacy within the academy (Mills 2002). Without this transformation, the entire project would have collapsed; anthropology had to emerge as a 'science,' or it would not receive government funding. This success increased the number of academic departments and positions in anthropology steadily during this period. By 1953, there were 38 teaching positions in anthropology, compared with only a handful prior to 1940 (Mills 2002). An entirely new professional association was spun off in 1946 to represent strictly *academic* anthropologists (i.e., the Association for Social Anthropology or ASA).

Significantly, however, tensions mounted between anthropologists based at the LSE and those at Oxford (see Pink in this volume). The latter believed that matters of academic policy should be under the control of academic departments, not the colonial office or research institutes funded by the CSSRC. The opposing sets of interests were institutional (Oxford versus LSE), political (anticolonial versus reformist), and philosophical (theory versus practice). It must be emphasized that, although the Oxford scholars did not hold practical anthropology in high regard, they still wanted to receive the CSSCR funding and control it themselves. While the academic factions battled over resources as well as against each other's institutional agendas, the British empire continued to erode. Its eventual demise was signaled by the outbreak of violence in Africa during the late 1940s and early 1950s. After the CSSRC wound up its affairs in 1961, it became clear that the British anthropologists were dependent on it for student training funds, as these went dry and there were no ready substitutes until later in the decade.

Mills (2002) argues that the relationship between theory and practice within the colonial context of Great Britain was a paradoxical one. The context for anthropology was decidedly pragmatic, at the very least, because the government needed the cover provided by intellectuals who appeared to be doing careful studies leading to colonial 'development and welfare.' At the same time academic anthropology was struggling to emerge as an autonomous profession from others that proffered ethnographic skill, such as colonial administrators, missionaries, and travelers (see Pels and Salemink 1999). The financial support and autonomy provided by the CSSRC enabled the discipline to legitimize itself. Yet British academia gained the upper hand in the production of anthropological knowledge, breaking the triangle of anthropology-subject-sponsor and leaving only the dyad of anthropologist and subject, sans sponsor. As the British stopped operating their colonies, applied anthropology was politically disgraced, and academic anthropology ended its use of the applied name. Theory thus became separated from practice, and the discipline became increasingly marginalized and lost its pragmatic value.

We suggest that the interaction of an imperialist economy and the British class system encouraged the split between 'pure' and 'applied' anthropology during the British colonial era. The imperialist system, particularly Indirect Rule as practiced by the British,[6] called for representatives of the colonial administration to observe the colony at arm's length (i.e., gather empirical data, but still be able to leave—a good fit with participant-observation). The hierarchical and paternalistic social system that flourished under colonialism virtually guaranteed that activity conceptualized by administrators in a top-down fashion, or detailed or technical work (in the field), would not be tolerated by the top men in the discipline. Thus, high-status theorists would conduct "pure science," and lower-status junior scholars or applied researchers would do task-oriented projects.

As Foster (1969) points out, anthropology as a discipline was not well-developed enough theoretically or methodologically in its early days (or even now, for that matter) to permit the hermetic separation of theorists and applied researchers into neat boxes, and sometimes it was not different people doing the work on the ground (i.e., theorists did applied studies). The point is, however, that 'pure' and 'applied' anthropology were reproducing an imperialist social class system. It was important to the continuity of the British society and empire that criteria be established and reinforced regarding superior and inferior roles in the anthropological status hierarchy, and it was also important that the identities associated with these roles be impressed upon individuals who might be filling them in the future. The theorist role was to be filled by someone capable to produce theory (read: educated 'properly'). This person could do applied anthropology if he so chose. The reverse was not to be the case, however. Consequently, we have the roots of a knowledge-based production role that was intentionally not capable (or not allowed?) to produce theory. We suggest that this structural model of theoretical– applied anthropology is the one in which applied anthropology was explicitly named, and it is this model that ultimately became the historical legacy for applied anthropology in the United States, though not immediately. As we will show, there was an important detour first.

What Happened to 'Applied Anthropology' in the Second World Case?

An interesting comparison can be made between colonialist Europe and the nations of the former Soviet bloc, especially Russia. Anthropology was an established discipline in that country during the late 19th and early 20th centuries.[7] Later, in communist Russia, anthropologists were encouraged to focus on understanding and administering the peoples of the internal colonies (i.e., indigenous people and ethnic groups), but with a subtle difference from colonialist Europe. The evolution of sociocultural forms had been incorporated into Soviet ideology via Marx and Engels' writing (e.g., *The Origin of the Family, Private Property and the State* [see Harris 1968]). Thus, anthropology came to be entwined with scientific socialism, and as a result its theories and methods were heavily politicized. For example, ethnology was considered by some communists to be more progressive than ethnography (which was deemed too bourgeois; i.e., knowledge of one society for its own sake, not for revolutionary purposes). This distinction led to the bizarre situation described by Yamskov (in this volume) in which certain approaches to anthropology were severely criticized (e.g., cooperating with geography), even though those advancing the criticism were later imprisoned and put to death and their textbooks banned. Russian anthropology (or ethnography) was rehabilitated in the 1930s, but only as a segment of the history discipline. It was compelled to avoid method-ological links with geography, following a dogmatic pronouncement by Stalin denying any environmental influence on the development of society (Matley 1966).

   Almost from the beginning of the Soviet era, the notion of 'applying' research results gained from academic studies was heavily promoted in the research academies. According to Yamskov (personal communication, 2005), Communist Party and state officials made direct and continual requests that anthropologists extract the 'applied aspects' of their academic scholarship and use this knowledge to benefit local populations and adminis-trations. Research institute leaders also stressed the practical outcomes of ethnographic studies as a means to justify the discipline's existence. Scholars were required to submit annual reports explaining how their work contributed to socialist objectives. In Russia, the focus of much 'applied' work was on indigenous people and ethnic groups; for example, alphabets and written languages were developed for Northern indigenous peoples. At times, the scholars were trying to introduce changes on their own initiative (e.g., teaching languages) that they believed would benefit local peoples, but at other times they were trying to stop or at least slow down other changes introduced by the state (e.g., collectivization in the North). Scholars also pressed their institutes' adminis-trators to pass their recommendations on to state or party officials (Yamskov, personal communication, 2005). While ethnic majority anthropologists (that is, not ethnic natives or minorities) might serve as consultants to the Soviet government, they had little real power. Later on, if ethnologists joined the government, they were to stop their research, with only a couple of exceptions (see Yamskov, in this volume).

In the Russian case, a notable segment of anthropology was (and is) 'applied' in the sense that anthropologists focused on practical uses and problems as defined by the state. However, there were (and are) very few instances of 'applied anthropology' in an institutional or formally named sense. Reasons for this can be examined from the standpoint of our hypothesis regarding the historical and cultural contexts of knowledge production. We suggest that (unspoken) political and ideological disagreements, both within anthropology and between the anthropological community and the state, prevented a consensus regarding the nature of anthropological practice, which mitigated against the adoption of a common linguistic representation for applied activity. As noted above, some Russian scholars were introducing changes to indigenous or other local populations on their own initiative, while others were acting to block or halt interventions sponsored by the state. Given the political conditions within the Soviet state prior to the 1980s, it was not possible to discuss openly the reasons for blocking state interventions; we assume that some of these actions were more or less covert. This was a tricky and risky business, not knowing whom one could trust. It was from these murky political and ideological waters that an explicitly named 'applied anthropology' failed to emerge. This name usually has meant delivery of practical value to a sponsor or community beyond anthropology. But in the context of Soviet-era politics and ideology, the anthropologists did not appear to have agreed with the state or party sponsors (or even among themselves) regarding the value of the pragmatic work that they were doing. Perhaps, they did not talk about the 'value' they were delivering, or they were halting the delivery of someone else's 'value' (i.e., as 'value' was defined by the state). Only after the fall of the Soviet Union could scholars openly disagree and oppose state-sponsored programs (see Yamskov, in this volume).

The Russian case suggests that in the triangle of anthropologist-subject-sponsor, which creates the context of applied anthropology, the anthropologist must have the professional autonomy to choose the relationships she forms with subjects and sponsors and be free to criticize or break these relationships if they are considered inappropriate or unethical. In the absence of this professional autonomy, the activity that is practiced should not be named 'applied anthropology.' Generally, we believe this case shows that if there is no 'community of practice' freely sharing its knowledge, methods, and values (Lave and Wenger 1991), then there can be no special name for practice. In the Russian case, our colleagues did not have the autonomy necessary to criticize openly the state for the programs of intervention propagated among indigenous people, but they resisted through their own means, at risk to themselves. Moreover, they did not name this activity 'applied anthropology,' and for that we may be grateful.

After the fall of the Soviet Union, the political and ideological reasoning against the naming of applied anthropology weakened, and we might expect formally named 'applied' structures to emerge. In fact, there have been efforts along these lines, as described by Yamskov (in this volume). However, resource scarcity, particularly among academic and research institutions in Russia after 1990, has prevented full-scale specialization. Many academic anthropologists and ethnologists have needed involvement in extra project work to supplement their incomes attained from academic institutions, due to resource reductions. Since project work usually has an 'applied' character, there has been a further blurring of demarcations between academic and 'applied' anthropology in Russia after 1990. However, there is still no naming of 'applied anthropology' in that country.[8]

What Happened to 'Applied Anthropology' in the Third World Case?

We must also examine the case presented by the so-called Third World nations prior to World War II. During this period, 'native anthropologists'[9] began to be trained and practice in their nations and regions. These anthropologists differed from those based in Europe, in that they focused on peoples and cultures within their countries of origin, and their work had policy impacts upon their own peoples. The major project of many 'native anthropologists' of the Third World during this period was the development and strengthening of the modern nation-state. Applied anthropologists typically followed a modernization theory of practice (e.g., acculturation theory) that supported policy aimed at strengthening the nation as a polity of citizens (Robeiro 2004).[10] Indigenous peoples or other ethnic groups often were marginalized and impoverished and did not participate as citizens (or, perhaps more accurately, were not allowed to participate). 'Native anthropologists' of the Third World sought to change this situation; they worked to make marginalized peoples full citizens.

Despite the significant engagement of Third World 'native anthropologists' in policy, as well as in practice-oriented research and intervention within their countries of origin, there was little or no institutionalization of 'applied anthropology' structures per se in the Third World prior to World War II (or more recently for that matter). The role of 'pure' theoretical anthropology in these nations was more or less reserved for anthropologists of the colonizer nations, who visited the colonies to make observations that enabled them to 'do anthropology' in the cause of science or theory.[11] The 'native anthropologists' of the colonies were trained by these colonizers to do 'applied' work, and the 'natives' embraced the notion of applying anthropology to address problems and to help build their nations. Virtually all 'native anthropologists' did applied anthropology in one form or another, even if they also held academic posts. However, there was no need for a special institutional designation for 'applied anthropology' since there were *not two classes of knowledge work internal to their societies*. The pure theorists were visitors, part of the imperialist wing of the world economy, based elsewhere. Also, it may be postulated that resource scarcity in the Third World precluded institutional structures that would support a class of knowledge work devoted strictly to 'pure' knowledge production. Only the colonizers could afford such luxury. If Third World anthropologists wanted to theorize, they would inevitably have to work on it in addition to their applying and practicing.

The Second Naming of Applied Anthropology in the United States

We have discussed above the cases of the U.K., Russia (Second World), and the Third World. Now let us return to the issue of the naming of applied anthropology in the United States. During the early part of the colonial era, and especially World War II, there was not a clear split between 'pure' and 'applied' anthropology in the U.S. (Chambers 1987; Bennett 1996). Few academic posts were available, theoretical anthropology was not well-developed, and most American anthropologists (with a few exceptions) did not have access to resources that would enable them to travel to foreign field sites. Their best opportunities for field research were struggling Native American communities. Anthropologists were employed via the U.S. Government in 'applied' roles related to the administration of the internal colonies. One of the early uses of the name 'applied anthropology' in the U.S. was by the Office of Indian Affairs, which established an Applied Anthropology Unit in the 1930s to halt resource depletion on Native American (designated) lands and encourage Native participation in the management of resources (Gardner and Lewis 1996).[12] At the time, American anthropology was hailed as a practical discipline that could contribute to Native American policies, although efforts were largely descriptive and had little effect on policy making. Anthropologists in this era had scant experience working in applied arenas and were often more interested in abstract problems and traditional depictions of Native American cultures before the arrival of Europeans, not as they existed in contemporary reality (Partridge and Eddy 1978). A result was that anthropology sometimes was characterized as favoring the preservation of traditional cultures, thereby drawing opposition from government administrators.

Yet, anthropology's involvement with Native American policies in the 1920s and 1930s, as well as the larger interdisciplinary orientation within the social sciences (see Bennett 1996; Kuper 1999), appears to have had an influence on the discipline as a whole. The willingness to engage—and *engage* is the key word here—in the problems of contemporary American society was reflected in the establishment of the Society for Applied Anthropology (SfAA) at Harvard in May 1941 (*prior* to America's entry into World War II).[13] The Society was founded by a group of distinguished anthropologists and others (e.g., psychologists, sociologists), including Conrad Arensburg, Gregory Bateson, Ruth Benedict, Elliot Chapple, Margaret Mead, George Murdoch, and William Foote Whyte, among several others. While the British colonial anthropologists *talked* about practice (while they delivered primarily theory), these American anthropologists 'walked the talk.' They genuinely were interested in the application of anthropological (and other sources of) knowledge to social problems, and they did the work. Their goal was to *integrate* scientific and pragmatic objectives, as was clear in the mission statement

> to promote scientific investigation of the principles controlling the relations of human beings to one another and to encourage the wide application of these principles to practical problems. [Arensberg 1947:1]

This statement appeared in their journal *Applied Anthropology* (later named *Human Organization*). They viewed theoreticians as interested primarily in the search for abstract laws or principles, yet they were more intrigued by concrete applications of knowledge in the modern world and what could be learned from such exercises. They recognized the intellectual synergy between theory and practice, and they wanted their own journal devoted to "attempts to appraise and use the agreed-upon core of knowledge or tested method," without being overridden by 'abstract' science (Arensberg 1947:1). The early issues of the journal demonstrate the commitment of these anthropologists to this goal.

There are significant parallels between the American anthropologists of the World War II era and their British counterparts at the London School of Economics. Both envisioned their brand of anthropology as a new kind of interdisciplinary practice that could *join science with application on equal terms* to solve important contemporary problems. Many disciplines and professions were invited to join; this was not an exercise in 'pure' anthropology. Attention was warranted by the most distinguished practitioners of the time, names that we continue to recognize today. However, in both locations, the majorities in the anthropological core did not embrace the notion of 'application' but still were more interested in abstract, theoretical pursuits. Ultimately, these mainstream colleagues became more dominant, even as the discipline was marginalized.

Several contextual factors in the U.S. encouraged the formation of a distinctive American model. The United States prior to World War II, unlike Great Britain, was not a hegemonic global economic power and was relatively isolationist (Partridge and Eddy 1978). The Great Depression and World War II presented immediate and compelling problems and shifted the attention of intellectuals toward contemporary troubles. In this atmosphere, we postulate that anthropologists developed a sense of responsibility toward addressing issues of their own society, as evidenced by the contents of the journal *Applied Anthropology* (e.g., industrial relations, mental health, social work, and social welfare), in spite of the continuing bias toward static analyses (i.e., not studying the effects of social change over time). The linkage of contemporary problems and theoretical interests (i.e., theory is needed to solve difficult social problems) might have enhanced the prestige of application and reduced the social distance between 'pure' and applied anthropology. In other words, if solving contemporary problems is important to society, and theory remains integral to anthropology, then the linkage of these two elements could heighten the importance of applied anthropology within the discipline.[14] The American case contrasts with that of the U.K., where anthropology by and large was divorced from contemporary problems of British society proper and became isolated by focusing on colonial subjects.

Other features of the American landscape encouraged anthropologists in the U.S. to experiment with both theoretical and applied pursuits simultaneously, thereby blurring distinctions between 'pure' and 'applied' roles. For example, the social class structure of the United States was not as formal and elaborate as that of Great Britain (Cavanagh 1990). An egalitarian ethos and interclass mobility were more characteristic of American society than was the case in Europe (Kerckhoff et al. 1985; Bennett 1996). In the U.S., these features might have encouraged more collaboration between various forms of knowledge work within the discipline. Moreover, pragmatism, America's only homegrown philosophy, likely influenced the definition and production of knowledge (i.e., truth is that which contributes to the most human good over the longest course). American entrepreneurs, for example, famously do not worry about organizational charts but rather assemble an organic team with everyone capable of doing multiple tasks interchangeably. Something similar might have been happening at Harvard in 1941. The founders of SfAA were, arguably, 'entrepreneurial anthropologists' who sensed an opening in the economic and political order prior to World War II. Indeed, the start of the war initiated the remarkable process by which American applied anthropology came to the forefront over the British, as is discussed in the next section.

The Redefinition of Applied Anthropology in America: 1945–1990

Between 1930 and 1960, independence movements grew in the former colonies and anthropology began to be criticized as a 'handmaiden of colonialism.' It was during this time that anthropologists of the European colonizer nations developed a tendency to reject anthropological application and practice altogether, rather than distinguishing between its use in the service of colonialism and its use toward other potential goals (e.g., see chapter on Portugal).[15] This tendency was fostered by the hierarchical status relationship between 'pure' and applied anthropology originating from Great Britain. Why engage in a kind of anthropology associated with a discredited and fading empire, in addition to its relegated second-class status?[16]

It is no coincidence that the Europeans' farewell to applied anthropology occurred just as the U.S. ended its international isolation through its entry into World War II. The war represented a major realignment of economic and political relations the world over. There was the end of colonialism, and the start of the Cold War, the effort of capitalism to find new markets, and the beginning of the era of 'development' policy as applied to the so-called Third World. These changes were reflected in disciplinary developments around the globe. It was after World War II that the United States emerged as an economic, political, and military superpower, and American anthropologists took the lead in institutionalizing applied anthropology. With this shift, a split between 'pure' and applied anthropology emerged in the U.S., this time taking a distinctly American form. Fiske and Chambers (1997:283) called it "a dance of distance and embrace" (more distance than embrace, in our view).

We suggest three primary factors contributed to a theoretical–applied split in North America, none of which were prominent prior to World War II. They are (1) an explosion in the demand for 'pure' (academic) anthropology and the subsequent rise of theoretical anthropology in the United States; (2) the emergence of epistemological, ethical, and political issues related to the application of anthropology, whose effect cast a shadow of doubt over the intellectual and moral legitimacy of application; and (3) job market growth for nonacademic practitioners in the U.S. with the rise of new institutional structures to support applied anthropology, which led to a subtle shift in the definition of applied anthropology (in America). The interaction of these factors restructured applied anthropology in the U.S. to the extent that the vision of the SfAA founders could not be realized. That is, anthropological theory and practice would not become partners trying to solve contemporary problems (Bennett 1996). We examine each of the three factors and their consequences below.

1. *The rise of academic anthropology in the United States.* During the 1950s and 1960s, university campuses in the U.S. expanded dramatically in size and scope, and anthropologists began to find significantly more academic posts (Partridge and Eddy 1978). We consulted the records of the American Anthropological Association (AAA) on degrees granted in anthropology during the 30 years between 1948 and 1978 (Baba 1994). In 1947 the discipline was very small with only 408 members of the AAA (Kuper 1999), and in 1948 only 24 anthropology Ph.D.'s were awarded. By contrast, in 1978, 414 Ph.D.'s were produced. This academic engine also increased its capacity to generate baccalaureate degrees in anthropology from 139 to 6,324 annually during the same period. In the early 1970s, the majority of the new Ph.D.'s were placed within the academy to produce the next generation of anthropologists. Data from the AAA Survey of Ph.D.'s shows that in 1971–72, 92 percent of new Ph.D.'s in anthropology found employment in academe, with 56 percent employed in anthropology departments and another 19 percent employed in joint departments (i.e., 75 percent of the total).

With this explosion in size and foreign fieldwork finding new sources of financial support (e.g., the National Science Foundation), theoretical developments in the discipline leaped forward as never before, with many intellectual advances in the 1960s and 1970s (see Ortner 1984). These advances, however, did not emerge from, or address, contemporary social problems. They were generated primarily by academic anthropologists in pursuit of 'pure' knowledge (albeit through intensive fieldwork), often framed at high levels of abstraction only applied to contemporary social problems with difficulty.[17] The American economic hegemony following World War II was accompanied by a theoretical ascendancy in American anthropology, similar to that witnessed in Great Britain during its days of empire. Imperial Britain, and then the post–World War II United States, possessed the economic resources to generate a dominant theoretical discipline.

2. *Epistemology, politics, and ethics.* The ascendancy of academic anthropology and knowledge advancement for its own sake were accompanied by an academic culture that increasingly guarded its own interests. Cultural forms arose that denoted the proper conduct of an anthropologist, and oftentimes these seemed to discriminate between 'pure' and applied anthropology. Whether in graduate student training, debates internal to the AAA, articles in the literature, or institutional policies, the effect of the emerging discourse during the 1960s and 1970s was to establish 'pure' (i.e., nonapplied academic) anthropology as the preferred category and to relegate applied or practicing anthropology to an 'other' category that implied it to be more dangerous, questionable, or even 'unethical.' The moves by which applied anthropology was placed in a secondary position involved Americanized conceptualizations of epistemology and ethics which were culturally and politically constructed. There is insufficient space in this chapter to explore these themes fully, but they are illustrated briefly below.

Situated epistemology. The rise of anthropological theory in the United States was accompanied by epistemological assumptions that tended to invalidate applied anthropology as a fully legitimate form of the discipline. A prime example was the widespread notion that 'real' anthropologists must conduct their ethnographic fieldwork outside the anthropologist's native culture and language (Schwartzman 1993; Freidenberg 2001; see also Messerschmidt 1981). It was assumed that an anthropologist could not think outside the categories in which she was enculturated, and thus took too much for granted in her own society and could not properly 'problematize' a given phenomenon at home. Such assumptions guarded the gates of professional status and served to devalue anthropology focusing on contemporary problems, both in the U.S. and abroad. It was categorized as inadequate for some purposes, such as theoretical production. Through such epistemological assumptions, "the criteria of what constitutes knowledge, what is to be excluded, and who is qualified to know" (Foucault 1971) were established, empowering the practice of 'pure' anthropology inside the discipline (a focus on abstract matters in small, relatively isolated ethnic groups) while disempowering 'applied' (a focus on contemporary problems). This created endless frustration for anthropologists working in the policy arena, where their work was viewed as that of 'accountants' or 'technicians' rather than producers of new knowledge (Hackenberg 1988). Anthropologists originating from the so-called Third World have sometimes criticized the 'view from outside' gained by nonnative anthropologists as narrow or biased (e.g., Puerto Rican anthropologists' criticisms of the U.S. anthropology of Puerto Rico; see Freidenberg 2001). Yet, Western anthropologists rarely observed or expressed the view that Western epistemological assumptions might be culturally constructed. Indeed, these assumptions were taken for granted. In this invisible state, we believe a vertical relationship between theoretical and applied anthropology was furthered in the U.S. These assumptions seem to have gone by the wayside today, as Rabinow's (1986:241) statement at the opening of this chapter suggests.

Culturally constructed ethics and politics. Prior to World War II, most American anthropologists, including applied anthropologists, skirted ethical concerns through their belief that they were scientists engaging in values-free research and also by avoiding direct intervention or policy implementation.[18] In this way, they resembled British anthropologists of the colonial era. American anthropologists did not always recognize their culture-specific values, such as not judging other cultures in the terms of one's own culture (i.e., cultural relativism), and their values might have been viewed by some as universal 'truth.'[19]

The situation began to change during and after World War II, as American anthropologists became engaged in a wider array of roles involving social change and intervention. Many social scientists came to realize that their research was not entirely objective or values-free (Holmberg 1958). The ethics of intervention in another person's culture, while maintaining one's responsibilities to multiple others (some with conflicting interests), was found to be fraught with moral contradictions. Minimizing the unanticipated consequences generally was the 'prime directive' (i.e., do no harm), but this invariably was the responsibility of the individual anthropologist, contingent upon circumstances of the case (Bennett 1996). Many anthropologists chose to avoid the inherent risks by avoiding practice altogether (thereby favoring 'pure' anthropology).[20]

Serious academic efforts at cultural intervention were undertaken during the 1950s and 1960s, and these sparked debates that contributed to the construction of applied anthropology as an arena of questionable politics and ethics. Examples are Sol Tax's Action Anthropology and Allan Holmberg's Research and Development Anthropology (see Holmberg and Dobyns 1962; Tax 1975; Bennett 1996). These academically based projects framed intervention within the context of a set of values that were stated explicitly. Ultimately, however, both projects met with strong collegial criticism and failed to thrive or reproduce. Many observers believed that these projects were tinged with paternalism; it was the anthropologist who told indigenous people that they needed help, not the other way round. This latter critique related to an emerging, postcolonialist view in anthropology portraying applied anthropologists as colonialist and elitist, a reaction to their extensive participation in international development projects (e.g., Thompson 1976; Bennett 1996).[21] A rift was emerging between applied development anthropologists employed by governments or international aid agencies and postmodern academic anthropologists focusing on 'development' as an object of study. The latter often charged the former with seriously misguided or even 'unethical' practices (e.g., contributing to a continuing cycle of impoverishment in the so-called Third World, enforced by developed economies and their agents; see Escobar 1995 and Gardner and Lewis 1996). Such criticisms had the tendency to reinforce earlier disciplinary biases against anthropological employment by powerful sponsors, lest the anthropologist become a target of attacks leveled against these employers (e.g., U.S. government or international aid agencies).[22] Again, 'pure' was the safest position.

Through the foregoing epistemological, ethical, and political discriminations, anthropologists who applied knowledge to 'real-world' problems, whether academic or not, were often treated as 'second-rate' or, even more harshly, as less worthy in bearing the name anthropologist (and, thus, some chose to leave their disciplinary identity behind). Applied anthropology in America had been transformed, from its potential role as an innovative and entrepreneurial partner of theory as envisioned by the founders of the SfAA, to the subordinate stepchild of a scholarly parent quick to criticize and slow to take responsibility for the consequences of its own intellectual production.

3. *Expansion of the job market for applied anthropology in the United States.* As the culture of American academic anthropology emerged during the mid–20th century, a series of parallel, but slower developments was shaping the community of professional practice associated with applied anthropology. As a result of the Great Depression and World War II, the demand for anthropologists grew beyond that of instructor/ researcher/consultant in the arena of internal colonial administration (i.e., Native Americans) and came to encompass other arenas and roles, including interventionist roles related to policy implementation, social action, and culture change (van Willigen 2002). There were not many anthropologists available for such roles immediately after World War II. There were not many anthropologists available in the first place, and those that did exist headed off to academic posts. Yet, the demand for applied anthropology was steady and growing due to numerous contextual shifts at national and global levels (e.g., the creation of new federal legislation that required anthropological expertise, the establishment of international 'development' policy, capitalism's search for new markets

overseas). New anthropology Ph.D.'s who chose not to seek academic employment, plus 'surplus' Ph.D.'s who could not be accommodated within academia, gradually became available to fill the demand for anthropological knowledge in government and the private sector.

There came an important turn of events in the 1970s and 1980s. The supply of new anthropology Ph.D.'s, who could not find academic employment, began to expand as a result of the shrinking academic job market. At their peak, anthropology departments in the United States produced 445 Ph.D.'s in 1976. Ten years later (1986), this number was 420; however, the number of new Ph.D.'s employed by an anthropology or joint department had fallen to 33 percent, and the percent employed by all of academia was only 51 percent of the total (as compared to 75 percent in 1971–72; Baba 1994). The rest found work in federal, state, and local governments (13 percent), the private sector (9 percent), museums (6 percent), and other venues (23 percent) [error due to rounding]. The 'other' category above likely included those who were unemployed or soon to leave the field entirely. The number of 'other' in 1971–72 was only 2 percent. Clearly, there was pressure on the discipline to shift its practices so that more graduates could find meaningful ways to sustain themselves beyond academe.

During the postwar era, many significant changes were introduced within anthropology to support the flow of practitioner knowledge to government and private sector applications. Although this flow still is not fully acknowledged as a mainstream activity within American anthropology, it was a key element of the disciplinary shift toward practice, including structural developments that brought practice to what had been a highly academic discipline. In this context, anthropology's institutional adaptation in the U.S. included various named structures that responded to the growing demand for applied anthropology, such as the establishment of numerous applied anthropology degree programs and departments, local practitioners organizations (LPOs), the AAA's founding of the National Association for the Practice of Anthropology (NAPA), the formation of the Coalition of Practicing and Applied Anthropology Programs (COPAA), new professional journals such as *Practicing Anthropology* and NAPA's *Bulletin* series, and the list goes on (see van Willigen 2002; Hill 1994). Importantly, the production of applied anthropologists for venues external to the discipline required a cadre of anthropologists within academia. So, there emerged a group of academic applied anthropologists who resided full-time in higher education and yet focused on the production of applied anthropologists for destinations beyond the academy.

With the expansion and institutionalization of this 'new applied anthropology' (Angrosino 1976) in the 1970s and 1980s, a subtle shift occurred in the meaning of the term 'applied.' While the SfAA founders had in mind an innovative linkage of theoretical and practical objectives, the 'new applied anthropology' of the latter 20th century became something else. Depending upon one's point of view, applied anthropology became a means to provide specialized knowledge to the policy realm, to train knowledge workers for employment, and to supply an established and growing source of knowledge for solving various practical problems. These new and expanded objectives are reflected in the definitions of applied anthropology appearing in the literature over the past two decades:

- Applied anthropology (is) the field of inquiry concerned with the relationships between anthropological knowledge and the uses of that knowledge in the world beyond anthropology (Chambers 1987:309).
- The term applied anthropology is used in both Britain and the United States to refer mainly to the employment of anthropologists by organizations involved in inducing change or enhancing human welfare (Bennett 1996:S25).
- We start out with our discussion of definition by simply saying that applied anthropology is anthropology put to use. . . . It is viewed as encompassing the tremendous variety of activities anthropologists do now and have done in the past, when engaged in solving practical problems (van Willigen 2002:8).

The objectives set forth in these definitions are significant and should be included within any conception of modern applied anthropology. What we question are the elements not found in the definitions. Only Chambers links applied anthropology to knowledge, and even then understanding is gained best through inquiry directed toward the uses of knowledge, apparently in venues beyond anthropology. Is there the possibility that applied anthropology could also contribute to the advancement of knowledge within anthropology and cognate fields, to the extension and revision of disciplinary theory, and to the development of innovations in social science methodology? Certainly, other applied fields in the social sciences (i.e., applied areas of economics, political science, and psychology) and clinical professions (medicine) contribute to the knowledge base of their respective disciplines. To what extent is this contribution a possibility, even a responsibility, of applied anthropology? As the above definitions reflected, contributions to anthropological knowledge no longer appear to be explicit within the extant meanings of applied anthropology, and we believe that this shift has come at a cost. Bennett (who indicates that he does not consider himself an 'applied' anthropologist) flatly states:

> The practical or applied side of academic fields in the human sciences is often viewed by scholars with ambivalence or even contempt. . . . Anthropology has traditionally devoted itself to the study of tribal or nonurban societies, and this has meant that it has with diffi-culty accepted a role of practitioner . . . practical anthropology in American anthropology generally lacks prestige in scholarly circles. [1996:S23–S24]

Indeed, a lack of prestige has translated into a lack of clout, which means that the 'new applied anthropology' has been weak as a policy discipline (Chambers 1987[23]).

The foregoing suggests that the split between anthropological theory and practice, which originally occurred in Great Britain under colonialism, reemerged in North America following World War II. While the British produced only an incipient version of the two-tiered model of knowledge production (since applied anthropology did not thrive in the U.K. after World War II), this two-tiered model emerged in its mature form in the U.S. In this model, the production of theoretical knowledge is reserved for disciplinary elites, and applied anthropology is positioned in the 'other' tier, where its knowledge is considered derivative, less prestigious, and not a contributor to disciplinary theory. Of course, theorists may 'apply' anthropology if they choose, but the theoretical community generally does not take notice of work produced by those who are considered (only) applied anthropologists. The hegemonic economic power of the day (i.e., the U.S. at the end of the 20th century) utilizes this cognitive and institutional structure as a means to produce applied and practicing anthropologists for the expanded neocolonial enterprise, while maintaining a 'pure' theoretical structure to produce ideology for export (see also Baba 2000). The primary difference between the British and U.S. models is that the American version has been able to maintain a distinctive identity that is not coterminous (i.e., confined or bound) with indigenous, ethnic, or tribal peoples, even though theoretical anthropology plunged into foreign fieldwork within exotic settings. The capacities to maintain a distinctive, named identity and a contemporary focus, in part, enabled applied anthropology's remarkable expansion in the United States over the latter half of the 20th century.

GLOBAL CONVERGENCE OF ANTHROPOLOGIES: 1990–PRESENT

During the 1990s, boundaries within and between nations and regions established after World War II began to shift, blur, or perhaps disappear, reflecting structural changes in the underlying economic and political relationships. These shifts were partially triggered by the dissolution of the Soviet Union and the end of the Cold War, which simultaneously disrupted the regional balance of powers and global political equilibrium since World War II. These shifts also opened up vast new areas of the globe for the advance of capitalism. The changes we describe here often are referred to as part of a process of 'globalization' (Robertson 1992; Chun 2004). Globalization theories predict that increasing economic and technological interconnections across nations will encourage *structural convergence*, meaning that institutional forms will become increasingly similar and resonant over time. For example, formal institutions charged with an educational mission may be expected to restructure their programs along lines that permit graduates to meet implicit or explicit global standards (i.e., leading to greater similarity in program content across nations). We suggest that we are experiencing the effects of a convergence process within our discipline, both globally and across the domains of theory and practice.

The anthropologist Jonathan Friedman discusses global change in his book entitled *Globalization, the State, and Violence* (2003; see also Friedman 2004). According to Friedman, the phenomenon popularly referred to as 'globalization' represents the latest cycle in a long-term historical process of capital accumulation. In this process, geographic centers of capital accumulation shift regionally, with older centers gradually losing their prominence and newer centers rising and gaining power. Although one may debate whether all that Friedman describes is part of the capitalist era, one can be certain that geographic centers of political and economic power or hegemony have arisen and collapsed over the past hundreds and thousands of years. These shifts can be traced from the great trading centers of the Middle East, to the Italian city-states, through the various nations of Europe, and lastly to the United States after World War II. Now, capital accumulation may be shifting to the Pacific Rim, especially the Asian side. We are quoting Friedman, at some length, given the importance of the subject:

> The rise of Europe itself was a process that can best be understood as in counterpoint with the decline of the Middle East at the end of the Middle Ages. Thus European capitalism did not simply evolve from feudalism. It was a product of the shift of accumulation from one world region to another. Europe was, in this argument, largely a dependent area in the previous Arab empires, a relation that was gradually reversed in the centuries following the Renaissance. The foremost mechanism in this process was and is the decentralization of capital within the larger system, a phenomenon that we refer to today as *globalization* (emphasis in the original). So the entire history of Europe, understood in global terms, can be seen in terms of a series of pulsations, expansions, and contractions, from the growth of the Mediterranean and Flanders as the Middle East entered into its terminal crisis to the shifts from the Italian city-states to Portugal and Spain, followed by Holland and then England. Each of these cycles was characterized by periods of centralized accumulation and expansive trade followed by decentralization (capital export or globalization) and a longer-term shift in hegemony. By the 1970s the entire West had become a major exporter of capital to much of the rest of the world and this might be seen as a major shift of accumulation from West to East. The formation of the Pacific Rim economy from the 1970s to the late 1990s represents a substantial redistribution of economic power in the world system. This phase corresponds to the rise of the globalization idea and its institutionalization in the West. [Friedman 2003:2]

In what appears to be a decline of the Western center and the rise of a new center in the East, the United States decreased its share of manufacturing from 40.3 percent to 24 percent between 1963 and 1987, while Japan increased its portion from 5.5 percent to 19 percent. The Asian Newly Industrialized Countries (NIC) countries of India, Spain, and Brazil were major benefactors of this decentering (Freidman 2004:76). Countries such as Taiwan, South Korea, and China have moved rapidly up the ranks of nations that export manufactured goods, at the same time that the Western nations have experienced declines, some by significant amounts. At present, the Pacific Rim nations have substantially higher rates of economic growth than the U.S. or Europe.[24] Of course, these rates reveal only one, potentially misleading, dimension of a complex situation. Still, it would be difficult to argue that the more mature (Western) economies are retaining their full sparkle for investment as they have become saturated with consumer products. Between 1978 and 1998, manufacturing imports into the U.S. increased from 17.8 percent to 31.8 percent. According to Freidman, the model is one where exported capital is used to manufacture products that are reimported to the older center, with a "trend toward increasing competition, decentralization, and a clear shift of capital accumulation to the East" (2004:76–77).

Furthermore, with the breakup of the Soviet bloc and socialism/communism's economic model morphing toward market-oriented forms, new arenas for capitalist expansion have emerged in places that heretofore were forbidden territory (e.g., eastern Europe, Russia, China, and their client states). In addition, starkly visible are the 'weak links' (e.g., failed African states) where order has basically collapsed and anarchy may rule (Friedman 2003). Abhorrent conflicts there have converted millions of people into armies of refugees, creating severe humanitarian crises that have riveted anthropological attention, as well as spinning off intercultural encounters that have created occasions for postmodern theorizing (Fischer 2003). Such processes link peoples, nations, and regions together across the globe and create compelling foci for anthropological practice in the world today.

Globalization processes are salient in the present context because they have implications for the structuring of applied and practicing anthropology in the United States and around the globe. Our essay argues that the production of anthropological knowledge within the global hegemonic power (Great Britain in the past, more recently the U.S.) is structured in a two-tiered format, including a theoretical and an applied/practicing tier. This structure emerged during a prolonged period of colonialism and neocolonialism, when the world had Western geographic centers. Only within this structure is 'applied anthropology' named as such. In this chapter, we have attempted to trace the historical developments surrounding the meaning of this name and changes in its meaning over space and time. We suggest that if the world is in the process of decentering—with Eastern or other non-Western powers on the rise, and the U.S. slowly losing its hegemonic status—then we might expect the structuring of anthropological institutions in the U.S. and elsewhere to reflect these shifts through a convergence process (particularly as resources are reallocated in a West-to-East pattern). Two tentative hypotheses regarding globalization and the naming of applied anthropology may be advanced: (1) other nations will begin to develop institutional structures that resemble applied anthropology institutions in the U.S. and will name them as such, or (2) institutional structures in the U.S. will evolve in a manner that moves closer to the global norm (i.e., a blurring of the lines between theoretical and applied anthropology).

We believe that tendencies related to the first hypothesis (i.e., the naming of applied anthropology in other countries) have been attempted rather unsuccessfully in other nations. Three chapters (Canada, Great Britain, and Israel) in this volume provide evidence of formal institutional structures created to support a separate applied or practicing anthropology activity over the past decade or more (and some were named 'applied anthropology' or a similar term). In each case, the experiment failed to thrive or has been ended.[25] At first glance, the failure of these models may appear contradictory since all of them arose in First World locales that seemingly should support a two-tiered system. However, we argue that only a global hegemonic power can support two tiers (e.g., Britain in the past, the United States at present). Each of the other national contexts (i.e., Canada, Israel, and Great Britain at present) is missing one or more critical elements needed for replication of a full-fledged, two-tiered institutional structure (e.g., economic or political resources to support two tiers, a large market demand for applied anthropology, and a varied role structure). The failure of institutional structures in supporting applied anthropology and the end of the 'applied' name does not mean that the application of anthropology ended in those nations; the activity goes on without the separate structure or name, just as it has everywhere else except within a power center. Some anthropologists (not Americans) have confided to us their relief that efforts to establish an applied anthropology 'apartheid' in their country failed, because they believe applied activity should be integrated with theoretical anthropology. While the term 'apartheid' may seem startling and alien in this context, perhaps it is an apt characterization for institutional structures that segregate and discriminate on the basis of (what some believe to be) 'inherent' characteristics.

This brings us to hypothesis two: the potential 'blurring' of theoretical and applied anthropology. We believe, based on the evidence in this volume and other literature, that hypothesis two is the more possible result of globalization. A new global model of anthropology appears to be emerging that situates our discipline squarely in the world, blurring (but not eliminating) the distinctions between academic ('pure') and nonacademic practice, as well as American and other national forms of the discipline. An argument for such a global model has been advanced by Fischer (2003) who has called for new conceptual and methodological tools needed because cultures of every kind are becoming more complex and differentiated as globalization brings them into exponentially increased interaction. He states that anthropology now operates in a series of 'third spaces' beyond the 19th- and 20th-century dualisms of us/them, primitive/civilized, East/West, North/South, or applied/academic. The opening of a 'third space' gives rise to a peculiar sense of 'oneness' or a blurring of boundaries that anthropology has not evidenced since the dawn of the discipline. From our perspective, this 'oneness' is expressed through three *dimensions of global convergence*, described across several chapters in this volume.[26]

These dimensions reflect aspects (i.e., features or outcomes) of institutional structures connected to anthropological practice in its broadest sense that appear to be emerging across nations and regions, including the United States. Three such aspects are described below: (1) a shift toward contemporary, problem-oriented interdisciplinary research, (2) participatory and collaborative methodologies, and (3) stronger profiles in policy making and political influence. We believe that these phenomena result from globalization processes and that they influence both academic and nonacademic anthropology and will transform the U.S. model of applied anthropology, as well as its name(s). We discuss each of these dimensions in the sections that follow.

A Shift in Academic Attention toward Contemporary Problem-Oriented Interdisciplinary Research

We have described some of the conditions that rivet anthropological attention toward urgent issues transcending national boundaries. This volume resonates with themes focusing our colleagues' interests, academic and nonacademic, toward research relating to the global troubles of environmental devastation, violence, disease, homelessness, and hunger. These issues cannot be analyzed with traditional 'pure' disciplinary concepts and methods alone. While traditional anthropological practice (solo, single discipline, abstract, 'exotic esoterica') has been marginalized, the epistemological heart of our discipline is being transformed through postcritical approaches to methodology and theory-building (Schweizer 1998), which encompass interdisciplinary forays across new intellectual frontiers. The potential synergy of problem-focused yet fundamental research is recognized across the natural and social sciences (Stokes 1997), and it is producing gains in cutting-edge areas such as environmental science, economic and 'institutional' anthropology, and complex adaptive systems (e.g., Moran and Ojima 2005; Jian and Young 2002; Agar 2004). Lines between theory and practice are blurred in such contexts because emergent problems are poorly understood and not well theorized. Those with access to the field may gain information crucial to new understanding, while those cloistered in the realm of 'pure' may risk failing to comprehend evolving realities, since old theory can be obsolete for dealing with contemporary issues. Importantly, gaining access to the field often requires an exchange of value (i.e., a problem orientation, a deliverable). Anthropologists need to transform knowledge gained in more pragmatic contexts into theoretical intelligence and not become disillusioned that such engagement is automatically 'impure' or represents a 'sellout' to the system.

This brings us to another consequence of global decentering and its tendency to prompt scholars' attention toward contemporary issues: The pursuit of knowledge for its own sake may be affordable only by members of wealthy institutions. The most exclusive academic institutions may continue such pursuits because they are more or less financially independent, but public institutions relying on tax revenues, tuition fees, and income from grants and contracts must heed constituents' calls for greater 'accountability and relevance,' meaning a shift toward agendas resonating with stakeholder interests (see Duderstadt and Womack 2003). These changes have fostered growing pressures on academic researchers to deliver 'products,' much as if they were in the corporate world, and the rise of an 'audit culture' in higher education (Shore and Wright 2000), which we believe is a mechanism for resource reallocation that accompanies the global decentering of power.

We believe these contextual forces will trigger an entrepreneurial impulse defining this as a moment of opportunity for anthropologists to lead in an interdisciplinary effort (much as that seen prior to World War II). Such opportunities come with numerous consequences, including the need for changes in the training or retraining of students (and faculty) and in the orientation of anthropologists' research goals and objectives. Over the long term, such influences may transform a discipline, bringing theorists closer to 'real-world' problems and blurring the lines between theory and practice (see Jian and Young 2002).

Meanwhile, the so-called 'institutional anthropologies' (Bennett 1996) have emerged during the latter part of the 20th century connecting anthropology to other disciplines and professions (e.g., medical anthropology, legal anthropology, educational anthropology, organizational anthropology, and so forth). Institutional anthropology has responded to the value of anthropological and ethnographic expertise across a wide array of modern professional domains (see Hill 1999, 2000). This 'diaspora of anthropology' has transformed many members of our discipline into intellectual hybrids coexisting simultaneously in anthropology and in other professional realms (e.g., medicine, business), from which they may come and go, being disciplinary and interdisciplinary at the same time. An interesting aspect of hybridity is that it requires knowledge integration from contemporary contexts to achieve competency, though a hybrid anthropologist may self-identify as theoretically oriented if she chooses (with respect to anthropological theory or to theory of another discipline). There is no requirement that an institutional anthropologist identify as an applied anthropologist, and many do not (though they focus on contemporary problems in other fields, as do applied anthropologists). We suggest that institutional anthropologies in the U.S. have evolved a practice that resembles the model of applied anthropology originally conceived by the founders of the Society for Applied Anthropology prior to World War II (i.e., Bateson, Mead, Warner et al.), except that the anthropologists now do not belong to one professional society. Institutional anthropology, by remaining outside the fold of the 'named' (or by taking on many different names), converges toward what is happening in other parts of the world, where applied anthropology also is not named, and consequently contributes to the blurring of the boundary between theory and practice.

Participatory and Collaborative Methodologies

In this volume, the power of collaboration is most clearly reflected in those chapters that discuss advances made in indigenous and aboriginal rights (e.g., self-determination, status recognition, jurisdiction, expansions of land, and treaty rights; see chapters on Ecuador, India, and Russia). Advances in this area are impressive and have involved collaboration among local peoples, anthropologists, NGOs, international agencies such as the World Bank, and transnational corporations. These advances are the outgrowth of a historical process, beginning with the social movements for equality and justice that traversed the globe in the 1970s and which ignited indigenous and aboriginal uprisings aimed at securing land rights and rights to self-determination. In some cases (e.g., Latin America), the uprisings had the effect of redefining the relationship between indigenous peoples and their states, often involving anthropologists in efforts to establish greater autonomy and more clearly defined economic rights for indigenous peoples (see chapter on Ecuador). Some of these efforts met with success, leading to legal and policy changes at the national level and improving the economic situation for indigenous peoples (see chapter on Russia).

A mechanism for diffusion of successful innovations surrounding indigenous rights has been documented by international agencies such as the World Bank. Toward the end of the 20th century, these agencies came under increasing pressure for positive economic results in the developing world. The chapters in this volume suggest that these agencies undertook projects focused on indigenous peoples and other ethnic groups, possibly as a means to demonstrate concrete results in limited cases, using methods adopted from applied anthropology (e.g., the case of 'ethnodevelopment' discussed in the chapter on Ecuador; also see chapter on Russia). Some of these 'win-win' strategies, once proven effective, were codified by the international agencies and made available for dissemination. Thus, collaboration among anthropologists, indigenous peoples, other ethnic groups, and international agencies may have contributed to the emergence of a world model for constructive economic change now being adopted as a global standard. Based on our observations, this process may be more theoretically sophisticated and ethically robust than anything utilized to 'manage change' in the private sector today.

Lamphere (2004:431) anticipated the convergence of anthropological practices in the U.S. toward that of other nations and how collaborative methodologies can represent convergence for academic and nonacademic researchers as well:

> Anthropology is in the midst of a "sea change." This is a culmination of three decades of transformation in the communities we study, the topics that command our attention, and the relationships we forge with the subjects of our research . . . the relationships we have established with communities have been reshaped from that of outside experts and scientists studying "others" to more collaborative and partnership arrangements.

Indeed, it is a "sea change," and an ironic one at that, when academically based anthropologists in the U.S. embrace participatory methodology, given the origins of this practice. While many streams of theory and practice contribute to the participatory tradition (Greenwood and Levin 1998; Wallerstein and Duran 2003), arguably the clearest commitment to the actual *practice* of community participation as a methodology arose from the work of Paulo Freire in Brazil. Through this, he intended to break the monopoly power of academic institutions over knowledge production and dissemination by changing the way in which poor people learned to read (Elden and Levin 1991; Taylor 1993). That this methodology would circle the globe and find its way into American academe as an innovative approach to anthropological research is certainly a case study in globalization and convergence if ever there was one.

Stronger Profiles in Policy Making and Political Influence

The century-long involvement of anthropology in public policy was a central theme throughout the historical tour conducted in this essay. In a world rapidly changing, public and private policy elites—especially Western elites whose hegemony is threatened—may experience unease and wish to get their hands on knowledge about the worlds beyond their immediate view. Anthropologists may lay claim to these unknown territories and, interestingly, they have become welcome in many corridors of power where they were seldom seen before. Because anthropological knowledge is necessary to elites in this era of massive global change, it is our belief that the 21st-century model of anthropology will enter the global centers of capital accumulation at higher levels of influence and authority than has been possible for almost a century. This shift is happening on a worldwide basis, as discussed in this volume (see chapters on Canada, Ecuador, Egypt, Great Britain, Israel, and Russia; for American examples, see Hackenberg and Hackenberg 2004). With this, a change is occurring within the discipline from the long-standing favored regard of abstract and esoteric knowledge, for its own sake, to a different focus on knowledge and practice that is more strategic and oriented toward the critical concerns of society.[27] Simply collecting knowledge of particular cultures leans toward isolation, while knowledge of urgent issues leans toward more connection and a global process. Because of these overall disciplinary shifts, anthropology will of necessity become more global in every aspect of our work (e.g., convergence toward global standards in literature, methodology, and practice). Those institutional structures and individuals who are capable of making this transition will be creating the anthropology of the future (e.g., preparing students with methodological skills via some mechanism, not necessarily within academia). It may be knowledge of domains of practice and complementary approaches that will segment future anthropologists (e.g., knowledge of medicine, educational or other forms of policy) rather than the dichotomies of the past, such as basic versus applied or commitment to a particular theory. Anthropologists will be allied with different kinds of cognate disciplines dependent on the defining issues and will concentrate on different regions of the globe and trans-global human communities where certain issues are more critical.

In summary, our overview of the evidence supports the view that anthropology in the United States is evolving toward a model of practice that tends to blur distinctions between 'pure' and applied, as well as one that creates new forms of the discipline with synergistic combinations of theory and practice in anthropology and cognate disciplines. Our explanation for this shift is turbulence in the global context, particularly the decentering of the world, and ensuing resource reallocations. We postulate that periods of high turbulence and uncertainty dislodge stable theoretical regimes and create crises that call for empirical investigation and action. The Great Depression and World War II were times such as these, and the present is such a time. The 'apartheid' of theory and practice, forged in the old centers of power under stable regimes, cannot stand under the present circumstances, for they block the global flows of knowledge needed to understand and act. Anthropology is challenged to re-form itself under the new conditions, and we must re-form ourselves to remain valid and dynamic (and to advance and, perhaps, become more valuable in the future).

TRANSFORMING OURSELVES: AMERICAN ANTHROPOLOGY IN THE 21ST CENTURY

In the past, anthropologists created niches for themselves within the contexts of colonization and its critique. From the time of Boas, the majority of anthropologists, especially those in the West, found a comfort zone for their liberalism in the confines of academia. Although Boas and his students were concerned with ethnicity and salvaging ethnographic descriptions of vanishing indigenous groups for the sake of knowledge preservation, anthropology remained a small and relatively powerless discipline. Boas and his students developed a conceptual framework (relativism) and ideology (liberalism) for the discipline that continued to underpin anthropology throughout the 20th century. Perhaps, it was Horton (1973) who best characterized anthropology's "romantic fascination" with traditional cultures. He stated that anthropologists, for the most part, are equipped with "liberal scruples" that allow us to avoid odious and invidious intercultural comparisons (e.g., cultural relativism). To maintain relativism, however, required anthropologists to avoid certain cultural comparisons or facts, creating (in our opinion) inadvertent disciplinary blind spots. For example, although anthropologists long have underscored the centrality of consumption in the production of cultural patterns (e.g., Sahlins 1976; Douglas and Isherwood 1979), much of the 20th century passed with anthropologists ignoring consumption as a proper object of study because influential members of the discipline wanted to 'protect' traditional societies from the 'contamination' that might accompany such goods, as well as protecting anthropology from extinction should these goods replace traditional material objects (Miller 1995). Now that the importance of consumption has been acknowledged, reflection upon this shift suggests that the unintended effect of our self-interested 'liberal scruples' denied, in part, social realities. Our scruples gave us a one-eyed view of the world (ironically, the 'self' eye; the 'other' eye was covered), which contributed to the intellectual and political marginalization of anthropology in local and global contexts.

A significant dimension of global convergence is reflected in the alliances and transnational networks forged by anthropologists that, in many cases, require a 21st-century ideology. Our theory and practice must reflect the new social and cultural restructuring of the world's political economy. While there is a place for 'liberalism' in our attitudes and actions, to advance we must recognize the emerging world's differences from the ones that produced the ideals of the 20th century. Globalization processes do not always originate in the West; thus not all aspects of globalization are harmful from the perspective of others. Values pertaining to the preservation of 'culture' or to the 'rights' of the underclass and the poor, for example, need to be shifted into other ideological frameworks more in tune with truly global processes, not only ones originating in Western societies. Global restructuring requires that anthropologists rethink their 20th-century ideology, values, and constructs within a 21st-century context. A major contribution of postmodern ideology has been the critiquing of the 'us–them' distinction and bringing the "other" more into the picture than did the older models permeating 20th century anthropology.

We contend that 21st-century anthropology will revive the innovative vision of the founders of the Society for Applied Anthropology, producing expert knowledge and skills that can integrate theory and practice, and in due course move the discipline away from a marginal position. Vital is the integration of theory and practice that will enhance our position in the global system and, we hope, counterbalance the tensions that threaten disciplinary integrity. We argued previously (Hill and Baba 2000), and vigorously reinforce the argument here, that the future of anthropology is firmly rooted in the theoretical and methodological issues that are emerging on the frontier of practice. This exciting and challenging frontier is rising now in a new global model that transcends our 20th-century ideals, incorporates the most innovative aspects of our past, and advances new ideas that are emerging from a decentered world.

NOTES

Acknowledgments. The authors wish to express their gratitude to Michael Angrosino, Erve Chambers, Sara Pink, Anatoly Yamskov, Tim Wallace, and three anonymous reviewers for insightful critical commentary and substantive suggestions on earlier versions of the manuscript. Any shortcomings, however, are strictly our own.

An earlier version of this paper was presented at the Ethnographic Praxis in Industry Conference, Redmond, Washington, November 14–15, 2005.

1. An exception was Foster (1969), who also reviewed the development of applied anthropology in Mexico and made limited mention of applied activities in Guatemala, Peru, Bolivia, the Philippines, India, and Italy. Gardner and Lewis (1996) discuss in some detail the development of applied anthropology in the U.K.

2. We hasten to point out here that we do not believe that the difference derives from any difficulty in translating the concept 'applied anthropology' into other languages and cultural contexts. The basic notion of using anthropological knowledge toward practical aims has proven remarkably fluid in crossing cultural boundaries, as made clear in observations by Foster (1969), Bastide (1973), Kuper (1983), Gardner and Lewis (1996), Freidenberg (2001), and virtually all of the chapters in this volume and the previous one.

3. Although these terms may now be obsolete, we deliberately maintain their use in this context for purposes of historical comparison.

4. Here, we use the term 'practice' in reference to the practices of the entire discipline of anthropology, including those of anthropologists who do not consider themselves practitioners in the sense of 'applied' practice (e.g., ethnographic fieldwork practices).

5. The British anthropologist Lane Fox Pitt-Rivers used the term 'applied anthropology' as early as 1881 (Gardner and Lewis 1996).

6. Kuper (1983) disputes the notion that indirect rule played any objective role in facilitating a 'functional' contribution from anthropology to British colonialism. However, he notes that the anthropologists themselves supported indirect rule, and that is the point in this context (i.e., that the anthropologists and the colonial administrators colluded in their belief that indirect rule was an effective approach, and that participant-observation was functionally suited to this approach).

7. The first ethnology departments in Russia were formed after 1917, showing the importance of the discipline to the Soviet Union.

8. Whether or not the hypothesis advanced for the Russian case also may be applied to the Chinese case is not known at this time.

9. The term 'native anthropologists' is used throughout the chapter to refer to anthropologists who study people in their own country or culture of origin. This term is problematic, however; for example, when used to describe anthropologists in the U.S., it incorporates at least two (and potentially many more) kinds of anthropologists: whites and Native Americans, in the case of this chapter. The point here is that European and U.S. anthropologists (outsiders) held a near monopoly on the study of peoples in developing nations, but that began to change as 'native anthropologists' from those nations were educated for this purpose.

10. In fact, these policies did not achieve their intended goals, as is noted in the next section. Freidenberg (2001) has pointed out that acculturation-based policies often had the effect of increasing class stratification in indigenous communities, by drawing indigenous people into labor-intensive industries outside the community.

11. Angrosino (personal communication, 2005) makes the valid point that First World academic or theoretical anthropologists often are not purely theoretical in the sense that physicists might be, since their grounding in fieldwork gives them a strong orientation to 'real-world' issues.

12. Later in the 1930s, the Office of Indians Affairs, together with the U.S. Department of Agriculture, engaged in a major natural resource survey involving anthropologists that emphasized the 'adjustment' of Native American attitudes to dominant American values (Gardner and Lewis 1996).

13. It is significant that the SfAA was founded *prior* to America's entry into WWII, since the war often is credited with crystallizing the modern form of applied anthropology in America. We suggest, however, that this modern form was crystallized before the war, out of conditions existing during the 1930s (e.g., the Great Depression).

14. Another potential factor influencing the SfAA founders could have been a 'multidisciplinary moment' within the social sciences, especially prominent at Harvard through the intellectual leadership of Talcott Parsons. Clyde Kluckholn, one of the major leaders in anthropology at the time, was involved in this effort, and according to Bennett (1996:S26), he "simply did not draw a clear distinction between applied and 'pure.' "

15. As a result of such criticism, some colonies and former colonies became hostile ground for anthropologists, even until recently in certain cases. Third World 'native anthropologists' also faced criticisms in their own countries for collaborating with the colonial project. Attacks on colonial anthropology do not acknowledge that some colonial-era anthropologists voiced sharp criticism against their governments (for examples, see chapters on India and Portugal in this volume).

16. In retrospect we can see that both 'pure' and applied anthropology in Europe were intimately associated with colonialism, although 'pure' attempted to distance itself by 'forgetting' its association with, and denying the existence of, the other 'applied.'

17. Some observers were harsh in their criticism of the turn taken toward theory: "something has obviously happened in the last two decades and not to the good. . . . Anthropology has developed its own restrictive taboos, its own little culture, and has been surrounded, if not strangled by it. It has developed status symbols which proliferate trivia and, even worse, the quest for trivia as a status symbol in the profession" (Nader 1975:31–32; cf. Bennett 1996:S27).

18. It should be noted that in the 1940s and 1950s some anthropologists (including a number of those who participated in the formation of the SfAA) were involved in the Human Relations School, where the research agenda focused on improvement of workforce productivity in American industry (Baba 2005). Because these projects required cooperation with company management, they often were viewed with suspicion in academic circles and even labeled "politically reactionary" (Bennett 1996:S24). Such views contrasted unfavorably with the "decent, liberal reformist anthropology" that supposedly was represented in the mainstream of the discipline (Bennett 1996:S37), and this further contributed to the cultural construction of application as a politically problematic category.

19. Indeed, cultural relativism is relative itself. We make ethical judgments about human behavior in our ethnographic fieldwork on a regular basis, and if we did not, we could find ourselves in conflict with institutional review boards. In a time when the world is rapidly changing, where boundaries are collapsing and people are thrown into close juxtaposition in unexpected ways, it is difficult to implement the principle of cultural relativism as if human beings lived inside hermetically sealed bubbles of cultural (in)difference. Such shifts in the context of anthropological practice mean that the willingness of applied anthropologists to suggest that some methods or outcomes may be preferable to others does not seem so alien now as it once did in the middle of the 20th century.

20. Of course, today we recognize that even 'pure' research represents an intervention if human subjects are involved, no matter how tangentially, and that we cannot avoid our ethical responsibilities in such research.

21. Following World War II, the concept of 'development' arose in the Western world as a means to address the perceived problems of economic 'underdevelopment' in Africa, Asia, and Latin America. Policy elites of the United States were leaders within the development movement, but soon the entire Western policy establishment joined, convincing newly elected leaders of independent Third World nations to sign on to the West's culturally constructed prescriptions for economic growth (Escobar 1995). As this movement developed force, American anthropologists gained opportunities to work jointly with international agencies and the U.S. armed forces to 'modernize' the nations of the Third World, an integral component of the emerging U.S. economic hegemony of the mid–20th century. As development agencies were evolving their policies, the peoples of the 'underdeveloped' nations became poorer and more desperate. Leading intellectuals in the Third World opened a strong critique of development, beginning in the 1970s with dependency theory. Dependency is a Marxist and world-systems-influenced theory that claims 'underdevelopment' is a direct consequence of peripheral nations' economic dependency upon capitalism and the exploitation of Western core nations (Peet 1999). While dependency theory itself has been severely criticized from various perspectives, the critique that it launched was only the opening round in a long and mounting global push-back against the concept of 'development,' which was gradually joined (later in the 1980s) by many other forces, including anthropologists who study development as a subject of inquiry.

22. Earlier, during the Vietnam era, the discovery that the United States military was attempting to recruit anthropologists to work in covert counterintelligence operations overseas created a furor and led to the American Anthropological Association's ban on conducting any research that could not be published openly. This ban, part of the AAA's Principles of Professional Responsibility (1971), virtually outlawed proprietary research in anthropology until the principles were changed during the 1990s.

23. Chambers (1987) notes several other factors that have inhibited the development of applied anthropology in America, some of which relate to culturally constructed views of ethics and values in the discipline.

24. For example, the *Economist* (October 29, 2005:104–106) shows that GDP (gross domestic product) rates for Pacific Rim and other Southeast Asian nations over one year previous were listed as follows: China (9.4% +), Hong Kong (6.8% +), India (8.1% +), Indonesia (5.5% +), Malaysia (4.1% +),

Philippines (4.8% +), Singapore (6.0% +), South Korea (3.3% +), Taiwan (3.0% +), Thailand (4.4% +). This compared with a GDP of 1.1% + for the Euro area and 3.6% + for the United States over one year previous.

25. In Canada, the Society for Applied Anthropology in Canada and its organ, *Proactive*, have ceased to exist. The applied anthropology graduate program that was piloted at the University of Saskatchewan also could not be sustained due to program downsizing. In Great Britain, the British Association for Anthropology in Policy and Practice and its successor have collapsed. In Israel, the applied anthropology track in the Department of Behavioral Science at Ben-Gurion University has been closed. It should be noted, however, that 'Anthropology in Action' still exists in Great Britain as an e-mail discussion group, and that since 2003 the ASA has initiated 'Apply,' which is an applied anthropology network that is active in promoting applied events and has its own website. In our view, these latter activities do not reflect the same degree of formalization as those institutional structures that have failed.

26. American examples of these dimensions of convergence may be found in a series of issues published by *Practicing Anthropology* (Hackenberg and Hackenberg 2004) and in our own work.

27. This shift perhaps only reinforces a long-standing tendency within anthropology to claim that increases in knowledge and awareness of 'other ways of being human' would enhance tolerance, mitigate conflict, and promote social well-being. From this standpoint, anthropology always has had a 'purpose,' albeit a secondary one after the pursuit of knowledge.

REFERENCES

Agar, Michael
    2004 An Anthropological Problem, a Complex Solution. Human Organization 63(4):411–418.
Angrosino, Michael
    1976 The Evolution of the New Applied Anthropology. *In* Do Applied Anthropologists Apply Anthropology? Michael Angrosino, ed. Athens: University of Georgia Press.
Arensberg, Conrad
    1947 Prospect and Retrospect. Applied Anthropology 6:1–7.
Baba, Marietta L.
    1994 The Fifth Subdiscipline: Anthropological Practice and the Future of Anthropology. Human Organization 53(2):174–186.
    2000 Theories of Practice in Anthropology: A Critical Appraisal. *In* The Unity of Theory and Practice in Anthropology: Rebuilding a Fractured Synthesis. Carole E. Hill and Marietta L. Baba, eds. Pp. 17–44. NAPA Bulletin 18. Washington, DC: American Anthropological Association.
    2005 Anthropological Practice in Business and Industry. *In* Applied Anthropology: Domains of Application. Satish Kedia and John van Willigen, eds. Pp. 221–261. Westport, CT: Praeger.
Baba, Marietta L., and Carole E. Hill, eds.
    1997 The Global Practice of Anthropology. Williamsburg, VA: College of William and Mary. Studies in Third World Societies #58.
Bastide, Roger
    1973 Applied Anthropology. New York: Harper & Row.
Bennett, John
    1996 Applied and Action Anthropology. Current Anthropology 36(Supplement):S23–S53.
Cavanagh, Gerald F.
    1990 American Business Values. 3rd edition. Englewood Cliffs, NJ: Prentice-Hall.
Chambers, Erve
    1987 Applied Anthropology in the Post-Vietnam Era: Anticipations and Ironies. Annual Review of Anthropology 66:309–337.
Chun, Allen, ed.
    2004 Globalization: Critical Issues. New York: Berghahn Books.
Douglas, Mary, and Baron Isherwood
    1979 The World of Goods: Towards an Anthropology of Consumption. New York: Basic Books.

Duderstadt, James, and Farris W. Womack

  2003 The Future of the Public University in America: Beyond the Crossroad. Balitmore, MD: The Johns
        Hopkins University Press.

Elden, Max, and Morten Levin

  1991 Cogenerative Learning: Bringing Participation into Action Research. *In* Participatory Action
        Research. William Foote Whyte, ed. Newbury Park, CA: Sage Publications.

Escobar, Arturo

  1995 Encountering Development: The Making and Unmaking of the Third World. Princeton, NJ:
        Princeton University Press.

Fischer, Michael M. J.

  2003 Emergent Forms of Life and the Anthropological Voice. Durham, NC: Duke University Press.

Fiske, Shirley J., and Erve Chambers

  1997 Status and Trends: Practice and Anthropology in the United States. *In* The Global Practice of
        Anthropology. Marietta L. Baba and Carole E. Hill, eds. Pp. 283–309. Studies in Third World
        Societies, No 58. Williamsburg, VA: College of William and Mary Press.

Foster, George

  1969 Applied Anthropology. Boston: Little, Brown and Company.

Foucault, Michel

  1971 The Order of Discourse. *In* Untying the Text: The Post-structuralist Reader. R. Young, ed. London:
        Routledge and Kegan Paul.

Freidenberg, Judith

  2001 Applied Anthropology/antropoligia de la gestion: Debating the Uses of Anthropology in the United
        States and Latin America. The Journal of Latin American Anthropology 6(2):4–19.

Freire, Paulo

  1970 Pedagogy of the Oppressed. Harmondsworth: Penguin.

Friedman, Jonathan

  2003 Globalization, Dis-integration, Re-organization: The Transformation of Violence. *In* Globalization,
        Violence and the State. Jonathan Friedman, ed. Pp. 1–34. Walnut Creek, CA: Alta Mira Press.

  2004 Champagne Liberals and the New 'Dangerous Classes': Reconfigurations of Class, Identity and
        Cultural Production in the Contemporary Global System. *In* Globalization. Allen Chun, ed. New
        York: Berghahn Books.

Gardner, Katy, and David Lewis

  1996 Anthropology, Development and the Post-Modern Challenge. London: Pluto Press.

Gellner, D. N., and E. Hirsch

  2001 Inside Organizations: Anthropologists at Work. Oxford: Berg.

Greenwood, Davydd J., and Morten Levin

  1998 Introduction to Action Research: Social Research for Social Change. Thousand Oaks, CA: Sage
        Publications.

Hackenberg, Robert A.

  1988 Scientists or Survivors? The Future of Applied Anthropology under Maximum Uncertainty. *In*
        Anthropology for Tomorrow: Creating Practitioner Oriented Training Programs. Robert Trotter II,
        ed. Washington, DC: American Anthropological Association.

Hackenberg, Robert A., and Beverly H. Hackenberg

  2004 Notes toward a New Future: Applied Anthropology in Century XXI. Human Organization
        63:385–399.

Harris, Marvin

  1968 The Rise of Anthropological Theory. New York: Thomas Y. Cromwell Co.

Hill, Carole E.

  1994 Professional Organizations and the Future Practice of Anthropology. Practicing Anthropology
        16:23–24.

  1999 Challenging Assumptions of Human Diversity: The Teaching Imagination in Anthropology. *In* The
        Social Worlds of Higher Education. Bernice A. Pescosolido and Ronald Aminzade, eds. Pp. 271–279.
        Thousand Oaks, CA: Pine Forge Press.

2000 Strategic Issues for Rebuilding a Theory and Practice Synthesis. *In* The Unity of Theory and Practice in Anthropology: Rebuilding a Fractured Synthesis. Carole E. Hill and Marietta L. Baba, eds. Pp. 1–16. NAPA Bulletin 18. Washington, DC: American Anthropological Association.

Hill, Carole E., and Marietta Baba

2000 The Unity of Theory and Practice in Anthropology: Rebuilding a Fractured Synthesis. NAPA Bulletin 18. Washington, DC: American Anthropological Association.

Holmberg, Allan

1958 Values in Action: A Symposium. Human Organization 17(1):2–26.

Holmberg, Allan, and Henry Dobyns

1962 Community and Regional Development, the Joint Cornell-Peru Experiment: The Process of Accelerating Community Change. Human Organization 21:107–109.

Horton, Robin

1973 Levy-Bruhl, Durkheim and the Scientific Revolution. *In* Modes of Thought: Essays on Thinking in Western and Non-Western Societies. Robin Horton and Ruth Finnegan, eds. Pp 249–305. London: Faber & Faber.

Jian, Guan, and John Young

2002 Introduction to the Investigation of the Present Situation and the Development of Ethnic Minorities in China. Practicing Anthropology 24(2):2–5.

Kerckhoff, Alan C., Richard R. Campbell, and Idee Winfeild-Laird

1985 Social Mobility in Great Britain and the United States. American Journal of Sociology 91(2):281–308.

Kuper, Adam

1983 Anthropology and Anthropologists: The Modern British School. London: Routledge and Kegan Paul.

1999 Culture: The Anthropologists Account. Cambridge, MA: Harvard.

Lamphere, Louise

2004 The Convergence of Applied, Practicing, and Public Anthropology in the 21st Century. Human Organization 63(4):431–443.

Lave, Jean, and Etienne Wenger

1991 Situated Learning: Legitimate Peripheral Participation. New York: Cambridge University Press.

Malinowski, B.

1929 Practical Anthropology. Africa 2(1):28–38.

Matley, Ian

1966 The Marxist Approach to the Geographical Environment. Annals of the Association of American Geographers 56(1):97–111.

Messerschmidt, Donald A, ed.

1981 Anthropologists at Home in North America: Methods and Issues in the Study of One's Own Society. Cambridge: Cambridge University Press.

Miller, Daniel, ed.

1995 Acknowledging Consumption: A Review of New Studies. London: Routledge.

Mills, David

2002 British Anthropology at the End of Empire: The Rise and Fall of the Colonial Social Science Research Council, 1944–1962. Revue d'Histoire des Sciences Humaines 6:161–188.

Moran, Emilio, and Dennis Ojima

2005 Global Land Project. Science Plan and Implementation Strategy. IGBP Report 33/IHDP Report 19. International Human Dimensions Programme on Global Environmental Change, International Council for Science.

Nader, Ralph

1975 Anthropology in Law and Civic Action. *In* Anthropology and Society. Bela C. Maday, ed. Pp. 31–40. Washington, DC: American Anthropological Association.

Ortner, Sherry

1984 Theory in Anthropology since the Sixties. Comparative Studies in Society and History 26(1): 126–166.

Partridge, William L., and Elizabeth M. Eddy, eds.

  1978 The Development of Applied Anthropology in America. *In* Applied Anthropology in America. William Partridge and Elizabeth Eddy, eds. New York: Columbia University Press.

Peet, Richard

  1999 Theories of Development. New York: The Guilford Press.

Pels, Peter, and Oscar Salemink

  1999 Introduction: Locating the Colonial Subjects of Anthropology. *In* Colonial Subjects: Essays on the Practical History of Anthropology. P. Pels and O. Salemink, eds. Ann Arbor, MI: University of Michigan Press.

Rabinow, Paul

  1986 Representations as Social Facts: Modernity and Post-modernity in Anthropology. *In* Writing Culture: The Poetics and Politics of Ethnography. J. Clifford and G. Marcus, eds. Berkeley: University of California Press.

Robeiro, Gustavo

  2004 Practicing Anthropology in Brazil: A Retrospective Look at Two Time Periods. Practicing Anthropology 26 (3):6–10.

Roberts, William

  1997 Introduction to Practicing Anthropology in Senegal. Practicing Anthropology 19(1):2–4.

Robertson, Roland

  1992 Globalization: Social Theory and Global Culture. London: Sage.

Sahlins, Marshall

  1976 Culture and Practical Reason. Chicago, IL: University of Chicago Press.

Schwartzman, Helen B.

  1993 Ethnography in Organizations. Newbury Park, CA: Sage Publications.

Schweizer, Thomas

  1998 Epistemology: The Nature and Validation of Anthropological Knowledge. *In* Handbook of Methods in Cultural Anthropology. H. Russell Bernard, ed. Walnut Creek, CA: Sage Publications.

Shore, Cris, and Susan Wright

  2000 Coercive Accountability: The Rise of Audit Culture in Higher Education. *In* Audit Cultures: Anthropological Studies in Accountability, Ethics and the Academy. Marilyn Strathern, ed. London: Routledge.

Stokes, Donald

  1997 Pasteur's Quadrant: Basic Science and Technological Innovation. Washington, DC: The Brookings Institution.

Strauss, Claudia, and Naomi Quinn

  1997 A Cognitive Theory of Cultural Meaning. Cambridge: Cambridge University Press.

Tax, Sol

  1975 Action Anthropology. Current Anthropology 16:171–177.

Taylor, P.

  1993 The Texts of Paulo Freire. Buckingham: Open University Press.

Thompson, Laura

  1976 An Appropriate Role for Postcolonial Applied Anthropologists. Human Organization 35:1–7.

van Willigen, John

  2002 Applied Anthropology: An Introduction. Westport, CT: Bergin and Garvey.

Wallerstein, Nina, and Bonnie Duran

  2003 The Conceptual, Historical, and Practice Roots of Community Based Participatory Research and Related Participatory Traditions. *In* Community Based Participatory Research for Health. M. Minkler and N. Wallerstein, eds. San Francisco: Jossey-Bass.

Biosketches of Authors

Ana Isabel Afonso (Ph.D. in Anthropology, 1997) lectures in the Department of Anthropology, RCSH–Universidade Nova de Lisboa, teaching anthropological research methods; ethics and anthropological practice. Her main research interests are anthropological methods and new technologies, social change and development, and risk and social impact analysis. She has done fieldwork in a peasant community in northeast Portugal and supervised a work team doing participant-observation in an estate neighborhood in Setubal (near Lisbon). Most recently she coordinates a project on Portuguese gypsies and collaborates in the collective project on the theme of road violence in Portugal (coordinated by M. J. Ramos and A. Medeiros, from DepANTISCTE, Lisbon). She has been an associate member of EASA since 1991, joined the EASA Teaching Anthropology Network in 1998, and from then participated in the EASA TAN/VAN joint meetings. Her recent main publications include *Terra, Casa e Familia* (forthcoming); co-edition of *Working Images* (with Sarah Pink and Laszlo Kurti, 2004, London: Routledge); *Retoricas Sem Fronteira* (with Jorge F. Branco, 2003, Oeiras: Celta); *Visual Teaching, Virtual Learning* (with Sarah Pink and Laszlo Kurti, 2002, special issue of *Anthropology in Action*). ai.afonso@fcsh.unl.pt

Marietta Baba is Dean of the College of Social Science and Professor of Anthropology at Michigan State University. She also holds an appointment as Adjunct Professor in the Department of Management at the Eli Broad College of Business. Previously, she was Professor and Chair of the Department of Anthropology and founding director of the Business and Industrial Anthropology program at Wayne State University in Detroit, Michigan. From 1994 to 1996, she was Program Director of the National Science Foundation's industry-funded research program entitled *Transformations to Quality Organizations*. Dr. Baba is the author of 70 scholarly and technical publications in the fields of organizational culture, technological change, and evolutionary processes. In 1998 she was appointed to serve on Motorola's global advisory Board of Anthropologists, the first of its kind in the United States. Dr. Baba was a founding member and past president of the National Association for the Practice of Anthropology (NAPA, 1986–88), a section of the American Anthropological Association (AAA). She served on the Executive Committee and Board of Directors of Anthropology for the *American Anthropologist* (1990–93). She holds an MBA (with highest distinction) from the Advanced Management Program at Michigan State University's Eli Broad Graduate School of Management and a Ph.D. in Physical Anthropology from Wayne State University (doctoral research conducted in the School of Medicine). She is listed in *Who's Who in America* (1992–present). mbaba@msu.edu

Alexander (Sandy) Ervin is Professor of Anthropology at the University of Saskatchewan. His specialties include medical, environmental, and applied anthropology. Fieldwork has taken him to Alaska, the Northwest Territories, and Saskatchewan, working with Inuit, Dene, farmers, refugees,

NAPA Bulletin 25, pp. 208–212, ISBN 1-931303-28-2. © 2006 by the American Anthropological Association. All rights reserved. Permissions to photocopy or reproduce article content via www.ucpress.edu/journals/rights.htm.

social service agencies, and the visually impaired. Publications include about forty articles and technical reports and four books; one is titled *Applied Anthropology: Tools and Perspectives for Contemporary Practice*. He has served on the board of the Society for Applied Anthropology as editor of *Practicing Anthropology*. Practice has also involved activities with local peace, social justice, and environmental groups and the Canadian Centre for Policy Alternatives. ervin@skyway.usask.edu

El-Sayed el-Aswad, currently Professor of Anthropology at Bahrain University, received his doctorate degree from the University of Michigan, Ann Arbor. Prior to this, he held the position of Chair in the Department of Sociology at Tanta University in Egypt. His most recently published book (2002) is entitled *Religion and Folk Cosmology: Scenarios of the Visible and Invisible in Rural Egypt*. He has published widely in both Arabic and English on such topics as Egyptian cosmology (modern and archaic), applied anthropology, mythology, Emirates University where he founded and served as Head of the Unit of Anthropological and Folkloric Resources. He has been awarded fellowships from the Fulbright Program, the Ford Foundation, the Egyptian government, the United Arab Emirates University, and the American University of Cairo. He currently serves as a board member of the American Anthropological Association. melaswad@hotmail.com

Carole E. Hill is Adjunct Professor of Anthropology at the University of North Carolina at Asheville and Professor Emeritus of Anthropology at Georgia State University. Her research and publications over the last 35 years have focused on applied medical anthropology in Central America and the American South. She has authored or edited 11 books and authored over 100 articles and technical reports. Her most recent research was located in Egypt and Jordan testing a model designed to measure the effect of culture on the technology transfer process. Throughout her career, she maintained an interest in linking theory and practice, culminating in a book, edited by Hill and Marietta L. Baba, entitled *NAPA Bulletin: The Unity of Theory and Practice in Anthropology: Rebuilding a Fractured Synthesis*. She is past president of the Society for Applied Anthropology and continues to be active in practicing anthropology. retch@langate.gsu.edu

Lorne Holyoak is Assistant Professor of Anthropology in the Department of Religious Studies and Anthropology at the University of Saskatchewan. He graduated from the University of Toronto with a doctorate in anthropology in 2000. His research involves religion and ethnic identity among minorities in northeast China and the ethnography and oral history components of cultural resource preservation in Micronesia, where he worked for three and a half years in the Palau Historic Preservation Office. lorne_holyoak@pch.gc.ca

S. Zev Kalifon was born in the United States and immigrated to Israel in 1970. He did his undergraduate work at the Hebrew University in Psychology and Social Anthropology. He served five years in the Behavioral Science Department of the Israel Forces before returning to the United States for graduate work. His Ph.D. is in applied anthropology from the Northwestern University Program in Ethnography and Public Policy. He returned to Israel in 1987 and is affiliated with the Inter-Disciplinary Department of Social Sciences at Bar-Ilan University. okalifon@bezquint.net

Pilar Larreamendy is a Human Geographer at the Department of Environmentally and Socially Sustainable Development, Latin America and Caribbean Region, at the World Bank.

Dr. Larreamendy has worked at the World Bank since 1999. Before joining the Bank, she worked in Ecuador for a decade in the Amazonian region in a number of environmental projects with nongovernmental and indigenous organizations. Dr. Larreamendy received her undergraduate degree in Anthropology at the Catholic University in Ecuador (1982) and her M.Phil. (1995) and Ph.D. (2004) at the University of Cambridge (U.K.). Her M.Phil. thesis, entitled *Agency and Culture among the Shuar in Ecuador*, is an analysis of a political indigenous organization when addressing the environmental depletion in the Amazonian region. Her Ph.D. thesis, entitled *Indigenous Networks: Politics and Development Interconnectivity among the Shuar in Ecuador*, is a case study of an Ecuadorian indigenous grassroots organization, focused on the nature of its networks (national, regional, and local) when defining politics and development agendas. Other publications of Dr. Larreamendy are *Mujeres y Flores* (C. Newman, P. Larreamendy, and A. Maldonado, 2002, Quito: Abya Yala); *Agency and Culture: The Shuar in Ecuador* (in press, Quito: Abya Yala); and *Gender and Development* (1996, Quito: Universidad Central). She was the field researcher for the publication *La Hacienda* (Quito: Ed. Mariscal) and *The Cacha Project* (1995, Quito: UNICEF). At the World Bank, Dr. Larreamendy is managing projects on indigenous and Afro-descendant peoples' development, biodiversity conservation, and community-driven development and is supporting issues concerning governance and social accountability. She is based in the Ecuador Bank office.
plarreamendy@worldbank.org

L. K. Mahapatra (born October 29, 1929) received his Ph.D. in (Hamburg) magna cum laude. He has had a long academic career since 1953 in research institutions and at five universities in India (Lucknow and Utkal Universities being the first and last ones) and as Visiting Professor at Hamburg University. A National Fellow of the Indian Council of Social Science Research and a Ford Foundation Fellow in Indonesia for research, he was Vice-Chancellor of Utkal and Sambalpur Universities, and at present he is Chairman of Nabakrushna Choudhury Centre for Development Studies under ICSSR. Senior-most professor in social anthropology, social historian, and folklorist, Professor Mahapatra had been a consultant to UNESCO and, for several years, to the World Bank in the field of Displacement, Resettlement, and Reconstruction in India. Pioneering teaching and research on a world area outside India among anthropologists, he had undertaken fieldwork in three Indonesian islands in the field of state–community interactions in rural development, besides conducting research on kingship, caste society, religion, and tribal affairs in precolonial, colonial, and present-day India and Southeast Asia.
lkmahapatra2001@yahoo.co.in

Sarah Pink is Senior Lecturer in the Department of Social Sciences at Loughborough University. She has a B.A. (1988) and Ph.D. (1996) in Social Anthropology from the University of Kent and an M.A. in Visual Anthropology (1990) from the University of Manchester. Her academic and applied research is mainly in Spain and England focusing on gender in public contexts and in the home, the senses, visual and material culture, and methodology. Her books include *Women and Bullfighting* (1997, Berg) and *Doing Visual Ethnography* (2005, Sage).
s.pink@lboro.ac.uk

Malka Shabtay was born in Israel. She did her undergraduate work at Haifa University in Social Anthropology and Education. She has a master's degree from Haifa University in special education and a Ph.D. in Anthropology from Ben-Gurion University. She has worked as an applied anthropologist with the Ethiopian Jewish Community in Israel for the last 20 years. She teaches applied anthropology at Tel-Aviv University and combines research, consultancy, and training for

various organizations who are interested in applying cultural and cross-cultural perspectives in their work. She has published four books and numerous articles.
mat@netvision.net.il

Jorge E. Uquillas is Senior Sociologist of the Social Development Unit, Department of Environmentally and Socially Sustainable Development, Latin America and Caribbean Region, at the World Bank in Washington, D.C. He has worked at the World Bank since 1993 on broad social and indigenous peoples' issues. Before joining the Bank, he taught at several U.S. and Ecuadorian universities and worked for various governmental and nongovernmental organizations on regional and agricultural development issues. Dr. Uquillas received his undergraduate degree in Sociology at Stetson University (1971) and his M.A. and Ph.D. in Sociology and Latin American Studies (1973 and 1976, respectively). He also did special studies in International Agriculture and Rural Development at Cornell University (1983–84). Dr. Uquillas has written extensively on agricultural systems, indigenous peoples, and socioeconomic development issues in Latin America. He has edited or is the author or coauthor of several publications, including *Exclusión Social y Estrategias de Vida de los Indígenas Urbanos en Perú, México y Ecuador* (2003, Banco Mundial); *Lessons of Indigenous Development in Latin America* (2004, Banco Mundial); *Traditional and Modern Natural Resource Management in Latin America* (1999, University of Pittsburgh Press); *Doce Experiencias de Desarrollo Indígena en América Latina* (1999, Fondo Indígena); "Including the Excluded: Ethnodevelopment in Latin America," in *Poverty and Inequality in Latin America* (1996, World Bank); "Are Modern Agroforestry Systems Economically Viable? A Case Study in the Ecuadorian Amazon," in *Financial and Economic Analysis of Agroforestry Systems* (NFTA-USDA/FS); "Social Impacts of Modernization and Public Policies, and Prospects for Indigenous Development in the Ecuadorian Amazon," in *The Human Ecology of Tropical Land Settlement in Latin America* (1989, Westview); "Indian Land Rights and Natural Resource Management in the Ecuadorian Amazon," *Cultural Survival* (vol. 16). His current duties at the World Bank include managing new projects on indigenous peoples' development and biodiversity conservation, coordinating various activities on indigenous peoples and community-driven development, and providing technical support on social issues to a variety of projects.
juquillas@worldbank.org

Wang Jianmin is a Professor of Anthropology in the Department of Anthropology, Central University of Nationalities, Beijing, China. He received his Ph.D. in Ethnology (Cultural Anthropology) from Central University of Nationalities. His main research fields are the history of anthropology in China, anthropology of art, and psychological anthropology. He conducts most of his fieldwork research in Xinjiang, northwest China. He is the author of *The History of Ethnology in China* (Part 1, 1903–1949) and *The History of Ethnology in China* (Part 2, 1950–1997) (1997, 1998, Kunming: Yunnan Education Publisher House). He is the editor of *The Research Methods and Methodology of Anthropology and Ethnology of China in the 20th Century* (2004, Beijing: The Ethnic Publishing House), and his English articles include "Last Nomads in China: Notes on the Everyday Life of Kazak Nomads in Xinjiang," in *China's Ethnic Groups* (2004, vol. 2, no. 1), and "Ethnonyms and Nationalism in Xinjiang," in *Exploring Nationalisms of China: Terms and Conflicts* (C. X. George Wei and Xiaoyuan Liu, eds., 2002, Westport, CT: Greenwood Press), among others.
multiculture@sohu.com

Anatoly N. Yamskov holds the position of Scholar at the Institute of Ethnology and Anthropology, Russian Academy of Sciences. He was appointed Associate Professor in Ethnology and Anthropology in 2003. He received a Ph.D. in Ethnography from the Institute of Ethnography, USSR Academy of Sciences, Moscow, in 1987. He has served on the Physical Geography Faculty at Moscow State University from 1980 and as a Senior Researcher in the Department of Ethnic Ecology at the Institute of Ethnology and Anthropology since 1998. He has been a member of the Russian Geographical Society since 1983 and been a member of the Commission on Anthropology in Policy and Practice, International Union of Anthropological and Ethnological Sciences, since 1993. He has coedited 12 books and authored 140 academic papers. His research has concentrated on field studies of traditional and modern economic activities, settlement patterns, present occupations and migrations, interethnic contacts, and conflicts in rural areas of the Transcaucasus, Southern Siberia, the Urals, and Central European Russia (totaling almost two years). He has been cited in *Annual Review of Anthropology* (1997, vol. 26, p. 246) and in seven other thematic reviews and has been listed in five different *Who's Who* publications (in Russian, English).

yamskov@iea.ras.ru

John A. Young is Professor Emeritus at Oregon State University where he served as department chair for 18 years. He is a past president of the Society for Applied Anthropology, 1997–99. His interests include bringing the work of Chinese anthropologists to a wider audience, most notably in two special issues of *Practicing Anthropology* referenced in this article. He has recently concluded applied research projects on alternative energy development and resettlement in Northeast China and Inner Mongolia. He is editor of a book series on Contemporary Social Issues for Wadsworth-Thomson Publishing.

jyoung@oregonstate.edu